The Rise of a Righteous Man Through God's Grace

STEVEN GAMBLE

authorHOUSE®

AuthorHouse™
1663 Liberty Drive
Bloomington, IN 47403
www.authorhouse.com
Phone: 1 (800) 839-8640

Published by AuthorHouse   10/19/2015

ISBN: 978-1-5049-2398-9 (sc)
ISBN: 978-1-5049-5733-5 (hc)
ISBN: 978-1-5049-2397-2 (e)

Library of Congress Control Number: 2015911580

Print information available on the last page.

KJV
Scripture quotations marked KJV are from the Holy Bible, King James Version
(Authorized Version). First published in 1611. Quoted from the KJV Classic
Reference Bible, Copyright © 1983 by The Zondervan Corporation.

NLT
Scripture quotations marked NLT are taken from the Holy Bible, New Living
Translation, copyright © 1996, 2004, 2007. Used by permission of Tyndale House
Publishers, Inc. Carol Stream, Illinois 60188. All rights reserved. Website

Contents

Preface

I would like to start off by saying; I am not calling myself a righteous man because of my own actions. My righteousness before God are like filthy rags the only way that I am made righteous is when I accepted and acknowledged Jesus Christ as my Lord and Savior.

This Book is an account of a certain segment of my time here on this earth.

Dedications

I dedicate this book in the memory of my eldest son Steven A. Gamble (July 24, 1983 – September 3, 2009) and my wife (Beautiful) Triscennea M. Gamble (December 10, 1965 – October 14, 2010).

Both of whom passed on to be with our Heavenly Father during this particular segment of my time on this earth.

Acknowledgements

First and foremost I give all praise, glory, and honor to my Heavenly Father for allowing me to have these life experiences and to see me through every step of the way. I am so grateful that my God saw fit for me to be used to write this book as it was given to me by the Holy Spirit.

I am truly grateful for my parents Henry and Lillian Gamble for their undying love and the many sacrifices that they have made. All that they have done helped to mold me into the man that I am today.

My God definitely showed me favor with the wife of my youth (Beautiful) Triscennea M. Gamble. This wonderful woman of God continued to love and honor me as I constantly ran from my God and His purpose for my life, while causing her a great deal of heartache and pain. I am so grateful that my God allowed Beautiful the opportunity to witness me take my rightful position and act in my authority as the head and spiritual covering for my family.

I thank God for ordering my steps and leading me to my Pastor Gerald L. Glasper and Co-Pastor Toni A. Glasper, my spiritual parents. Beautiful and I searched for many years, visited many churches before finding the Pastor that was meant to lead us forward in our walk with Christ. I also couldn't ask for a better family of believers to be joined with than my Rhema Word Kingdom Ministries family, whom all I love and appreciate dearly.

A special thanks to my neighbor and dear friend of fifteen years, Dr. Debra Burt-Frazier for performing the task of editing this book. It was fit for God to call her to do this for she was a witness to these life changing events that occurred and became a catalyst for me becoming who I am today.

My God is an awesome God!!! I have been blessed with the wife of my latter years Fanita A. Gamble, we were married after I finished writing this book and before having it published. So many people go through their entire lives without experiencing the true love of a spouse and best friend; I get to have that experience twice. Fanita has become my best friend, cheerleader, motivator, and partner. Through our union our God will accomplish great works for the advancement of His kingdom here on earth. I have given her the name Phenomenal for that is what she is to me.

Introduction

I must begin by stating as long as I can remember; I have always had this inherent Love for my Heavenly Father. In other words, before I was taught that I was to Love God more than anyone and anything else, I already did. God has always been first and foremost in my life. Also, all my life I have never worried about anything, which used to drive my wife crazy. I don't remember exactly when I was saved, but it was after watching a television evangelist program and I repeated after him my confession of faith out loud. He then stated "If you repeated these words out loud and believed in what you said then you are saved." Then I realized after speaking those words I was saved.

I first met my wife Triscennea in grammar school, but was reintroduced to her by a mutual friend named David. We started hanging out, all of us, on the weekend while smoking weed and drinking. Occasionally, other friends would join but, mainly it was the three of us. This went on for months, some flirtatious activity occurring between me and her. We all were just friends hanging out on the weekends. The thought of a union did not occur until our mutual friend, David told us of a dream he had regarding Triscennea and I, and in that dream we were a couple.

Now at that time, Triscennea thought she was "Miss It" dating older dudes who was giving her money, and I "Mr. Playboy Extraordinaire" always had at least four through six females I was with almost daily one at a time. The two of us seemed to be the most unlikely of individuals to become a couple. In fact, her response to David's dream was I couldn't handle her and my response was it would just be a one-night stand.

I will never forget the day our union began because it was on the day the world was supposed to end. I suggest anyone reading this book to verify this date and prediction by many renowned scientists. On March 10, 1982, there was a planetary alignment that occurred that should have caused a cataclysmic action that should, according to them, end this earth's existence. This was stated in the Chicago Tribune and Sun Times Newspapers one or two days before March 10, 1982. In fact I used to joke with Triscennea saying had we not gotten together that day the world would have surely ended.

Now I had always been the romantic person in our relationship. For instance every year we celebrated March 10th as an anniversary date even after we were married on July 30, 1988. We then began to celebrate two equally important dates for us.

It took only approximately a month or two after we began our relationship that I knew I loved her. My love for her was not birthed from any sexual or lustful attraction. In fact, I did not tell her for a long time that she was so beautiful to me. We were 16 when we began our relationship March 10th. On November 30th of 1982 we found out she was pregnant, which just happened to be my 17th birthday. Tracy, which was the name I called her then, turned 17 ten days later. I was born November 30, 1965, she was born December 10, 1965. I was only ten days older than her.

Tracy became very ill shortly after Steven, our first child, was born and was hospitalized for approximately 3 weeks before she was diagnosed with the disease, Lupus. We were informed that she was born with it, and that the stress put on her body from the natural child birth of Steven brought out the disease.

Steven was born July 24, 1983. The following year shortly after his birthday and his baptism, I was posed with a question by a priest I worked with at the time. He asked me if I loved Tracy, I immediately answered yes. Then he asked me if I can imagine my life without her, I immediately answered no. That same priest informed me of an engagement ceremony that existed in the Roman Catholic Church. On December 14, 1984, we participated in that ceremony and became engaged.

I told Tracy then that after we were married that I would no longer address her as everyone else did. I would from that day forward only call her by the name, "Triscennea". A few years after being married, she expressed a need for me to tell her how I thought she looked because in all those years I had never told her. So from that point on I would either address her as "Triscennea" or "Beautiful" because she was so beautiful to me on the inside as well as the outside.

Triscennea had to battle with her Lupus for approximately a decade before it went into remission. The Lupus she had attacked her kidneys. To sum up her medical history as quickly and neatly as I can throughout our 28 years together she had been hospitalized at least 20 times. The reasons varied from kidney rejection, infections, fever, removal of one of her native kidneys (because it was cancerous), 2 kidney transplants, and the removal of her second native kidney due to cysts being found on it and the history of cancer with the other one.

My beautiful wife, Triscennea, was a fighter. She was truly blessed to recover through all those adversities and bouts with illness she always had victory over them. You see, Beautiful always had a praying husband by her side, she also had faith in knowing she was already healed by Jesus' stripes and that no weapon formed against her would prosper.

My eldest son, Steven, was battling with the judicial system as well as with cancer during the time of his passing. I remember this one particular conversation with a doctor that was a specialist in infectious disease. There was only four of us in the room at the time; Steven, the doctor, my Aunt Carolyn and myself. The doctor was trying to convince me that my son couldn't be healed and that he would surely die soon.

I immediately told him that my son would be healed and made whole again by my God. He excitedly asked me (while raising his voice considerably) then why did my God give him cancer? I stated that He didn't, but, He would heal him from the cancer. The doctor became infuriated and he began to raise his voice even more stating that it wasn't possible for Steven to be healed. I told him very calmly that He will surely heal my son and that I had witnessed God's healing power before.

You see the doctor simply stated his claim on the outcome of Steven's condition on what he learned from his medical books. I was stating the truth from what I had witnessed prior and what the Word of God (The Bible) had told me, that Steven was already healed by Jesus' Stripes. I have prayed for people that the doctors have sent to hospice facilities to die and witnessed them being healed and coming home. All the miracles I have been a witness to with Triscennea's medical history alone was enough to convince me of my God's healing and miraculous working power.

So, as I stood before the doctor with my sword (Bible) in hand, I was able to tell him with all confidence that I believed the report contained within the pages of this book verses my sons medical chart that he held in his hand. Even though he was very angry and was still yelling at me, I remained calm. I calmly told him that at this point in time we should agree to disagree because, there was nothing I could tell him to convince him of my God's healing power and that he would never convince me to believe a lie.

When I told Beautiful (my wife) what had occurred she thought that I should report him. I simply told her that wasn't necessary because he didn't upset me. Actually, his lack of faith saddened me, for he couldn't take my peace because he didn't give it to me. During the last few months of my eldest son Steven's time on this earth, I truly learned how and was able to walk by faith and not by sight. For it mattered not to me however bad it may have looked I trusted and believed that my God was more than able to heal my son and that He would.

You see, I praised God throughout this whole situation with my son from beginning to the end, always trusting God to heal my son. In the midst of my praying to and praising my Heavenly Father all during this situation He gave me a peace that surpassed all understanding. I learned the true power and benefits in praising God in the midst of what may seem to everyone else as the worst possible situation in life that I was facing.

I remember being in Steven's hospital room one week and one day before he left this earth to go home to our Heavenly Father, it was on a Wednesday. Triscennea and I was in the room alone with Steven we watched as his vital signs started failing his nurse came in and asked us what we wanted to do, in other words should we let him go. Triscennea looked over at me and asked should we just do nothing and let him go? I stated that we should honor his wishes and do everything we humanly possible can do to save his vessel on this earth. I will expound on this incident in greater detail later within the pages of this book; however after the code blue was announced and we were instructed to leave the room. The Code Blue Team worked on Steven for over an hour until they got him stabilized.

We were informed by the doctors and other medical staff members that the next few hours were very critical and that he probably wouldn't make it through the night. They asked us if we would be spending the night so they could tell us where on the floor we could wait and slumber until morning. I immediately informed them that we wouldn't be spending the night because it was Wednesday and our church had bible study on Wednesdays which we attended regularly and that we would be attending tonight as usual. I knew my God didn't need me present to keep and heal my son and I trusted my God fully and completely.

CHAPTER 1

STEVE'S ARREST

Beautiful and I had an estranged relationship with our eldest son Steven. We really hadn't spoken to him in about nine months because of his disrespectful behavior towards his mother, which is one of thing that is totally unacceptable for any son of mine.

One afternoon, in the early part of January 2008, we received a call from Steven's fiancé' stating that he had been arrested for shooting a young man who broke into his truck and threatened his life.

We were informed by her that the young man had died from the result of the shooting and Steven was being officially arrested. I was very upset to find out that the incident occurred around 5 a.m. that morning and we were just being notified.

Steven lived in an apartment complex in Griffith, Indiana just 20 minutes away from us. I immediately called my wife to inform her of what had happened to our son. We both expressed our anger of being notified so late in the day; because we were both awake at the time of the shooting.

Triscennea had forged a friendship with a woman whom she had worked with who happened to be a lawyer. My wife called her at the place where she was recently employed, and made her aware of Steven's arrest. She knew that we needed a lawyer that lived and practiced in the state of Indiana, so she immediately began to make some calls and said she would get back to us.

When we arrived at the police station we were informed that the arresting officer, a detective, was out to lunch and that's who we needed to speak with. They wouldn't allow us to see our son.

While we were waiting to see the detective before seeing our son, my wife's friend, Debra, called us back with the name of an attorney who happened to be an active professor of law in Indiana. After we spoke with him he agreed to meet with our son that same evening. This was truly a miracle in itself because we had not yet met him nor had we given him any money to retain his services, besides the fact that he was found by a friend of my wife in a matter of hours and was available to take the case.

The detective tried to convince us that he was on our son's side, which I knew was a lie, but I played along so I could see our son. As the detective sat and talked with us he informed us that Steven had waived his right to have an attorney present during questioning. He went on to tell us that our son felt he had done nothing wrong, but there were some inconsistencies in his statements made in comparison to the evidence that had been collected. The detective also informed us that the young man my son shot was dead.

When my wife and I went to the holding cell to see Steven, he immediately informed us that the man he had shot was dead. Steven was visibly shaken and saddened by that fact; we acknowledged that we already knew. We asked Steven how he was doing, had he eaten anything. We advised him to ask for his lawyer to be present before being questioned further. We talked with David, Steven's attorney, later that evening. He informed us that he had met Steven several hours after we left the police station and he agreed to take the case. Keep this in mind this was all done prior to us talking about any money being paid to the lawyer for defending Steven.

Both of us met David for the first time briefly, the next day we asked him about a retaining fee for his services thus far, he immediately told us we could talk about that later but first he needed to speak with the detective in charge and Steven again. Later he would meet with us. The shooting occurred early in the morning on a Tuesday in January 2008, so they could hold Steven for 72 hours pending an investigation of all the evidence before officially charging him. My parents, Triscennea, and I met with David again on that Friday and discussed the statement the police had gotten from Steven. We, finally, talked about a fee for representing Steven which David acted reluctant to discuss, almost as if he were embarrassed!

We were able to see the transcript of the questioning and saw while we sat waiting to see the detective that first day, he wasn't out to lunch; instead he was actually interrogating Steven, while going back and forth on the phone with the District Attorney's office. We knew today was Friday and the 72nd hour was rapidly approaching and that they had to either officially charge Steven, or let him go because they could no longer, legally, hold him.

Upon leaving the courthouse where we met David, per his instructions, we began trying to get in touch with the detective in charge. We were, finally, able to contact him and were informed that Steven was officially charged with murder and was transferred to Lake County jail early that morning. After a few moments of devastation and trying to come to grips with the seemingly surreal news, I informed my parents, who had just entered their vehicle several yards away from us in the same parking lot.

Then we proceeded to call Steven's attorney with this ill fated news of Stevens' murder charge. He stated that he had to get in contact with the District Attorney's office to get more information and that he would get back to us as soon as possible and we hung up. I began to pray to my Heavenly Father to protect and continue to watch over my son and for him to be found innocent, as soon as possible. But more so for his immediate release from jail so that we could stand as a family, confront the enemy, and have victory over this apparently desperate attack; by the evil one.

I knew then after praying that I needed to contact a true, man of God, a true prayer warrior, the one name that was dropped in my spirit was DaShaun, who is a minister at my church Rhema Word Kingdom Ministry, which I hadn't attended in approximately 2 years or more. I still had DaShaun's number in my phone even after switching my phone, due to upgrading, and although, I hadn't used it in well over a year I was compelled to keep it. I called him, reminded him who I was, and informed him of my son's situation. He immediately reminded me of my responsibilities as the head of my household and the power of my prayers because I am the head.

DaShaun told me that this was a time to pray, diligently, and he told me to fast. He asked me whether I had ever fasted before. I informed him that I had not. Although, I've had plenty of reasons to in the past. He went on to explain the purpose for fasting and the benefits from doing so, and then we began to pray for my son.

From that moment on I began to pray diligently and promised God I would fast (no eating from 6 a.m. until 6 p.m.) until my son was set free from jail. I talked and prayed with DaShaun several more times via telephone, he asked me had I returned to church, I responded not yet. He told me that I needed to go to church somewhere; I told him I would only go back to the Body of Christ I joined and where I had met him at, Rhema Word Kingdom Ministries.

I returned to Rhema Word immediately and sought out DaShaun so that we could get reacquainted. We had forged a relationship years ago when my family and I first joined. He was over the Men's Ministry. He made an announcement one Sunday that he would start conducting a men's bible study every Tuesday evening in which I attended, faithfully, that's when I got to know him. I remember after one of the Men's Bible Studies, DaShawn was giving away some of his old books. I raised my hand several times to receive one of the books. I didn't receive my top choices but I was able to get a daily devotional book entitled *God Calling*, which I read daily for a while.

After attending and finally joining Rhema Word for approximately eighteen months or so I returned back to the life I led prior to joining, so in turn, I stopped attending and my family did, as well. I have recently been reflecting on everything I went through to even find out about Rhema Word Kingdom Ministries. I went through years of using drugs back and forth, rehab after rehab. Doing all these things trying to escape from a world I never felt I belonged in. My wife and I attended church after church never finding one we both wanted to join, until we attended Rhema Word Kingdom Ministries.

I use to be a binge user of drugs, in other words, I didn't use every day except when I went out on a binge. It was after one particular time I binged, I was so broken and tired of living my life that way, that I was agreeable to any condition my wife wanted in order to save my marriage. Triscennea asked for my keys to our home and told me I could no longer live with her while leading the life I was leading. She told me that I needed to go to rehab, to get my life back and to save my marriage, I, of course, agreed.

My wife wasted no time after I cleaned up a little she drove me to a Department of Human Service facility where they processed me to be transported to the Haymarket facility downtown. I was already familiar with the facility because I was there a couple of years prior to this.

They fed me and assigned me a pallet to sleep on, in a room with approximately, forty-nine other men. The next day I spoke to a counselor, a gentleman who spoke very brash to me. He simply told me that I wasn't sick or going through any drug withdrawals because I had been smoking crack and I was just tired. As he looked over my file, he reminded me that I was there a couple of years ago and he asked me was I finally tired of using drugs and ready for a change. This man spoke to me with authority, telling me that I needed to go to the Salvation Army for their six month program where they would put me to work for them while I worked on my recovery, I agreed.

When I met with the same counselor the next day his demeanor was totally different, he went from being forceful and authoritative to being calmer and more caring. He asked me what I wanted to do, I reminded him that he told me where I needed to go already and I had agreed. He acted as if he didn't recall our conversation, from the previous day, and I truly believed he didn't have any recollection of having spoken to me previously.

It wasn't until very recently that The Holy Spirit revealed to me that He spoke to me through that counselor. He needed to guide me to the correct path, because at that very moment I stood at a crossroad. I was given a bus card and directions to get to the next facility and a time frame in which to arrive. I arrived there within the given time frame and before I could enter the facility I had to pass a breathalyzer test, which of course, I did.

I was assigned a dorm room with fourteen other men for a six-month period of time. It was there that I met my now Pastor, and Spiritual Father's older brother, Jimmy. He had a very tough and unapproachable demeanor about himself; he basically kept to himself and only conversed with a few men, in our dorm room. I wasn't intimidated by his toughness or his unapproachable behavior. On occasion, we would be in the dorm room by ourselves. I would sometimes begin a conversation with him, the very first time I did this, he informed me that he usually didn't talk to the new guys, because he didn't know if they were serious about their recovery or if they would last the six month period required. He would only talk with someone who had been there three months or more. I had only been there a little over a month when we began talking to each other.

During the next few months we talked more, sharing our past experiences with one another and, of course, talking about our faith in God. He informed me that his little brother was a Pastor of a church not too far from where I lived. Jimmy went on to tell me how anointed his brother was and if I would attend his church one time, I would surely join. He was right! His brother is truly anointed, a true follower of Jesus Christ, and my family and I did join.

When I reflect back on everything I had to go through to be in that dorm room at that particular space in time, to meet with Jimmy so he could tell me about his brother's church; the Body of Christ that I was predestined by my Heavenly Father to become a part of, I count it all as joy.

Chapter 2

OUR QUEST FOR A BAIL HEARING

In the State of Indiana, where Steve was living and where the shooting occurred, there is no bail for anyone charged with murder. So that placed us in a precarious position, because we couldn't just simply request a date for a bail hearing. We were faced with the dilemma of requesting a court date to come before a magistrate or judge to present a reason why Steven should have a bail hearing. In other words, we had to provide enough evidence to cause reasonable doubt in the mind of the magistrate or judge that Steve shouldn't be charged with murder.

This process began with the scheduling for the first hearing before the court's magistrate and formally requesting a bail hearing. We were informed by the magistrate that the State of Indiana didn't give bail for the charge of murder. We informed the magistrate that he shouldn't be charged with murder because his life was threatened. Steve was simply defending himself from the young man that was in his truck illegally at the time of the shooting and had stated that he too had a gun when Steven (with his hand gun drawn) told him to exit his vehicle. Steven, repeatedly, told him to exit his vehicle that he had broken into and was in the process of stealing his radio.

The prosecution was also given an opportunity to attempt to refute our evidence supporting our claim of self-defense. Another court date was scheduled to start presenting our evidence supporting our case to defend Steven on the grounds of self-defense. During the time between the court dates we talked and prayed with Steven over the phone when he was allowed to call us. We, of course, visited him every time he was able to have visitors.

It was very difficult and so upsetting to have to see my son behind that glass and talk to him over a phone while he was held captive at the Lake County Jail Facility. We never denied the fact that Steven had shot the young man who had broken into his truck and threatened his life with a gun of his own and that the young man had died as the result of the shooting.

The charge of murder implied that my son, who, first of all, when approaching his truck didn't expect to find a thief still inside, had not come outside with the intent to cause anyone hurt, harm, or danger. The charge of murder implied that his intention was to confront someone, which is totally incorrect, because after his alarm had been going off for such a long period of time it wouldn't have been feasible to even assume that a thief would still be present.

When we received our first bail hearing it was our burden to convince the court magistrate that Steven wouldn't be a flight risk. We presented Steven to the magistrate as a good, solid and stable young man who had never been in trouble before. He had graduated from college (Devry Institute of Technology) with an Associate's Degree in Electronics and Computer Technology. Steven has always worked even while attending Devry full time and was currently working for Tyson Foods. The challenge we were facing would seem like an impossible situation to overcome for an unsaved person. However, I knew that I serve The Almighty God and through Him, all things were possible to those who believed in Him and placed all their trust in Him.

Throughout this whole ordeal I had been fasting, praying, and praising God for delivering my son out of the hands of the enemy. I had no doubt in my mind that not only was my Heavenly Father able to free my son from the hands of his false accusers, but that He, indeed, would do so. We were able to get Steven a sword, a Bible, while he was in jail, through

The Rise of a Righteous Man Through God's Grace

his attorney, David. Steve began to read the Word of God every day, as he sought to know God better. Through the instructions of The Holy Spirit, I had already told Steven the accounts of a few of the Mighty Men in the bible; such as Joseph, David, and Meshach, Shadrach and Abednego, this latter trio from Daniel 3:1-14.

Upon receiving his Bible he was able to read the accounts of these men and so much more. I informed my son that I would stand in the gap for him as much as humanly possible, meaning the gap between him and his relationship with our Heavenly Father (The Almighty God). I also informed Steve that he had to work hard at establishing his own relationship with God and that my faith alone would only take him so far, he had to learn to trust God more and his faith had to increase. My Daddy, The Almighty God, is so wonderful and wise; He used this time alone with Steven to not only increase his faith in Him but to increase mine as well. God allowed my son to be placed in a situation where he was isolated from the rest of the world and was in a state where no one else could save him; but God.

Often I would share with my son about my relationship with God more fully than ever before. Because, now he was ready to listen and to learn, like never before. I prayed with him daily and began giving him the instructions from The Holy Spirit whenever I was instructed to do so by The Holy Spirit. I remember during the first month of Steven's captivity, I was praying to God on my son's behalf. My prayer was regarding the increase of his faith and trust in God and the removal of any hindrance to that increase occurring. During my time of meditation, after praying that prayer The Holy Spirit had revealed to me, that Steven had unforgiveness in his heart, that he needed to release.

That spirit of unforgiveness had to be released from Steven's heart before he could go any further in his relationship with God. At that point, in my relationship with God I wasn't fully convinced of the origin of that revelation, because I had already felt that way in my heart but hadn't told him. I prayed to God two more times regarding that revelation I had received, so I could be sure that it indeed came from The Holy Spirit and not from my own thoughts. Both times, God confirmed that it came from Him and I needed to tell my son immediately.

I was very reluctant to tell Steve because I knew that he probably would choose to be offended by the revelation and that it may cause strife between us. At this point in Steven's relationship with God, and with me he wasn't fully convinced that The Holy Spirit would speak a Word to him through me. I chose to be obedient to The Holy Spirit regardless of how he might react. The next time he called me I told him what was revealed to me by The Holy Spirit; that his unforgiving spirit was blocking the way to his freedom. Upon hearing this he became very angry, cursed at me and hung up the phone.

Steven called me back a few moments later asking why I would tell him something like that while he was being held in captivity. I explained to him that when it was first revealed to me; I had doubts from where it originated. I informed him after further prayer and meditation, it was confirmed to me that it, indeed came from The Holy Spirit and that I needed to tell him immediately.

During this point of Steven's spiritual journey with God he wasn't convinced that The Holy Spirit could and does talk through me; that came later. I told him that he needed to release any unforgiveness that he held in his heart. I knew that he held unforgiveness for his mother, because of me. He couldn't understand why she put me before him in spite of the fact that I would hurt her, repeatedly, by my going away for days using drugs. Many times my son saw his mother cry herself to sleep and become majorly depressed when I would be absent from her. He saw the suffering that I caused her, by my continual disregard for everyone and everything, as I pursued drugs. I never purposely set out to hurt my wife or my children, but the end result was the same every time.

I used drugs as a means to escape this reality that I was in. I never felt like I belonged anywhere in this world. I didn't think as others thought, I didn't have the same value system of others, behaviorally, or morally. I knew that I wanted to serve my God any way He saw fit and I wanted to truly give my life to Him; but, I didn't know how so I became frustrated and used drugs.

Steven didn't feel that his mother loved him the way that she should. That was the source of his constant disrespect to her and the cause of our estranged relationship with him. This resentment Steve held onto for years and allowed it to grow until it nearly consumed him. I informed my son that God wouldn't forgive him if he wouldn't forgive others. Steve knew that I loved God, but he also knew that my actions didn't always line up. He had no idea of the depth of my relationship with my God. He couldn't understand.

As time went forth, I continued to reveal more to Steven about my relationship with my God. I told him how I was able to build my trust in God, how my faith increased as a result of that building up of trust. I told my son that it didn't happen overnight it was gradual. I promised Steve that I would continue to stand in the gap for him; but I couldn't fill a gap as wide as the Grand Canyon. I told him that he needed to start closing the gap by building and strengthening his relationship with God.

Steven continued to read his bible daily while in captivity and I would read to him from my daily devotional book called, *God Calling* by A.J. Russell, as well as, another daily devotional that I received from, televangelist Joel Osteen via his internet website. My son was frequently amazed at how these daily devotionals spoke to him and his current situation, personally. I also began to inform him of the revelations The Holy Spirit was giving me regarding him. As a result of these events occurring so accurately his faith began to increase.

I remember reading to Steven what Joel Osteen had written a few days before he was granted bail. To briefly summarize it, he said always have faith in knowing that God is working behind the scene even when we can't see anything being done in the natural world. I had a dream that my son was granted bail and was being released the morning of his release. I only told my wife of this dream; I went to work that afternoon before it came to pass in the natural. I was informed in the evening that bail had been granted and he was coming home that very evening. My prayers had been answered. My son was coming home on bail.

Now remember, we were informed in the very beginning that the State of Indiana doesn't grant bail when an individual is charged with murder. Not only was he granted bail that was less than $10,000.00, he found a job within two weeks of his release from jail. The position, Steve acquired within the company, required him to be trained out of state, the court granted him permission to leave the state whenever necessary for job training without having to inform them of every occurrence.

This was truly the work of my God; He made a way out of no way. These true occurrences spoken of in these first two chapters establishes to the non-believer, as well as, the believer that my God is able to do all things. In addition, there is nothing that He won't do for those who trust and believe in Him.

Chapter 3

THE BEGINNING
OF STEVEN'S TRIAL

We all knew there was a lot of work to be done to prepare for the actual trial, so my family and David, our attorney, decided we needed another lawyer to be added to the team, to help out. David had an attorney in mind, his name was Scott and he was based in Chicago. Because the trial was occurring in Indiana we needed a lawyer licensed in Indiana which was David, the lead attorney however we were allowed to have the secondary attorney come from Illinois.

Triscennea, Steven and I went to Scott's office in downtown Chicago to meet with him. We briefly discussed the case, his views of how to proceed with the defense and we hired him. We had to make sure everyone on our team believed in our son's innocence and would work hard to prove it. I never had a doubt in my mind, or heart, that Steven would be found innocent and not be required to spend another day imprisoned. As it is written in Psalms 62:2, "He only is my rock and my salvation; He is my defense; I shall not be greatly moved." Psalms 91:14-15 reads "Because he hath set his love upon me, therefore will I deliver him: I will set him on high because he hath known my name. He shall call upon me and I will answer him: I will be with him in trouble: I will deliver him, and honor him."

I knew that we had a fight ahead of us, even though victory was already promised; we still had to fight. So we did not fight as those who knew not what the outcome would be, but as believers fighting victoriously. The prosecution's case was built on false witness statements. The main witness being the deceased thief's partner in the crime wave they were partaking in on the morning of the incident. They burglarized, approximately, a dozen motor vehicles, stealing radios, speakers and whatever else they thought was of value from the vehicles.

According to the partner in crime they were about to call it a night when they saw Steven's truck. His truck was adorned with 24" inch chrome rims and limo tinted windows, they just couldn't pass it up. The other false witness was a police officer who claimed that Steve told him that he looked out of his apartment window saw a guy breaking into his truck, so he grabbed his gun; went out and shot the guy. This false claim of the officer was easy enough to invalidate. Steve lived in a basement apartment that didn't even have a clear line of sight to his vehicle; let alone to enable him to see if anyone was in his truck or not.

We were unaware of all the things it would take to build a proper defense for our son, or how costly it would become. Our limited surplus of cash was rapidly being exhausted, so we had to do a lot of the leg work ourselves. We could not afford the luxury of hiring investigators to run down leads or to find additional witnesses. Steve had lived in a large building complex in Griffith, Indiana, which housed a little over a thousand residents. Steven told us that while he had his gun drawn and pointed at the thief in his truck, telling him to get out; a car had driven up, stopped observed him, and then drove off.

My wife and I spent weeks canvasing the apartment complex looking for that particular witness whose statement would immediately refute the prosecution's key witness' statement that Steve came out shooting without warning or saying a word. We never found that particular witness who may have been a visitor of someone who lived in the complex. We did, however, locate two witnesses in the same building as Steven who heard him yelling prior to the shooting.

One of the witnesses lived in the apartment directly above Steven's and she was acquainted with our son's fiancée. The other witness lived on the floor above the first witness; his apartment faced the courtyard portion of the complex, which is in the opposite direction of Steve's and witness number one's apartment. With some effort, we were able to obtain a signed deposition from both witnesses. They both agreed to testify in court on Steve's behalf. David told us to make sure we keep in contact with the witnesses because people do on occasion change their residences over a period of months. Well, wouldn't you know that both of our witnesses moved from the apartment complex prior to the time of receiving their court order to come and testify!

The young lady actually relocated to a different state and was difficult to get in contact with. But, by the Grace of God, and with much effort on our part, we were able to contact her. We gave her the court date and time that she was scheduled to appear and testify. We were instructed by David to offer to pay her plane fare and to compensate her for any lost wages she may incur as a result of appearing in court. She stated to us that this wouldn't be necessary because it was her pleasure and duty to come to the defense of an innocent man.

The other witness, a gentleman, who lived on the second floor of the same building in the apartment that faced the opposite direction of the complex, had also moved without leaving a forwarding address. He was the most difficult witness to track down between the two, because we absolutely had no idea of where he had moved. Since, we didn't have the funds to hire an investigator to track him down we did the work ourselves and trusted God for a positive outcome.

The two of us didn't just sit around wondering what to do, we prayed to Our Father, The Almighty God for direction then we proceeded to do the foot work. My wife and I knew that faith without works is dead, in other words praying to God and sitting around doing nothing wouldn't work. We searched the phone book for anyone with the same last name as our witness. David came up with a gentleman who lived in a suburb not far from us. We ended up going to that residence several times before catching anyone home. It turned out that was our witness' father's home. We left a message with his father for him to contact us, after explaining the situation to him and how vital it was for him to get in contact with us, as soon as possible.

Almost a week had past and he hadn't contacted us. The date he was to appear in court was drawing near. We went back to his father's house to see if he had heard from his son and if he was able to pass on our urgent plea for him to get back to us. By The Grace of my Daddy, The Almighty God, when we arrived at that residence this particular time our witness, the homeowners' son, answered the door. Triscennea and I were so elated to see him! We were so grateful that our faithfulness and persistence had paid off.

Immediately, we greeted him, reminding him who we were and our purpose for searching for him so diligently. He remembered who we were and knew why we were seeking him. Per David's instruction we offered to reimburse him for any lost wages that he may incur for appearing in court. He jokingly told us that we didn't want to do that because he currently earned close to two hundred dollars a day. He also stated that it wouldn't be necessary because, it was his civic duty to come forward and testify on behalf of an innocent man.

Our first witness, the young lady from the apartment above my son, testified on the night in question that she had heard yelling outside, then quiet, more yelling and finally gunfire. Her testimony agreed with Steve's statement that he yelled at the guy to get out first and only after the young man stated he had a gun also and began to reach for it, only then did Steven shoot him because he feared for his own life. The prosecutions witness, the partner in crime stated that Steve had run out of the apartment building and upon arriving at the middle of the parking lot began shooting, without uttering a single word. Their witness painted a picture of Steven running outside with the intent to shoot someone that was in the process of stealing his vehicle, which couldn't have been further from the truth.

Our second witness was the gentleman from the second floor apartment, which faced in the opposite direction of the parking lot. The position of his apartment played a key role in the importance of his testimony. Also, the fact that he served in America's Armed Forces added to the credibility of his testimony. He testified that he heard yelling, then concentrated gunfire approximately six shots, then he heard more yelling. His testimony also agreed with our first witness and with Steven's statement that he verbally confronted the now deceased young man before any gunfire occurred.

When the prosecution was given the opportunity to cross examine our first witness she tried to infer that she was friends with Steve's fiancée and they could have collaborated a statement for her to repeat on the witness stand. Our witness countered with she was acquainted with her by only seeing her in and around the apartment complex. She also stated that they had no prior conversations regarding her testimony before coming to court.

When the state's prosecutor cross-examined our second witness, she first attempted to imply that since he lived in the same building that somehow they all had collaborated on their statements before testifying. He simply stated that he only saw them in the building or parking lot before once or twice. He went on to say, other than greetings hello or like goodbye that they had no verbal contact. He ended his statement by saying he wasn't a talker. It was plain to see by his demeanor that was a totally accurate statement.

The prosecutor then asked for an explanation of the term concentrated gunfire, which meant three or more shots fired consecutively. In this case six shots fired consecutively. She proceeded to question his ability to even make such a claim. He referenced his time spent as a soldier in the Armed Forces and his own experience with firearms, specifically, automatic weapons. Apparently he was well aware of what concentrated gunfire sounded like.

We must remember as believers, or learn as unbelievers who want to believe how faith works. We must put forth the effort, we must work, sometimes very hard, and always trust God for the outcome.

Chapter 4

ADDITIONAL CHARGES FILED

When Steven was originally arrested in January of 2008 he was officially charged with murder. That would have made our defensive strategy much easier had it remained the only charge. The prosecutor filed additional charges such as; manslaughter, involuntary manslaughter, and illegal use of a firearm, to name only a few off the long list of charges that they had come up with. In doing so, they were increasing the number of charges that Steven would have to be found not guilty.

We all must be aware of the strategy of our enemy. Although, our enemy knew he was already defeated and that there was absolutely no chance of victory, he was determined not to just concede defeat. He was committed to fight to the bitter end. We as followers of Christ, should take note of the commitment of our enemy to fight to the end, never to give up no matter how bad things get, or look. We should remember, however that although we have been promised victory we still have to fight and never give up, or give in to the adverse circumstances that often times may arise.

Since the prosecution decided to file additional charges, we were forced to modify our defense strategy. In the midst of any battle; conditions and circumstances may dictate an abrupt change. We must remain unshakeable and unwavering in our resolve that the victory is ours. Our defensive strategy was modified primarily due to the additional charge of illegal use of a firearm. The prosecution knew that if Steven was found guilty of that charge, then we couldn't go forward with our defense claim of self-defense.

The prosecution knew that our whole defensive strategy hinged on self-defense, Steve's life was being threatened, and he acted in self-defense. As a result a young man, while in the commission of a crime, was shot dead.

If Steve was found guilty of committing a crime by using his firearm for his personal protection, he would be unable to claim self-defense. Our son, if found guilty of that charge, would be in the midst of an unlawful act himself, which would automatically negate our claim of self-defense. Steve had been living in Indiana for approximately one year prior to this incident. He had retained an Illinois driver's license and a FOI (Firearms Owners Identification) card while being a resident of Indiana.

In Indiana a resident can apply for and obtain a license to legally carry a firearm on their person. When Steve went to apply for a license to have a firearm in Indiana he was asked what was the purpose of owning a firearm. He stated home defense. He was then informed that he didn't need a license for that purpose. Steve never desired to carry a firearm on his person wherever he went. He had never left his residence carrying a firearm on him. The shooting occurred within the confines of the building complex where he lived. He never left the private property of the building complex, so therefore he was never among the general public when the shooting took place.

The prosecution tried to claim that once Steve crossed the threshold of his apartment door that his legal right to defend himself with his firearm ended. They claimed he was in the general public even while still being in the apartment building where he resided. The extremely large building complex was totally fenced in with a security guarded booth at the entrance, along with a barrier blocking the entrance which had to be lifted by the security guard on duty. In other words, this complex was nothing short of a gated community.

As a property owner in the state of Illinois, I have the right to defend myself with my firearm if my life is threatened by an individual, who claims to have a gun and reaches for it, while on my property. My property consists of my dwelling place as well as all the land surrounding it. Had the same identical situation with my son occurred in Illinois it would have been deemed self-defense, according to the police officers we questioned here in Illinois. My cousin, Shirley, also explained the situation to a judge here and they concurred that it would be a case of self-defense.

The internet news media reported the story and allowed the public to post comments on their website. The reporters conveyed the incident as if it were simply a shooting over the attempted theft of property. Our family and Steve's friends began to flood the website poster board with the true facts.

The young man had been shot and killed while in the process of committing a theft. However, the shooting occurred because he threatened my son's life with a gun he claimed to have had of his own. The fact that he didn't really have a gun was inconsequential because he stated that he did have one and began to reach for what Steve thought (by the assailants own admission) was a gun. Originally, the detective in charge of the case just stated that there wasn't a gun found on the deceased. It wasn't until later that we discovered he did have in his possession two very large, menacing knives. One knife was over 7 inches long, doubled edged with a serrated surface on one side and a hook on the end used for gutting animals. This was lying in his lap 3 quarters of the way opened. He was more than likely reaching for the opened knife in his lap, not a gun.

When viewing the toxicology report we discovered that the deceased had several drugs in his system. Three of which were marijuana, alcohol and Xanax; this could explain his nonchalant behavior while Steven had his weapon drawn and pointed at him, while commanding him to exit his vehicle. Upon hearing my son yelling at him to exit the vehicle, he just simply turned and looked at Steve starring at the drawn weapon and stating that he, also, had a gun. He then turned calmly back to continue the process of stealing the radio from his truck. Again Steve yelled for him to exit the vehicle. Only after the young man reached for something at his waist; did Steve fearing for his life shoot the young man.

The expert we hired on drug interactions reported on the assailant's possible state of mind due to the many drugs in his system. Due to the combination of alcohol, marijuana, and Xanax they most likely caused a state of euphoria, reckless and irrational behavior. Also according to a sworn statement from the partner in crime he was known to customarily carry a gun on him. Possibly in his drugged state he actually thought he did have his gun with him and that's why he wasn't afraid of Steve's gun pointed at him.

After the shooting occurred several residents exited their apartments and came outside to see what had happened, one of them was Steve's fiancée. He yelled to her to call the police as he laid his firearm down on the pavement, at the rear tire of the driver's side of the vehicle and awaited the arrival of the police. He informed one of the officers that arrived first on the scene as to what had happened. Steven told the officer that his fiancée woke him because she heard his truck alarm going off, he immediately turned it off and waited for it to reset. When the alarm reset, it went off again. This time he looked out of his basement apartment window to see if he could see why. He was unable to establish a clear line of sight to his vehicle from his basement window; because of the row of vehicles parked on the apartment side of the parking lot.

The parking area was designed, as such; there was a row of parking spaces right in front of the rear entrance of the building, which is where Steve's apartment window faced. Directly behind that row was a two- way driveway to allow traffic to come in and out of the complex, after the driveway was another row of parking spaces. Steve's truck was parked in that second row of parking spaces to the left in proximity to his basement apartment window. Therefore, when he looked out of his window he was unable to get a clear view of his vehicle; which forced him to go outside despite the fact that he was extremely tired and was just a few moments ago, asleep.

Due to the rash of recent apartment break-ins and robberies occurring in and around his apartment complex and the early morning hour, Steve brought his firearm with him for protection. When Steve exited his apartment he never anticipated that he would have to use his firearm or that he would even have to take it out of his pocket. These facts stated in the past few paragraphs should have been enough. We thought to refute the sworn statement of the one officer that was first on the scene. Normally, in cases like this it would simply be Steve's word against the police officer's. In most cases the jury would lean towards believing the officer.

Just to repeat what one of the first responding officers claimed that Steve told him regarding the shooting. He claimed, Steve said his alarm was going off, so he looked outside saw a guy breaking into his truck grabbed his gun to go outside to shoot him. Our facts clearly proved that Steve's line of sight was severely restricted from his apartment window, due to distance and proximity of the parking space his truck occupied. Because of these undeniable, easily verifiable facts, it wasn't just a case of Steve's word against the officers, it was a case of what was possible and what was impossible.

As I reflect back on this, despicably, weak case that the prosecution was presenting to a judge and jury; I sigh in amazement. A case built upon lies, false witness statements from credible and non-credible witnesses, yet, the prosecution moved forward boldly. Steadily acting as if they were seeking justice.

Chapter 5

CANCER DISCOVERED

A year had gone by since Steven had been charged with murder. He had moved back at home with us for about eight months, and working full time. I had been working just under a year on a part time temporary assignment that was supposed to last only ninety days. Because of the grace, mercy and favor of my Heavenly Father my temporary assignment was extended just shy of four times the length it should have lasted.

It was because of my Father in Heaven that I found favor with the corporation to which I was assigned. In a matter of months, I was promoted from being a Proxy Account Representative to a Peer Monitor/Proxy Account Representative. The story behind that promotion was actually pretty amazing because of how strangely it occurred. If my memory serves me correctly, I was informed that my name was chosen by the Head of the Quality Assurance Team, which was located in Dallas. I was pulled from my team, in the Call Center, to an office for a conference call with an officer over the Quality Assurance Team. I was asked my name, I replied, "Steven Gamble". The person on the other end of the call asked me to repeat my name which I did. I was then asked to get the person who called me into the office for the conference call, which I did and I was asked to leave the room and wait right outside for a moment.

In a few short moments, the lady exited the office and she informed me that a mistake had been made and profusely apologized for the mix up. They were looking for someone with the first name Steven, but not me, Steven Gamble. I did however, meet the quality standards that were set in place for the position, I just wasn't the one chosen. I returned back to my area and informed my supervisor, Naoni, of the misunderstanding and began to work again. She seemed surprised that a mistake like that had occurred and she asked me would I have been interested in the position, I replied yes.

I worked evenings, during the week, on this temporary assignment. The next evening, Naoni informed me that I needed to attend a meeting for Quality Assurance. I reminded her of the previous evenings misunderstanding with the same named employee who they really wanted. She reiterated that I was scheduled to attend, so I went. I attended the meeting; however, when they were distributing system access information there was nothing inputted for my name. The supervising agent in charge stated that my access would be forthcoming. When I inquired about the mix-up that had occurred, previously, she confirmed that it was indeed a mix up.

The supervisor conducting the meeting further informed me that when a certain individual heard about the situation they felt I would be an excellent candidate for the position and recommended me for it. When I inquired about the identity of the individual, I was just informed it was someone with enough influence to get my name added to the list after it was already released and approved.

I started this assignment in February of 2008 shortly after Steven was arrested and charged with murder. All of the people that I came in contact with there knew me as a joyful and happy person, who didn't appear to have a care in this world. Should the truth be told, I didn't because I had given the whole situation with Steven over to my Daddy, God. I simply placed it in His, more than capable Hands and left it there for Him to handle. When the people that I was closest to found out about my son being jailed for murder, prior to me starting this assignment, they were astonished. They asked me how I could walk around being happy and joyful while I was going through such a horrific situation. They simply couldn't understand it. I informed them that my God was in control of this situation and I trusted Him, completely.

I elaborated further by stating that He could and would handle this situation that I placed in His Hands, because He loves me and I trusted Him to do so. Therefore, since I had faith in Him to take care of it, how could I be anything other than my normal joyful, happy and carefree self? My God didn't give me a spirit of worry, so I never did, all the days, of my life and I wasn't about to start now. I know that my Daddy is The Almighty God, creator of the heavens and the earth, and everything therein. There is no problem, or situation, too small or too large that He can't handle.

I learned a long time ago, that my God can and does increase or promote you even when you don't ask or inquire about such advancement. It is simply called favor and the people who aren't the recipient of it will always say favor isn't fair. I purposely traveled back to when I started my temp assignment to illustrate what my circumstances were at that time. To show everyone that is reading this book how my God used my faithfulness to Him in the midst of a difficult situation to confound the wise.

I am so grateful that my testimony was used to draw people closer to my Heavenly Father. I was blessed to see and feel the power of my testimony's effect on the individuals I gave it to. I was so amazed how much of an affect this small thing I was going through and my reaction to it could have on people. I don't want anyone to get confused by me calling this a small thing, for if I was leaning on my own understanding, and depending on my power to handle it, I would have viewed it much differently. If I were to take on this situation by myself it would have been too heavy for me to handle. Believe me, that is a fact that I am in no way confused about.

My Father in Heaven loves us all so much that He requests us to cast all of our cares, fears and worries upon Him. He expects us to place all of the things in His Mighty Hands and to leave them there. We are to trust Him and believe that He has taken care of it already.

It is very important that when we leave it in His, more than capable Hands that we have the faith and patience for Him to work it out on our behalf. A lot of times, we believers think because it didn't occur in the time frame that we feel it should, we can take it back out of His Hands and try to handle it ourselves. In doing so, we take the responsibilities from God's Hand and return these heavy burdens on to ourselves. Granted, these are the same burdens we knew we were unable to handle in the first place.

When we assume this action of inaction our condition actually worsens. We were actually in a better state when we first, had the good sense to hand it over to God. In taking these things back, we allowed them to frustrate and to weigh us down, even further. Unfortunately, when we do come to the realization that we need to return these things to God's Hand because they are much too much for us to handle, we are usually so broken down, dismayed and weary. Very often, we re-approach God begging Him to take these things away from us. In acting in such a fashion, we are coming to God as if He doesn't want to, or perhaps He won't take the problem back, when, in fact, it was always His intention to handle it for us in the first place.

In the last week of January 2009 Steven was laid off from his job on Monday and my assignment ended on Friday of the same week. My wife noticed a lump on the left side of Steve's neck and inquired about it. He stated that it had been there a little over a month and when he would press on it mucous would be released into his throat. We convinced Steve that he needed to see a doctor about the lump. He was reluctant to go so I volunteered to accompany him to ensure that he would, indeed, go. Since, he didn't have any health insurance I suggested that we go to the county funded hospital on the west side of Chicago. He stated that he would prefer going to a closer facility, so we found one on the south side of Chicago.

Since we were both out of work we went there on the following Monday, at 8:00 am. A staff member informed us that Steve couldn't be seen without an appointment. They suggested that we go to the emergency room in order to be seen by a doctor. The two of us waited over twelve hours for his name to be called, and approximately another six hours to receive the results from the tests that were run. We were informed that the tests were inconclusive and they made an appointment to see a doctor at the west side facility. They informed us that the other facility was more advanced in technology and in addition, the specialists were located there.

They gave us an appointment for the following week along with a list of the tests that were run. I inquired would the test have to be repeated since we were going to a different facility. I was assured because it was another Cook County facility that they were connected by the same network and could access the results. Needless to say, they couldn't; so the same tests were run there along with several others. This went on a little over a month because after each battery of tests we had to make another appointment to receive the results. I accompanied my son for each visit, especially after he informed me that if I had not been with him that first time, which ended up taking a little over eighteen hours, he surely would have left.

A biopsy of the growth on Steve's neck was included in the last battery of tests that they ran. We returned for the tests results on March 5, 2009, which just happened to be my middle son's eighteenth birthday. As usual, I waited in the waiting area when Steve went back to see the doctor. When I saw him return from the examination room I realized that his whole countenance had changed. I immediately knew that something was very wrong. I swiftly left my seat and approached my son who was now at the reception desk making another appointment.

I gently, caringly asked my son what was wrong. He could barely respond while trying to fight back tears. He was finally able to utter the word "cancer", he then said, "Dad they said I have cancer". I threw my arms around my son and assured him that he would be fine because, my God is greater than cancer. I reminded him that he was already healed by Jesus' stripes. From that moment, I touched and agreed with him that we would fight this unwelcomed intruder and reminded him that victory had already been decided. You see, we weren't fighting as those who don't know the outcome, we knew we had already won.

Most unbelievers and some believers would look at this unfortunate turn of events along with his present legal battle, as much too much to bear. I personally viewed it as yet another opportunity for my God to get the glory as He takes on all attackers and defeats them with His Mighty Hand.

Chapter 6

TREATMENT PLAN
FORMULATED

When Steven and I returned for his appointment with the oncology physician, this time I went back with him to see the doctor. I vowed to do so from that day forward. I knew that the enemy would try to attack him more so if I, the Head of the family, wasn't present. Steven, Triscennea and I had done some research on the type of cancer the doctor said he had. We then comprised a list of questions for the doctor regarding his treatment plan, ratio of recovery, what stage the cancer was in, and what was his general prognosis?

The type of cancer Steve was afflicted with was nasal pharyngeal carcinoma, which is a very rare form of cancer not seen in the United States. This particular strain of cancer develops deep in the nasal cavity and can only be detected by a specialized series of tests. This cancer is most prevalent in parts of Africa and Asia where they actually conduct screenings for the disease, just as we, in America, perform routine mammograms on our female population of a certain age group. In Africa, as well as, in Asia it usually affects males from the ages of 18 – 30 that's when the testing occurs.

So, of course, the oncologist asked Steven had he recently done any traveling abroad. He had not. We were informed that the cancer was in stage 4 because it had already spread from his nasal cavity to his neck when it was first discovered. The doctor discussed the treatment plan he had devised, he planned to attack, this unwanted and uninvited intruder, most aggressively. We agreed completely with this attack strategy. His prognosis was very favorable, because of Steve's young age and his strong support system.

Even this man of science knew the best way to confront an enemy intruder was to attack, with a full arsenal. The doctor knew not to forge a passive attack on this formidable intruder that could prove ineffective and possibly recover from it. In any war, and be not mistaken, that's exactly what was going on within my son's body a full-fledged war. A war was raging between these cancer cells and his healthy cells. These cancerous cells didn't rest, slumber, slow down, or divert from their primary objective to seek, kill, and totally destroy the healthy cells. They were adamant in seeking new territory to take over and inhabit.

This enemy, cancer that Steve was at war with is actually a type and a shadow of our enemy satan. The aggressive mannerism that the cancer exhibits is the same manner that satan exhibits when he attacks. We, as believers are in a full-fledged war, constantly battling an enemy that doesn't rest, slumber, slow down or divert from his primary objective to seek, kill and totally destroy us. He is very adamant in seeking out new territory in our lives to take over and inhabit. The warfare that we are engaged fully in is fought on a spiritual plain; therefore, our weapons that we must fight with are spiritual.

In the New International Version Ephesians 6:12-17 explains our warfare and the weapons we are to use. "For our struggle is not against flesh and blood, but against the rulers, against the authorities, against the powers of this dark world and against the spiritual forces of evil in the heavenly realms. Therefore, put on the full armor of God, so that when the day of evil comes, you may be able to stand your ground, and after you have done everything, to stand. Stand firm then, with the belt of truth buckled around your waist, with the breastplate of righteousness in place, and with your feet fitted with the readiness that comes from the gospel of peace. In addition to all this, take up the shield of faith, with which you can extinguish all the flaming arrows of the evil one. Take the helmet of salvation and the sword of the Spirit, which is the word of God."

The warfare that we are engaged in, and our spiritual weapons as described in the passage above, with prayer, perseverance, praise, unwavering faith and fasting is more than enough to fight the good fight. Truly as believers we already have the foreknowledge that victory is ours as long as we fight the good fight of faith.

The oncology doctor set a schedule for Steve's treatment which consisted of a very strong dose of chemotherapy and radiation treatment. Over approximately a 12 week time frame he would receive radiation 5 days a week for 10 weeks and he would go for chemotherapy once every 3 weeks over the 12 week time frame. The radiation treatment was concentrated at the area of the bridge of his nose just under his eyes, all the way down to his chest area just below his collar bone. They directed the radiation at the origin of the cancer; which was in his nasal cavity and covered the area in which it had spread, to his neck.

These men of science knew exactly how to combat an invading force. They knew first to attack at the source of the invasion and then to pursue this enemy combatant in the direction that it was headed. The medical team knew they had a higher probability of success by using this formula to destroy this cancer that had invaded my son's body.

There is a very close correlation between the manner in which cancer attacks the body of an individual and how our enemy the devil chooses to attack The Body of Christ (The Church). Our enemy, first of all, finds a weak spot for his point of entry, more so often using a person or persons in the body to invade the body. Maybe, it is someone who allowed themselves to come under the subjection of the spirit of offense. He then waits patiently for that spirit to grow within that person or persons and, then, for it to spread to others. For he knows if it goes unchecked it can potentially spread throughout the entire body. The spirit of offense never works alone it will proceed to usher in other spirits such as un-forgiveness, strife, jealousy, judgmental-ness, self-righteousness, and rebellion. His goal is to cause in-fighting and complete chaos within the members of The Body of Christ. He knows, if he accomplishes his goal, we will be too busy fighting each other to fight him. Instead of praising God and waging war against him; which we were originally gathered together to do.

Be not confused our enemy, the devil, is very wise and has been waging this war long before any of us were born. He knows if he were to try a frontal assault on a unified Body of Christ that he would lose that battle most expediently. That's why he chooses to formulate an attack from within our ranks; it has been proven as an effective method in the past for him. He chooses wisely whom he will concentrate his forces on, within the body. Anyone who has been engaged in warfare before knows the quickest, most effective; way to stop an enemy force is to chop off the head (the leader). When the leader is removed from his seat of power and authority the rest of the body becomes ineffective and will often scatter in defeat.

So within the Body of Christ the enemy sets his sight on the Pastor, a person whom The Almighty God has appointed and anointed to be the Shepherd over a particular flock of believers. A person that He has given the authority and responsibility to preach, teach, and lead them forward, by example in serving God in the mighty way that He has called them to serve Him. When my Father in Heaven appoints a person to be a pastor it is an awesome responsibility. He gives them everything they need to be successful, in other words, my Daddy doesn't set anyone of us up for failure. There is a particular anointing, grace, measure of faith and a divine must that has to be imparted on such an individual.

This chosen individual is made aware ahead of time that this call to Pastoral Ministry comes at a great cost to them, their spouse and their children. Oh!! This great calling to become a Shepherd over a particular Body of Christ comes also with a great reward. To be chosen by God to serve Him in this capacity is such an honor, great privilege and responsibility; to be used by God to increase His Kingdom by leading a multitude of followers to go forth and witness to the unsaved, leading them in their confession of faith.

The enemy also uses this formula of waging war on our families. He first concentrates his forces on the head of the household which is the husband. God appointed and anointed man to be the Head, the covering for his wife and children. Being the head of the family is an honor, a great responsibility and comes at a cost. As the head, and as a husband we are to love our wives just as Christ loves the church, we are to love our wives as we love our own bodies. For he who loves his wife loves himself.

As the head it is our awesome responsibility to be the spiritual covering for the whole household and to lead by example. Because of this great responsibility placed on man God designated a helpmeet for us, a woman (wife) to assist with the raising of the children and management of the household, but the full accountability falls on the man. Therefore, the enemy attacks the man first, trying to remove him from his seat of authority by any means necessary. One method that the enemy uses against the head is to send a seducer his way. He has studied the husband and has seen what he likes and tries to lead him astray.

We as husbands should take heed to the Word of God in regards to this matter. As it is written in (NIV) 1 Corinthians 7:3-5. "The husband should fulfill his marital duty to his wife, and likewise the wife to her husband. The wife's body does not belong to her alone but also to her husband. In the same way the husband's body does not belong to him alone but also to his wife. Do not deprive each other except by mutual consent and for a time, so that you may devote yourselves to prayer. Then come together again so that satan will not tempt you because of your lack of self-control." We, men are the head and must realize that our enemy, satan, has us under constant surveillance looking for a way to infiltrate our household. His first choice is the man always, as I stated before to chop off the head then the household's strongest line of defense is gone.

If he can't get to the head; he then focuses his attack on the woman. He attempts to cause strife between husband and wife. At the same time he will attack the children so that he might cause total chaos in the household. We men as the head must remember that we are fighting a spiritual war. We must remember that our enemy is just using our wives and children to wage war against us. In reality they are just casualties of war to him, pawns being used and sacrificed, collateral damage.

If this battle was fought out on a game board it would be a Chess game, not Checkers. Our enemy plans his moves very carefully he always plans 4 to 5 moves ahead and he is constantly observing and studying his opponent.

Chapter 7

THE BATTLE BEGINS

The treatment plan had already been formulated; now, it was time for the battle to begin. When I stated it was time for the battle to begin I was referring to the battle on the medical front. I knew from the beginning when we were first informed of this intruder that had entered my son's body uninvited that we were going to wage the battle on two fronts medically (physical) and spiritually. We began the fight on the spiritual front as soon as we identified the intruder. We weren't burdened with the activity of having to formulate a battle plan on this front. The men of science formulated their plan of attack from the knowledge found in their medical books. Our plans of attack as well as the weapons we were to use were already formulated. We simply had to refer to Ephesians 6:12-17 located in the sword of the spirit, which is the word of God which was stated in the previous chapter.

We also had specific instructions on calling for reinforcements in this battle, found in James 5:14-16 which states "Is any one of you sick? He should call on the elders of the church to pray over him and anoint him with oil in the name of the Lord. And the prayer offered in faith will make the sick person well; the Lord will raise him up. If he has sinned, he will be forgiven. Therefore confess your sins to each other and pray for each other so that you may be healed, the prayer of a righteous man is powerful and effective."

For those of us who choose to trust and believe in the word of God. We will find everything we need to know about living in this world and the proper preparation for entering into the next one, within the pages of the Bible (God's word). In approximately a week or so after the medical treatment plan had been formulated, my son and I began our journey back and forth from the hospital. Monday through Friday we were there approximately 4 hours a day. We spent those hours mostly waiting for his radiation treatment, which only took 45 minutes or so to complete.

On the days he had to receive chemotherapy we were there 10 to 12 hours. My Heavenly Father allowed us to have this time together to strengthen our relationship with him as well as with each other. We took this time that we had to do just that, our relationship with each other progressed and strengthened to a much higher level than I had ever anticipated. I was so blessed to see God working in his life by increasing his faith in Him and strengthening him as we fought this battle together. Steven never complained even as our week of traveling back and forth for his treatments continued.

My son would become so sick and weak every time he received his very strong doses of chemotherapy, but remained strengthened in his faith in our God. He moved forward past those physical feelings because he knew, he was already healed by Jesus stripes and that victory wasn't something that we hoped for, it was already promised. When the oncologist performed a biopsy of the growth on Steve's left side of his neck it caused it to grow further and it spread to the right side of his neck. So he ended up with a larger growth on the left side and almost equally large growth on the right side. Before he ever got started with the radiation treatment they had to take measurements of the area where the radiation would be concentrated, so that they could create a mask for the particular dimensions. The mask fit very snugly over the growths on his neck in the beginning. After 4 to 5 weeks into the treatment the mask didn't fit snugly anymore. The tumors in his neck had shrunk so much that they weren't even visible to the eye on the outside of his neck any longer. Steve had to be measured again so he could be refitted with the newly designed mask for his radiation treatments.

The team of doctors in charge of his radiation treatment informed us in the beginning that 6 to 8 weeks into his treatment would be the most difficult period for him. They knew beforehand that after so many weeks of concentrated radiation it would cause severe damage to his throat and his saliva glands; making it extremely difficult and painful for him to swallow. The radiation caused his saliva glands to produce very little saliva and it literally cooked his throat; making it almost unbearable to swallow. That being said, coupled with the nausea from receiving chemotherapy he immediately began losing weight, rapidly. The weight loss was a major concern for all of us; we knew he had to have enough nutrients so he could remain strong enough to continue with those grueling treatments. The doctor gave him medication to assist his saliva glands in producing more saliva and he also received medicine to help with the nausea. We as human beings know we need to eat in order to live and be strong. When we are fighting any sort of sickness it is imperative that we not only eat for strength; but may have to consume certain nutrients more abundantly so that we can be stronger for the battle.

This method also applies with fighting any sort of sickness on the spiritual plain. We knew it was equally, if not more imperative that we feed our spirit man, as well. Some may ask how do we feed our spirit man. (NIV Matthew 4:4) "It is written: man does not live on bread alone, but on every word that comes from the mouth of God." We began to increase the diet of our spirit man as well. We extensively increased our consumption of the word of God; we also took our praise and prayer life to a height that we never experienced before.

We as a people know that our physical bodies (man) weaken day by day, year after year as we grow older; it is simply the law of physics. We as believers know that as our physical man weakens by time, our spiritual man can and should grow stronger with time. In order for this metamorphosis to occur, we must continue to grow in faith with the reading of the word of God, trusting God, exercising our faith by praising God in the midst of our trials and tribulations.

The enemy knows it is more probable to break us down by attacking relentlessly on the natural plain, our physical bodies. He hopes that we will concentrate all of our efforts in strengthening our physical man that we leave our spirit man weakened from malnutrition and vulnerable for his next wave of attacks on the spiritual plain. We as believers who have been called specifically for spiritual warfare, such as I, must always be prepared to defend on all fronts that the enemy chooses to attack from, not only to defend, but to launch a retaliatory attack on the enemy at any given moment.

We must remember that our enemy, the devil, is well-versed in the art of war. He knows one of the first, if not the most important rule is to know your enemy. He has spent his time observing and studying man since our time of creation. He has discovered our strengths, weaknesses, likes, dislikes and where we are most vulnerable. The devil uses our emotions, and or feelings, as a focal point for his attack. The most popular feeling he uses against us is our anger, jealousy, low self-esteem, guilt, hurt, abandonment, rejection and blame. The enemy knows that this particular set of feelings can in a lot of cases lead us to sin and sin leads to death (separation from God). He knows if he is able to separate us from God; who is the source of our strength and power that we become weakened and vulnerable for his wave of attacks. The enemy always attacks in waves; just as a boxer attempting to win a title match uses a specific combination of punches in order to achieve a knockout.

Steve's body required him to consume much more fluids after his chemotherapy treatments. He had to be hydrated in order to flush out the chemicals he consumed through chemo. That became more of a challenge as the treatments went on because of his difficulty with swallowing. We ended up spending many more additional hours at the hospital so he could receive fluids via an IV drip. We even had to take additional trips on the weekends to the emergency room because of his dehydration. So now we were engaged in a battle against dehydration and rapid weight loss; which left him in a weakened, vulnerable state. We knew not to concentrate all of our time, strength and efforts to fight on this physical front alone.

There was still a battle being fought on the spiritual front in which we had to increase our efforts in order to achieve victory. We began to increase our time spent reading the word of God, praying, praising and worshiping God we actually took our efforts to the next level. I thank my Heavenly Father that our family wasn't engaged in this battle on the spiritual front alone. My Daddy (the Almighty God) already knew that this time was going to come to pass, so he already made provisions for us to fight the good fight of faith.

My God planted us in the body of Christ (church) called Rhema Word Kingdom Ministries where we are under the anointing, authority and covering of a mighty man of God, Pastor Gerald L Glasper. He is the Pastor that Beautiful and I searched for our whole adult lives; a man that is a true follower of Jesus Christ and has such a grace and anointing on his life. Being a member of this particular and peculiar body of Christ, I had a legion of prayer warriors to touch and agree with, to engage in this battle with and to declare victory with. My Rhema Word family was with us from the onset of this battle all the way to the declaration of victory.

Chapter 8

APPROACHING
THE BRINK OF VICTORY

I had faithfully been there with my son through the eight weeks of his radiation treatments except for the last day. I know now that all while we were in battle with the enemy that he constantly and consistently searched for a chink in my armor, any opening, no matter how small, and he found one. I was so concerned with strengthening my son Steven and the rest of my family, making sure everyone else was fit for battle, I allowed an opening for the enemy to attack me. He has studied me for years and knows how he has been successful in mounting an attack against me in the past, so when he saw an opening he simply went to his old playbook and waged a successful attack against me.

I had made a serious error while being engaged in battle with the enemy much older and wiser than myself. I allowed pride to enter my being, at some point I felt I was strong enough and decided to pray for everyone else. To fight in this battle and I stopped praying for myself to be strong enough to go forward. I stopped relying on God to strengthen me when I stopped praying for myself in this battle. I provided the enemy with an opening. Most people have heard the phrase that pride comes before a fall; well, I am here to verify that it is so true. Pride had me thinking that I was strong enough and I had to concentrate my prayers for everyone else's strength except my own. I instantly became weakened and vulnerable to the enemy's attack and sought my usual means of escape through the use of drugs. I abandoned my son on his last day of his radiation treatment because I allowed pride to enter into the equation. Condemnation soon followed, I was so angry with myself I couldn't see how I could be forgiven for such an act of selfishness. Earlier on, in my history of escapism through the use of drugs it wouldn't take so long for me to come to myself and come back home. In time, I soon learned of the disease theory of my actions stating that I had a disease called addiction and that I wasn't responsible for my disease. The leading authorities informed me through their literature that I had an incurable disease that if left untreated that it would lead to jails, institutions and death.

Throughout many years of my life I have learned all that I could about this aspect or opinion of my unseemingly destructive behavior. At first, I was relieved to hear that it wasn't my fault I had a disease and that I was not responsible for my behavior once I started using drugs. They told me that I was powerless over my addiction and they would equip me with tools to combat the disease. The clinical staff taught me the only way to have victory over this disease is not to pick up in the first place because I was in battle with an enemy that was greater than myself. They taught me that I had to choose a higher power to rely on to assist me in this battle and that it could be anything such as the 12 steps of recovery, recovery meetings, group sessions or a God of my own understanding. They stated that these methods for recovery, from the disease of addiction which they diagnosed me with having, have been proven to be effective for decades in helping other addicts. I would like to state first of all; that I am not an authority on the disease of addiction. I can't advise anyone on a clinical level how to combat this disease of addiction. I am in no way stating or refuting that their methods, which have been proven to work for thousands of people are incorrect, however, these methods aren't effective for me nor have they been anything but a temporary relief of my symptoms.

My brothers and sisters, in Christ, there has always been a battle waging within me, a strife of two natures which the apostle Paul best describes in Romans 7:14-25 as, "We know that the law is spiritual; but I am unspiritual, sold as a slave to sin. I do not understand what I do. For what I want to do I do not; but what I hate I do. And if I do what I do not want to do, I agree that the law is good. As it is, it is no longer I myself who do it, but it is sin living in me. I know that nothing good lives in me, that is, in my sinful nature. While I have the desire to do what is good, but I cannot carry it out. For what I do is not the good I want to do; no, the evil I do not want to do-this I keep on doing. Now if I do what I do not want to do, it is no longer I who do it, but it is sin living in me that does it. So I find this law at work: when I want to do good, evil is right there with me. On my inner being I delight in God's law; but I see another law at work in the members of my body, waging war against the law of my mind and making me a prisoner of the law of sin at work within my members. What a wretched man I am! Who will rescue me from this body of death? Thanks' be to God Jesus Christ our Lord! So then, I myself in my mind am a slave to God's law, but in the sinful nature a slave to the law of sin."

I always knew deep down in my spirit that my issues with escapism through the use of drugs were rooted in sin, my sinful nature. I never agreed with nor did it ever feel right to follow the protocol of the recovery meetings which requires everyone to state their names and to label ourselves as addicts or alcoholics. I refuse to give myself a false label, to identify myself as an addict or an alcoholic is simply a lie. I am a son of the Most High God, not a God of my understanding, not a higher power that I devised and made up as I go along. My God is God, and He changes not, He is the same yesterday, today and forever more.

A lot of times, I will put the blame on the enemy (the devil) when in fact the true enemy I was battling was in me; my sinful nature. The whole drug scene was an effective tool used by the enemy to keep me away from becoming who God has called me to be and the feeling of condemnation kept me away from fulfilling my purpose longer and longer. I am and always have been my greatest critic. I use to place myself at a much higher standard than everyone else because of the spirit of pride. Whenever I failed, I convicted myself so severely and condemned my actions as unforgivable. Condemnation began to keep me away from my loved ones longer each time I would fail. The spirit of condemnation kept me from praying to my Heavenly Father for forgiveness because I couldn't forgive myself, so I couldn't see how God, or anyone else, could forgive me either.

The apostle Paul provided us with a solution to our struggle with our two natures and addressed the feeling of condemnations in Romans 8:1-11, "Therefore there is now no condemnation for those who are in Christ Jesus because through Christ Jesus the law of the Spirit of life set me free from the law of sin and death. For what the law was powerless to do in that it was weakened by the sinful nature, God did by sending his own Son in the likeness of sinful man to be a sin offering. And so he condemned sin in sinful man, in order that the righteous requirement of the law might be fully met in us, who do not live according to the sinful nature but according to the Spirit. Those who live according to the sinful nature have their minds set on what that nature desires; but those who live in accordance with the Spirit have their minds set on what the Spirit desires. The mind of sinful man is death, but the mind controlled by the spirit is life and peace; the sinful mind is hostile to God. It does not submit to God's law; nor can it do so. Those controlled by the sinful nature cannot please God.

Paul goes on to say, "You however are controlled not by the sinful nature but by the Spirit, if the Spirit of God lives in you. And if anyone does not have the Spirit of Christ, he does not belong to Christ. But if Christ is in you, your body is dead because of sin, yet your spirit is alive because of righteousness. And if the Spirit of him who raised Jesus from the dead is living in you, he who raised Christ from the dead will also give life to your mortal bodies through His Spirit who lives in you."

I am fully aware that if I rely on my own power and strength that I can't effectively go into battle with the enemy (the devil). It, however, took longer for me to learn this same fact when battling the enemy in me, my sinful nature. I have to rely on the power of my God and constantly pray for strength whenever my flesh rises up against me because I am unable to kill off the fleshly desires by myself. Steven had his last radiation treatment without me being present with him which I truly regret not being there with him to the end. He had one more treatment of chemotherapy to go to and I was present to take him there for that. The way his treatment plan was scheduled he had a two or three week rest before he had to return to be x-rayed to find out how effective the treatments had been. However, my son and I ended up having to go back to the hospital during the course of those weeks because he suffered from dehydration as a result of his last chemo treatment. We did have a must needed rest from our grueling traveling schedule and his body had a much-needed rest from his intensely grueling treatments.

We thank our Heavenly Father for getting us through this difficult stage in our battle with the enemy through prayer, worship and praise. We gave our God all the glory for seeing us through thus far, for we knew that if it had not been for the Lord being on our side we wouldn't have been able to make it through this ordeal. Steve was extremely weakened physically from all those weeks of treatments and his body showed significant evidence of the stress he had endured during that time frame. The swelling on both sides of his neck were completely gone, which was a sign that the radiation was successful.

We took this time to assist Steven in the process of recuperation. We knew it would take time for his throat to heal and for his saliva glands to start functioning normally again. We knew we had to make sure he received the proper nutrients to help strengthen and build him back up, physically. Steve's spirit man, however, was as strong or stronger than it had ever been before, so we all continued to praise and glorify our God for all he had done and all he was going to do. We continued to celebrate our impending victory over our enemy.

Chapter 9

THE DOCTOR'S REPORT

Steve and I returned to the hospital so he could be tested for the presence of cancer. We had to set an appointment after the tests were completed to return for the results. While we were waiting to receive the results back we continued to praise, glorify and magnify our Heavenly Father for keeping us, strengthening us and for giving us the victory over this enemy called cancer. The date finally came for us to return to the doctor for the test results. We were looking forward to receive a favorable doctor's report however, when we were called to the back to see him I could tell by his demeanor that he didn't have good news for us.

The doctor proceeded to give us the test results. He stated that the cancer was gone from his nasal cavity and from his neck. He then reported that the cancer had metastasized to Steve's liver which was very serious. The doctor went on to state that he had hoped that the aggressive methods that were used to battle the cancer would have eradicated it totally. When Steve heard that the cancer had metastasized to his liver a look of devastation came over him. When I saw my son's expression concerning the doctor's report I immediately started to confront his disappointment and fear.

I knew when engaged in warfare, when the enemy has lost ground in a particular battlefield he doesn't just give up and concede defeat. It is strategically smarter to pull your offenses away from that position and move to another territory as your point of attack. We all were surprised to hear that the enemy invader cancer had moved to another area to attack.

The treatment plan formulated by Steve's doctors was supposed to have had that possibility covered. The radiation portion of his treatment was devised to attack and obliterate the cancer at the point of this attack. The chemotherapy portion of his treatment was designed to stop the cancer from spreading to any other area and the doses were so strong it should have been able to do just that.

I reminded Steve that our God is greater than cancer and for him to remember that he was already healed by Jesus' stripes. I attempted to have Steve look at the positive side of this report we had defeated the cancer at its origin and we will proceed and attack it where it had relocated. We are more than conquerors through Jesus Christ who strengthens us. I proceeded to ask the doctor what our next move was, in other words, what was the next plan of attack going to be? He expressed his surprise and disappointment with the fact that the first treatment plan failed because we attempted to defeat this cancer so aggressively. He felt it should have been successful.

The doctor stated that the only weapon we could use medically now since it moved to the liver was chemotherapy. He needed to confer with his fellow physicians to develop a new treatment plan. I asked the doctor what was the percentage rate of successfully defeating this cancer in a case such as ours. The doctor actually informed us that our best opportunity to defeat this cancer had passed when we failed to do so with our first aggressive plan of attack. He went on to inform us that the percentage rate for successfully defeating this cancer now was less than 5%.

I then looked at my son, then turned back to face the doctor and told him that was good. I went on to inform him that it really didn't matter if the percentage rate was 0% because I actually wasn't depending on him to heal my son nor have I truly been since the very beginning. I turned back to my son, held his hands, looked him straight in his eyes and told him that we would fight this enemy together and defeat it. I told him as we touched that we needed to agree at that very moment that we would trust our Heavenly Father, the Almighty God to give us the victory that he had already promised us. The oncology doctor informed us that he would contact us in a few days or so with a new schedule for Steve's next round of chemotherapy treatments. Upon leaving the doctor's office I informed my wife of the doctor's report.

Triscennea didn't take the news of the doctor's report, or his prognosis, very well. She experienced a range of emotions the first one she expressed was sadness. She asked how Steve took the news? I informed her that he too was saddened by it and showed vivid signs of disappointment and discouragement. I also told her how I attempted to encourage our son not to give up, that he wasn't in this fight by himself and that I would be there by his side until we're able to claim victory. My wife then expressed her feelings of disappointment, discouragement and outrage. She was so angry at the medical team for their failure to contain and eradicate the cancer; she felt that they didn't do enough or even try hard enough to cure Steven.

I reminded her that in the beginning of all of this that we touched and agreed that we were putting all of our faith and trust in our Heavenly Father, the Almighty God to heal our son and make him whole again. I told her that the doctor's report hasn't changed anything because they were never in control of this situation, our God was, always has been and continues to be the final authority. I told Beautiful (Triscennea) that I didn't care how bad it looked in the natural, that my faith in my God's healing and restorative power would not waiver. I reminded her that our son was already healed by Jesus' stripes and I told her that she should stand in agreement with me.

My faith and trust in my Father grew, exponentially, during the course of this battle. I learned the importance and the practice of praising God in the midst of this battle no matter if it appeared like we were losing or gaining ground. It simply didn't matter to me, I knew that my Daddy (the Almighty God) had the final say. My Father made it so easy for me to walk by faith and not by sight it was truly amazing to me and to those who encountered me. I remember praying to my God while relaxing in a hot tub of water about how grateful I was that He increased my measure of faith so much. The Holy Spirit immediately reminded me that I asked for this increase in my faith long ago and He brought it back to my memory with crystal clear clarity.

I remembered about thirty or so years ago I was watching a movie on television, there was a woman of God who encountered a man who was just in a gunfight and was shot; he pointed his gun at her and attempted to take her hostage. This mighty woman of God refused to be taken so he threatened to kill her; she still refused and stood her ground unafraid. The gun man saw that she wasn't afraid even as he proceeded to take aim and pull the trigger; so he asked her why she wasn't afraid. The woman informed him that he couldn't cause her any harm unless her Father in Heaven gave him permission to do so and she was more than willing to die if that was His Will. I sat there, in my seat in awe of this woman's faith and how she was able to stand her ground unafraid and trust in God's Will for her no matter what the outcome would be. I said in that moment, "Now that's the kind of faith that I want to have." As I lay there in the tub remembering I began to weep heavily with joy; just as I am right now while writing this.

Steve and I proceeded home; on the way we prayed to God to strengthen us for this next phase of the battle we were entering in. Steve's body was still in a vulnerable and weakened state, the doctor's report struck a blow at his spiritual man also. I know during this waiting period for the next treatment plan that we had to provide nourishment for his natural man as well as his spiritual man. We remained aware that we were still battling this enemy on two fronts; there were two battlefields we had to defend one in the physical realm and the other in the spiritual realm. They were both critical areas so we took this time to strengthen Steven as well as ourselves, physically and spiritually.

My son Steven continued to lose weight even though he was eating because he wasn't consuming enough calories to maintain a constant weight. His throat wasn't healing as quickly as we had hoped and his saliva glands still weren't producing the necessary amount of saliva. We sought continually to find ways for Steve to get more calories into his system. We knew his body wouldn't effectively be able to fight this battle if he continued to become weaker and weaker due to malnourishment. As a family we continued to pray and trust God for strengthening Steve physically and to restore his bodily functions back to the state that he had created it to function. We knew no man could know more about how the body should function than the one who created it from dust, the Almighty God Himself.

We knew that if our God chose to He could instantly heal Steve's throat and restore his saliva glands back to their full functioning capabilities, as well as, cause the cancer to be removed with one word from Him. Being aware that our God is all-powerful and yet our son was still going through this battle with an already defeated foe, we trusted in our God's Will that this was necessary to fulfill His purpose to bring glory to His name. My family and I didn't waste any precious time asking God why he allowed this to happen to our son; we more wisely spent our time praying, praising and trusting God to see us through this battle to its victorious end.

Chapter 10

PHASE 2
OF THE BATTLE BEGINS

A few days had passed when we were contacted by the oncologist, he informed us that Steve would begin receiving a lower dosage for his chemotherapy treatment than before due to his decreased weight and weakened state. The doctor also informed us that Steve had to start gaining his weight back in order to be strong enough to withstand the chemotherapy treatments. The first day of his first treatment came around; we arrived at the hospital at the scheduled time. I remained with Steve until they started the IV line to administer the treatment. I decided to walk to a store which was approximately 5 blocks away; after I had traveled 3 ½ blocks into my journey I received a call from my son asking for me to return, immediately.

I quickly turned around and hurried back to be with him. When I arrived back a few moments later they had already stopped the treatment because Steve had become extremely ill after only a short time of receiving the chemotherapy treatment. My son had begun to have problems breathing and felt as though he was going to pass out so they stopped the administering of the chemotherapy because of these symptoms. They began giving Steve fluids right after stopping the treatment so they could flush out the chemicals from his system that were making him ill. The chemicals used in the chemotherapy treatments are nothing less than poison to the person's body that they are treating. This method of attacking cancer is very crude at best because of the severe damage that it causes to the whole body.

The doctor cautioned us that if Steve didn't start gaining his weight back that he possibly wouldn't be strong enough to withstand the treatments. He also told us if Steve couldn't withstand the treatments of chemotherapy there was nothing else he could do for him medically, to combat this cancer. In the beginning of this battle with this enemy invader cancer my faith and trust had been and still remains in my God for the healing and full restoration of my son. I knew that my God who is God has all power and that He would heal Steve by whatever method He chose to use. He could heal Steve through the doctor's treatment or simply speak a word and he would be healed, instantly. Since we weren't aware of what method our God would use, we of course prayed, praised and glorified God and used the doctor's method of treatments in case that was the way He would heal him.

As it is written in the book of James 2:26 b) "Faith without deeds is dead," so we put forth our efforts with the doctors prescribed treatments and prayed to God for a favorable outcome. My Heavenly Father did bless our efforts because the radiation treatments Steve received eradicated the cancer at its origin, which gave us the victory in Phase 1 of the battle. Phase 2 of this battle ensued as a direct result of our victory in the first phase, the enemy invader lost the battle at the point of invasion. The enemy (cancer) had jumped borders and had invaded a new territory to wage a new attack against Steve's liver.

Some people may pose the question how we could claim victory in our initial battle with this enemy cancer. Well it's simple, because after Steve's radiation and chemotherapy treatments there was no trace of cancer found in the areas where the initial invasion occurred. The fact that this enemy had to re-concentrate its forces in a different area to wage a new attack is evidence that it lost the first battle; but hadn't conceded defeat in this war. Our family would never concede defeat in this war because we knew that our God is all-powerful and we were already promised victory. We took our prayers and praise to our Heavenly Father to an even higher level than previously, in full confidence of victory.

While Steve was engaged in this battle against cancer, he still was fighting yet another battle, a battle for his continued freedom. When we initially informed the court system about his battle with cancer; they exhibited some compassion and leniency. If for a medical incident or reason he couldn't be present for court hearing they wouldn't produce a warrant for his immediate arrest. The last time Steve was in court he was required to stand but he was so weak he was unable to do so, so they allowed him to sit instead. We all knew that the prosecution's case was ridiculously weak at best. If Steve will be found guilty of even one of the charges it probably would have been the least severe one and should be constituted time served from the three months he spent in County jail.

I knew in my heart in the very beginning when Steve was released from jail that my God would not allow his freedom to be taken away again. That was already decided and I was standing firm in the fact that my God is all-powerful and once He freed Steven from the hands of his false accusers, that was it. So it didn't matter to me how bad things appeared in the natural I would continue to stand on God's word as found in Psalms 62:2, "He only is my rock and my salvation; He is my defense; I shall not be greatly moved." Psalms 91:14-15 says "Because he hath set his love upon me, therefore will I deliver him: I will set him on high because he hath known my name. He shall call upon me and I will answer him: I will be with him in trouble; I will deliver him and honor him."

Most of us have heard the saying: "It's always darkest before the dawn," well things definitely appeared to be very dark at this point. But I knew that my Heavenly Father has the final say over everything. I knew that the doctors and the judicial system weren't in control of Steve's destiny, God was. We as a family of faithful believers had a choice to place our trust in the doctors and the judicial system or continue to trust the word of the Almighty God no matter how bad things may have appeared. We chose God. We exhibited our choice by continually praising God with all of our might; declaring victory over all adversaries. The enemy (satan) sought to use the seemingly unwinnable situations to break us and became very confused when we were strengthened in spite of them and we continued to praise the Almighty God.

We learned earlier on in these battles that we were engaged in that praising God in the midst of them served a twofold purpose. First, we showed God that we trusted him no matter how bad things appeared to get. Secondly, we confused the enemy because he was hitting us with everything he could think of to break us and it failed. His attempts not only failed miserably, we had the audacity to continue to praise God, joyfully, as he unloaded his arsenal at us. I truly learned more about my responsibility as the head and being the spiritual covering for my family. I knew there was a certain grace attached to this huge responsibility. I have the authority to lead my family in our reaction to these adverse situations; I was the head praise singer, dancer and motivator of our family.

I know now that my household is the first church that I have the awesome responsibility to serve as Pastor. Giving praise to my Heavenly Father, the Almighty God is a daily occurrence in my household and so is prayer. To be totally honest, that wasn't always the case; it truly started when we began battling the enemy for my son's freedom from false imprisonment and then from the enemy invader, cancer. It is strange how God can use two seemingly devastating situations, such as ours, to be a catalyst to move us forward in our walk of faith with Him. It's equally amazing to measure the very different rates of growth by my individual family members. Logically, one would assume that the different growth rates would primarily depend upon where the individual was in their walk of faith in the beginning.

I can testify that was not always the case because I have been a witness to it. You can have two siblings who have just experienced the passing of their mother who raised them both in the same household. Their walk of faith is seemingly equal, I use the term seemingly purposely because I am but a man, therefore, I am unable to truly know the intricacies of another person's heart or measure with accuracy a person's walk of faith; only God knows an individual's heart and with accuracy knows where a person is in their walk with Him. At any rate, two siblings who appear to be at the same point in their walk of faith experienced the exact same loss and it causes one of them to draw nearer to God; the other to become so angry that he withdraws from God totally.

One sibling increases his dependency on and faith in God. The other retracts from God and truly questions his faith in Him. The first attends church, faithfully, and even starts attending Bible study and finally commits to joining a ministry. The other becomes very bitter and stopped praying to God and stopped attending church altogether. There were two other siblings same case scenario, however, these siblings walk with God was outwardly at very different stages. Both of them were saved. One of them hadn't attended church regularly since being saved many years ago. The other after being saved was on fire for the Lord, he attended worship every Sunday, Bible study every Wednesday and joined a ministry shortly after becoming a member of the body of Christ he was meant to be planted. Shortly after faithfully serving in a ministry he answered the call on his life and began training to be a licensed minister He was seemingly well on his way and fulfilling the destiny God had for him.

Then, suddenly without warning, their mother went home to be with the Lord. The two siblings were devastated over the passing of their mother, but they were able to keep it together until after the home going celebration for her. The first sibling, who hadn't attended church regularly since being saved many years ago, started praying to God fervently for strength and peace to see her through this very difficult sense of loss that she was feeling. She began attending church every Sunday and Bible study every Wednesday seeking peace and strength in the presence of God. One particular Wednesday at Bible study they taught about God's sovereignty; she truly received that message and a miraculous peace came over her. This teaching didn't occur until after several months of her attending Sunday worship and Wednesday Bible study, faithfully.

Sometimes God will use the passing of a loved one to draw us nearer to him. A lack of patience could have spoiled her deliverance in this situation because it took several months for her to hear just what she needed to receive the peace she so diligently sought. Her perseverance paid off. We as human beings are impatient by nature, to a fault. Too often, we Christians pray to God for something and when it doesn't happen within our expected time frame we even try to accomplish the thing we prayed about ourselves or become angry with God and stop trusting in the power of prayer.

The other sibling who had been on fire for the Lord since being saved and shortly thereafter answered his call to ministry reacted to the passing of his mother very differently. He became very angry with God after attending his mother's homegoing celebration. He felt that he was doing everything right since he got saved. He attended Sunday worship and Wednesday Bible study faithfully from the beginning and he even answered the call to ministry. He couldn't understand why God would take his mother from him while he was serving him so faithfully and diligently. His anger soon turned to bitterness so he stopped praying to God, going to Sunday worship, Wednesday Bible study and stopped his training to become a licensed minister. Had he not severed all his communication with God, he could have been present for that Wednesday Bible study with his sister to receive the message on God's sovereignty. He could've received that miraculous peace as she did if he had persevered to the end.

The Gamble Family

My "Beautiful" wife Triscennea

and our sons

Steve, Tremont and Centarious

In Loving Memory of Steven

*I have fought a good fight, I have finished my course,
I have kept the faith: Hencefourth there is laid up for me
a crown of righteousness, which the Lord, the righteous judge,
shall give me at that day: and not to me only, but unto all them
also that love his appearing. ` 2 Timothy 4:7*

Triscennea Gamble

Simply "Beautiful"

"Beautiful"
My wife and best friend.

Tre' - Steve - Centarious   *Me and my Sons*

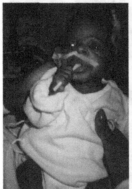

Tremont "Our Miracle"

Tremont welcomes baby Centarious

Triscennea was a "Beautiful" mother.

Steve our beloved #1 Son

In Loving Memory Of

Our Big Brother

Never would have made it without my parents.

The Gamble boys best friend. Our dog "Deja".

Tre' came home with a fade.

Proud Parents

Chapter 11

THE POWER OF PERSEVERANCE

Despite our efforts to ensure Steve received enough calories to start gaining his weight back we were unsuccessful. In fact we weren't even able to stabilize his current weight; he kept losing weight despite our best efforts. The damage caused by his radiation treatments to his throat was healing but not as rapidly as we anticipated or hoped for. His salivary glands still weren't producing a sufficient amount of saliva coupled with the severity of the damage to his throat it was very difficult for him to swallow.

We had another appointment to see the oncologist, so we went. When the doctor spoke to Steve he would respond without fully opening his mouth. The Doctor was very disturbed by this. He told Steve that he had to open his mouth fully to talk before he experienced a condition called lock jaw. He explained that lock jaw occurs when a person doesn't use their muscles required for opening and closing their mouth for a long period of time. He expressed his concern about Steve's continual weight loss and asked him why he wasn't eating more. Steven informed him that it was still so painful to swallow because of the lack of saliva and his extremely sore throat.

The oncologist then examined Steve's throat after finally getting him to open his mouth wide enough. Upon the completion of his examination he stated that his throat had healed considerably but not totally. In other, words with the medicine that he was taking for producing saliva and the state of healing his throat was in, he should be able to eat and swallow much easier now. He reminded Steve the only way to battle this cancer that moved to his liver medically was with chemotherapy. He further informed him that if he were to be hospitalized because of this continuous weight loss he wouldn't be able to receive the chemotherapy treatments. He would have to be physically strong enough to come into the clinic to receive the treatments.

He encouraged Steve to press pass the pain and discomfort he felt while swallowing so he could take in enough calories so he could start gaining his weight back. He stressed the fact that he was at an extremely critical stage in this battle and if he was unable to use the only medical weapon (chemotherapy) to fight, it all would be lost. Steve and I listened to the doctor's report that he was at a very critical stage in this battle with cancer. We still knew what God's report said, that Steven was already healed through Jesus' stripes. We were still fully aware that we were fighting this battle on two fronts medically and spiritually.

I began to encourage my son by reminding him how much our Heavenly Father loved him and that He, and, He alone had the final say. We touched and agreed that we would continue to trust God no matter what the doctor's report said no matter how bad things may look in the natural because our God is Supernatural, All-knowing, All powerful and He is the only one in control of the outcome of this battle and victory has already been promised to us. I reminded him that the tide could change in the blink of an eye with just one word from the Almighty God he could be healed and made whole again, instantly. It was our responsibility to do whatever we could do on the medical front in this battle; but our faith and trust is and will remain in the healing and restorative power of our Heavenly Father, the Almighty God.

As a unified family we continued praying to and praising God for strength to continue on in this battle. Steve continued to lose weight and became weaker and weaker in spite of our best efforts. One evening in the month of June, 2009 Steven was taking a bath in our upstairs bathroom which has two entrances; one from the hallway and the other from the master bedroom. My wife and I were in our bedroom (master bedroom) lying down in the bed watching a movie on television when we heard a loud thud. The noise sounded like it came from the back she hopped up out of the bed and rushed into the bathroom calling for our son, Steve, while in motion. She arrived in the bathroom just before I did to find our son on the floor he apparently passed out while attempting to exit the tub.

Triscennea told me that Steve was nonresponsive and totally motionless when she arrived just a few seconds before I did. She had lifted his head up to try and communicate with him only to find a blank stare upon his face. I also tried to make him regain consciousness, after a few minutes he finally did. He had no recollection of what just occurred, the last thing he remembered was lying in the tub. My wife and I rushed him to the hospital's emergency room. Upon arriving there I procured a wheelchair so I could transport my son into the building. Upon entering the emergency room we explained our reasons for coming there to the attendant. We also provided a brief history of Steve's present condition regarding his treatments for cancer. They immediately took his vital signs and found that his blood pressure was low and his pulse was high; which was a definitive sign of dehydration. They immediately began administering fluids to Steve via an IV drip to combat the dehydration. We remained there for approximately 12 hours or so until his vital signs reached an acceptable level. The attending emergency room physician informed us that Steve fainted due to extreme malnutrition and dehydration. He cautioned us that his condition would worsen if Steve didn't begin consuming more calories and fluids.

As human beings, we have the power to think rationally and in most situations we do just that. I thank God that I really never was like most human beings. I was born with a very analytical and rational mindset like some other people. The difference in me was the initial measure of faith that was imparted in me at birth, which caused me never to worry a day in my life. Being human, I also have the ability to choose any course of action in any given situation, freedom of choice. I can choose to use my analytical and rational mind to draw a course of action or come to a conclusion. I learned earlier on in my life that, that type of boxed thinking limits the power of my God in my life. I learned that I must abandon that form of thinking and start thinking outside of the box because the box has limitations and the power of the Almighty God is limitless. Only boxed thinking and a lack of faith can limit the manifestation of God's power in my life.

Beautiful and I possessing these very rational and analytical minds had a choice to use that methodology to formulate a course of action or to draw a conclusion regarding Steve's present condition. Thinking rationally and analytically one could postulate that we were surely looking at defeat in this battle. As the head and spiritual covering of my family, I had already decided that we as a family would persevere until the very end. The course of action that I formulated from the very beginning of this battle was simplistic. We were to trust God to heal Steve and to make him whole again, no matter how bad things may appear to get in the natural.

I knew at the onset of this battle that it could be a long drawn out fight and I was prepared for it. I trusted my Heavenly Father to the extent that there would never come a point in time that it would be too late for Him to heal Steve and make him whole again. I even had the audacity to trust and believe that my Father, the Almighty God would awaken Steve upon my request if the doctors were to pronounce him dead. My seemingly audacious believe wasn't unfounded, it indeed was founded on the word of God (the Bible). As recorded in the Gospel of John, chapter 11:1-44 the account of Lazarus being raised from the dead. John 11:11b "Our friend Lazarus has fallen asleep; but I am going there to wake him up." John 11:17 "On his arrival, Jesus found that Lazarus had already been in the tomb for four days." Upon hearing the fact that Lazarus had been buried for four days; already many would state that it's too late to do anything about it; but it is never too late for my God to act on the behalf of those who love, trust and believe in him.

When we brought Steven home from the hospital we continued praying to and praising Our Heavenly Father for our impending victory in this battle with cancer. We worshiped God first of all for who He is and then for all He had done and is going to do for our family. Most people and even some believers would find it hard to believe at this point my trust and faith in my God grew, exponentially. My joy didn't decrease; neither did my expectation of the tide turning at any given moment. My God empowered me to such a great extent that I was able to walk effortlessly by faith and not by sight.

We continued to try to get Steven to increase his consumption of nutrients and fluids. I thank God that his throat was healing and his salivary glands were producing more saliva. We kept pressing him to eat and drink more fluids, but he informed us that he was getting full faster now. Just as we were clearing one hurdle that stood in our path another one materialized. The enemy always attacks in waves as I previously stated, he's relentless in battle. The radiation treatments had caused such extensive damage to Steve's throat and his salivary glands that he was hardly able to ingest food or fluids for long period of time. The aftereffect of that was Steve's stomach had shrunk considerably. Our next logical course of action was to have our son eat smaller meals, but increase the frequency of them.

This next logical course of action didn't fare very well, either, besides the fact that Steve wasn't at all hungry; his body wouldn't accept the increase in the frequency of nutrients and fluids. Steve began to feel frustrated along with his mother he felt as if his own body was turning on him. We knew we had to try everything we could to fight this enemy invader cancer, while still expecting a supernatural breakthrough. My expectation of victory never lessened or changed through the course of the battle thus far and wasn't about to now.

Chapter 12

THE CALL TO GLORY

When a human body consistently is malnourished from lack of eating it seeks alternative sources for nourishment it begins with the fat cells until that source is depleted. When the excess body fat is completely depleted it starts on the muscular system. Steven had been malnourished for such a long period of time; despite our best efforts his body fat was depleted. We knew the next biological step was for his body to seek nutrients to sustain it would be from his muscular system. My family and I have always made a point to barbecue for every holiday during the warm seasons. I actually (the barbecue King) do all the grill work and have done so for twenty-some years. It was July 3, 2009 which fell on a Friday that year; I barbecued that day for the Independence Day celebration. That particular day Steve barely left his room, he mainly stayed in the bed all that day. We had a lot of company, as usual, whenever we barbecue a lot of family members come by to eat our excellently prepared food. Everyone that came asked how Steve was doing and traveled down the hallway to the last bedroom on the right to see him. So many people had come to the room that my son asked me to stop them because he was tired and didn't feel like having any more company.

The next morning Saturday, July 4, 2009 Steve needed help walking down the hall to get to the bathroom because of his weakened condition. Once I got him seated in the bathroom I brought him a portable dinner tray table for him to lean on while he was seated. I instructed him to call me when he was done so I could assist him in returning to his room. I just want to be perfectly clear before I go on any further, at no point in time was I ever in a state of denial or oblivious to everything that was going on around me. Walking by faith and not by sight doesn't mean that one goes into a serious state of denial or becomes oblivious to the current situation or conditions. What it does mean is that your perception actually becomes more crystal clear; even your understanding of the current circumstances is heightened to an immeasurable level. With all that being said your faith is raised to an even higher elevation, which allows one to walk by faith and not by sight.

A little while later Steve called for me to help him back to his room, so I went to the bathroom to do just that. When I arrived, I immediately removed the table from in front of him and helped him to his feet. We were only able to take a couple of steps before his body went totally limp as he fainted. My bathroom is long and narrow barely enough room for two full-sized adults to walk side-by-side in it. When he fainted suddenly I didn't have much room to maneuver so I had to lay him down. I yelled for my wife and I was trying to get Steven to regain consciousness. She arrived a few moments later to see that blank stare on our son's face.

Triscennea then called 911 to have an ambulance dispatched to our location. Several minutes had gone by and he was still unconscious, my wife and I tried to move him but we were unsuccessful. I yelled for my youngest son Centarious, who was right outside with his friends, to assist me in moving Steven out of the bathroom. When he and his friends heard that Steve had passed out they all rushed in to help. When Centarious' friend Bobby saw Steven on the floor he immediately yelled out, "I got him." He hoisted him up over his shoulder and carried him to the couch in the living room. Shortly after being transported to the couch he regained consciousness.

Just as he was regaining consciousness the emergency medical technicians (EMT's) from the ambulance were coming up the stairs. Steve was still slightly dazed, while asking us why were they here. When we informed him that he fainted in the bathroom while I was helping him up, he denied that fact. Then I asked him how did he think he got from the bathroom to the couch in the living room, he replied that he walked.

Just as before when he fainted he had no recollection of the event. They took Steve's vital signs and discovered that his blood pressure was low and his pulse was high, which were signs of dehydration. We informed the ambulance medical team of our son's battle with cancer and of his most recent treatments. One of the attendants asked us if we wanted him to be transported to the hospital via ambulance. We asked where they would be able to take him. They informed us that they could only take him to one of the two nearest hospitals, which was unacceptable to us. We know the only logical hospital to transport him to would be the county hospital where his oncology doctor practiced medicine. The EMT attendant then provided us with a waiver to sign stating that we didn't want them to transport him and that we will do it ourselves to the hospital of our preference; so I signed the form.

Beautiful (my wife) and I started preparing Steve to be transported to the hospital. My youngest son Centarious and one of his friends assisted me in carrying Steve down the stairs; while my middle son Tre'mont cleared a path and held the door so we could exit our home. We were obviously very concerned with Steve's most recent fainting spell because he stayed unconscious for a much longer period of time than before. So as we partook in our journey to the hospital we did so in an atmosphere of praise to our Heavenly Father with music and songs of praise playing as we went on our way.

I stated that we were obviously concerned by this current event, but never was I worried. Being worried would constitute a lack of faith and trust in the healing and restorative power of my God and that just wasn't the case. I would just like to reiterate on the importance in the continual trust, faith, prayer, praise and worshiping God through the entirety of your time of tribulation. We as true believers in the one true God and His only begotten son, Jesus Christ should never waiver just because of how our current situation appears in the natural.

REFLECTING BACK

I would like to digress for just a moment; it will become clear to you why when I am finished. Triscennea and I had three sons together, which happened to be the only children we have, period. Our eldest son Steven was born after we had been together a little over a year we were both 17 years old at the time of his birth. Steven was our only son born naturally. As many people know natural child birth places an enormous amount of stress on a woman's body. Triscennea wasn't immune to the stress factor just like all other women, accept shortly after having our son she lost an enormous amount of weight. Three days after giving birth you couldn't even tell that she had been pregnant in the first place, and that she was now skinnier than she had been in her life and she became very ill.

I am unable to recall all of her symptoms; but the few that come to mind were the rapid weight loss, fatigue and a high fever. She was, of course, immediately hospitalized. There I was a 17-year-old young man with a newborn son and the young lady I loved and planned to spend the rest of my life with had become violently ill after giving birth to our son, all within a week's span of time. Beautiful (Triscennea) remained in the hospital as they ran test after test trying to figure out what was wrong with her. They continued to treat her with a wide spectrum of antibiotics, for the possibility of a viral infection, but they just didn't know.

Three weeks had gone by before they discovered the cause of her illness which was Lupus Erythematous. We had only heard of one other person having Lupus before, a childhood friend of ours mother and she died from it. We only knew that the word Lupus meant wolf. We had a lot of questions for the doctor regarding their diagnosis; such as where does it come from, how did she get it and how do you treat it. The doctor informed us that they didn't know how a person contracts the disease but that she was born with it. As it was explained to us, it can lay dormant inside of a person for a lifetime and never be activated.

It places an extreme amount of stress on the body, and takes something like natural child birth to cause it to leave its state of dormancy. The doctor also told us if it had to surface in her lifetime this was the best time because she was young, strong and better fit to combat it. They told us that they would treat it with high doses of steroids at first, and then taper down the dosage. Beautiful and I battled with this Lupus for several years before it caused her to have renal failure. Her particular strain of Lupus persistently attacked her kidneys only; which actually was a good thing because it could have affected other organs, as well. So after it caused renal failure her Lupus went into remission; but it caused her to be on dialysis for a period of time while she remained on a kidney transplant list.

Many of my older family members and friends were sympathetic to what they called the hand that life had dealt Beautiful (Triscennea) and commended me for staying with her. They further stated that that was a lot of responsibility to shoulder even for a more seasoned adult let alone someone of my young age. I must state that I was very confused by their ideology. I have to say that from the beginning I looked at the present situation as our situation and that she would never have to deal with it alone as long as I lived. I actually was very grateful to our Heavenly Father that the Lupus surfaced at this young stage in our lives and in our relationship. I never felt burdened by it or sought to use it as a way out because I was truly in love with her.

When we began our relationship we were too young to get married. Our first son Steven was born out of wedlock. However, he was produced from the genuine love we shared for each other, at present we were just too young to get married, not too young to be in love or to know what love is. Triscennea remained on the transplant list for a kidney for approximately 4 years before receiving one. We were married six years after the start of our relationship six days after Steve's fifth birthday, at the age of 22 on July 30, 1988. My wife was informed that she would remain on antirejection medication for the entirety of her life; we both accepted that possibility if that was our God's will.

In September 1990, we discovered that we were going to have another child. The transplant physicians asked Triscennea if she wanted to terminate the pregnancy. In light of the fact that she harbored a transplanted organ (a kidney) and was taking so many antirejection medications; although her lupus had gone into remission they feared the possibility of it being reactivated during the strain of the impending childbirth. Our first question for the doctor's was would the medications she was presently taking harm the baby? They said no. We then asked of the probability of the Lupus resurfacing from the impending birth of our child, they were unable to give us a definitive answer. They did, however, tell us that it was possible that the Lupus had burnt itself out after it was done attacking her kidneys.

The transplant doctor's also postulated that if we were to go forth with the pregnancy that because of the medication she was taking that it could affect the growth and development of the fetus. They stated because of this possibility they would monitor her pregnancy very closely. Beautiful and I had a very brief discussion after hearing all the information given to us by the doctors. I do mean a very brief discussion because neither one of us ever believed in abortion. However, we did want to be informed of the different possibilities of the outcome of this pregnancy that the doctors could provide.

We already knew that our Heavenly Father, the Almighty God was in control of the situation and of the outcome. We had witnessed irrefutable evidence of our God's will being manifested in our lives from the beginning of our relationship. Our Heavenly Father had already predestinated for us to start our 28 year relationship at the age of 16 for our first son to be born at the age of 17 and for her lupus to be revealed at this early stage of our lives and relationship so we would be better equipped to combat it.

I would like to be very clear on a few points that I wrote about concerning the beginning of Beautiful's (Triscennea) and my relationship. I am not in any way condoning or promoting sexual promiscuity; nor am I inferring that my Heavenly Father does either. I am simply stating the facts and conditions present at the onset of our relationship. I am also not stating or promoting that a 16 or 17-year-old individual has the mindset or level of maturity to know what love is. When I stated that I knew I was in love with Beautiful it wasn't based on any physical or sexual attraction to her. It wasn't even based on how she made me feel when I was with her.

It's difficult enough for many adults to distinguish the difference between love and infatuation, especially if they are solely basing it on how the other person makes them feel when they are with them and when you add being sexually active with the other individual it truly becomes confusing. I was born with a discerning spirit; shortly after beginning my relationship with Triscennea, we were embracing each other one particular occasion and I felt a powerful stirring of my spirit during this embrace. It's very difficult to describe precisely; but it felt as if my spirit ran ten one mile laps in a circle in 2.5 seconds and ended with a triple somersault.

Beautiful didn't have the same feeling at the time of our embrace that I did, which didn't matter because I know what I had felt. I know that I had never felt my spirit react in this manner during an embrace with anyone before her. At that point I knew that my spirit had found its mate, some people would use the term soul mate. I just knew that at that point in time I held in my arms the female that I was to spend a lifetime with. The embrace I speak of was a long hug nothing sensual occurred during this embrace such as kissing or touching, what did occur at the end of the hug was the very first time I knew and told her that I was in love with her.

Some of you may feel what I based knowing that I was in love is no more certain than basing it on how I felt when I was with her. I disagree, adamantly, because unless you had that sort of spirit stirring event occur in your life and have felt how powerful it was, you could never draw an accurate conclusion to the argument. I can provide irrefutable evidence to support my basis on how I concluded that I was in love. My proof simply is our 28 years together, 22 years of which we were married, we remained together in love through sickness and health, good times and bad, for richer or poorer till death did we part. May I remind you that was a relationship that started when we were 16 years old and only ended because of her being called home to be with our Heavenly Father at the age of 44 at this point in the presentation of the facts I feel confident enough to rest my case.

The doctors monitored my wife's pregnancy very closely especially the transplant medical team; they always keep close tabs on any transplanted organ. The first trimester went well the fetus was growing at an acceptable rate and continue to do so through the second trimester. During the course of the third trimester is when a problem arose, our child's growth slowed down considerably. The doctors felt that he wasn't getting the proper nutrients and they felt he would do better outside of her womb. The doctors made the decision and set the date for the cesarean birth of our son. I was present for the birth of our first son Steven and planned to be present for this son, also. They scheduled the operation for the birth to occur in the evening so I could make it there after work. I remember arriving at the hospital and inquiring whether they were still on schedule for the procedure. A representative from the surgical team led me to a room and provided me with covering to go over my clothes so I could be present in the operating room. Approximately an hour had passed and no one came to collect me so I could be brought to my wife.

I began calling for someone to come and take me to my wife on the phone provided in the room which resembled a portion of a hotel suite minus the sleeping area. I couldn't get a definitive answer from anyone about when someone would accompany me to be with Beautiful. Approximately 10 to 15 more minutes had passed without any one ringing that phone with the information that I required. I undoubtedly was getting upset by this time and had to pray to my God for peace before I became too upset and acted with irrational behavior. Moments after praying for peace the phone rang and I was given instructions on where to go. Upon arriving at the destination I was greeted by the anesthesiologist who was part of Beautiful's surgical team she informed me that they had forgotten all about me waiting to be brought into the room but my wife was persistent and relentlessly charging them to go and get her husband so I could be there with her.

Just as I was ready and prepared to start searching each and every delivery room until I found her. She wasn't going to allow them to go forth with the cesarean birth of our son without me being present. By the time I arrived the doctor had already made the initial incision, my wife was visibly very elated to see me as I was to see her. The anesthesiologist gave me specific instructions on where I was to stand at prior to entering the room. She told me that I could be in a position almost at her side slightly back but that I would be close enough to hold her hand. She instructed me to be in that position so I couldn't see Beautiful's open incision for fear that I may become sick from the sight of the opening of her abdomen and all the blood, they thought I might pass out.

They didn't know me at all, that was my wife's body which meant that was my body that they were operating on and also my son that they were retrieving from it. They had given Triscennea an epidural injection. Due to the numbness the injection caused she couldn't feel the physical manifestation of the breathing process, in short she couldn't feel the sensation of her chest moving while breathing. Beautiful became distressed over the inability to feel that sensation and she felt as if she was having difficulty in breathing. In her moments of distress she asked me to look if I could see her chest moving. I repositioned myself so I could see beyond the veil that they had lifted, so that I could reassure my wife that she was breathing steadily and that her chest was moving up and down as it should.

The anesthesiologist gazed at me with amazement as I witnessed the opening made by the incision and how they literally had Beautiful's skin peeled back and held open resembling a banana peel. I continued to observe after looking back reassuring my wife she was breathing normally and looking into the eyes of the anesthesiologist assuring her I was comfortable with the events that I was witnessing. When they retrieved our son from my wife's womb he was covered with a thick fluid, blood and had a bluish tint. They immediately handed him over to another team who cleared his airways so he could begin breathing and eventually let out a cry and they continue to clean him off, wrapped him up and placed him in an incubator.

I continued to observe as they removed the placenta and began stitching my wife back together again. The doctors worked on her for approximately 30 minutes before getting back to the point of the original incision which only took a few moments because they just stapled that skin back together and they were finished. Our son's birth weight was less than 2 pounds he was so small that I could comfortably hold him in one hand. His face resembled that of a partially wrinkled old man with an oh so serious look upon his face. Tre'mont Montrale Gamble had arrived successfully in this world and we were very happy. Tre'mont contracted jaundice a day or so after being born he was kept in the incubator under special lighting, to combat it. His condition became better after a day or so then one of his lungs collapsed. His skin tone changed considerably he went from a caramel tone to dark brown overnight. An intensive care unit nurse told us that drastic change occurred because of lack of oxygen.

We were informed when a baby is born premature and under 5 pounds they usually remain in the (ICU) intensive care unit until they reach at least 5 pounds or more. Because Tre' was born six weeks prematurely some of his organs weren't fully developed yet and the fact he weighed well under 5 pounds made his situation critical at best. Beautiful and I knew that Tre' wouldn't have been born in the first place if it wasn't in our Heavenly Father's will. We knew since our God called him to be born into this world He would take care of him no matter what the situation may be.

During this same timeframe with my son having difficulties, I contracted a severe case of strep throat. Almost overnight, after the onset of my condition I couldn't swallow my own saliva without experiencing excruciating pain. I dropped my wife off to be with our son Tre' while I went to the emergency room to find out what was wrong with me (I didn't know it was strep throat at the time). This was the first time we didn't visit Tre' together since he had been born. When my wife arrived at the neonatal intensive care unit she learned that one of his lungs had collapsed again and that his abdomen had become extremely distended. Beautiful immediately became distressfully worried at the discovery of Tre's current set back.

As I have already previously stated in this book that the enemy attacks in waves. He is always observing and testing the integrity of our defensive front searching for any weakness in our defensive structure so he can capitalize on it. Well, he found one that day because the circumstances beyond our control we were forced to go in separate directions. My wife was left to go visit our son without me (her spiritual covering) her husband and was faced with a tumultuous turn of events. The enemy took this opportunity to bombard her with false thoughts of doom and gloom; she actually began envisioning the worst possible outcome. I was in the emergency room of the same hospital so she was unable to contact me for support.

The enemy (satan) knew he had a golden opportunity to launch a successful attack on the weaker one of us. He also knew his window of opportunity would soon be closing so he proceeded to sow those seeds of doubt, fear and dismay in my wife's mind while I was absent from her side. We as believers should take note of the enemy's tactics during battle so we can be better prepared to combat him. There is an old saying that rings very true "forewarned is forearmed." In other words if we are warned beforehand we should be better prepared or armed for the impending attacks of our enemy. In total I spent approximately 5 hours in the emergency room. I was examined by an attending physician looked at my throat and decided to refer me to an ENT (ear nose and throat) specialist because of the redness and inflammation he had discovered.

The ENT specialist examined my throat and swapped it for a culture. He then informed me that I had an extremely bad case of strep throat. He wrote a prescription for antibiotics to treat the infection and told me to gargle at least three times a day with warm salt water. I informed him that I had an infant prematurely born son in the ICU of this hospital and I asked if I was contagious because I needed to join my wife in visiting him. He informed me that I wasn't extremely contagious, but because of the environment I was going to be in that extra precautions would have to be taken and he suggested that I didn't visit that day. He suggested that I should wait at least a couple of days until the prescribed antibiotics were in my system.

I had no choice but to go to the ICU to inform Beautiful of my condition because no cell phones were allowed to be on while in the ICU. Upon my arrival and prior to attempting to enter the unit, I informed one of the nurses of my condition and who I was there to visit. The nurse informed me that I couldn't enter because I was contagious and that the environment was too volatile to take the risk. I then asked the nurse to retrieve my wife so I could speak with her and she did. When beautiful entered into my presence I noticed right away she was visibly shaken and upset. I immediately asked her what was wrong, she began to inform me of Tre's current condition; that one of his lungs collapsed again and that his abdomen had become extremely distended (swollen).

Upon seeing how distressed my wife was and hearing of the seriousness of my son's condition; I knew I had to see him. I asked the nurse to put me in contact with someone with a higher authority because I had to see my son and I wasn't taking no for an answer. A few moments later I was in the presence of an ICU physician; I informed him of my current condition and told him what the ENT specialist told me about taking extra precautions before entering the ICU. I then informed him of the current condition my son was in and how imperative it was for me to see him today.

He informed me of the extra precautions that would have to be in place in order for me to visit him for a few moments today; I agreed and proceeded in to see my son. I knew at that point it was important for my wife and me to be there together so that we can hold hands while touching our son and praying for healing and restoration for his body. The enemy had many hours while my wife faced our son's current condition without me being present with her to sow seeds of doubt, fear and dismay in my wife's mind. I on the other hand had only a few moments with her in the presence of our son to pray over him and to speak the truth about his current situation we were faced with. I wonder how many of you reading this book know that all I needed was a few moments in prayer to undo the many hours of work our enemy had put in. The word of God (the Bible) states in the book of James 15:16b "The prayer of a righteous man is powerful and effective."

Shortly after Triscennea and I prayed for our son we had to start heading home, we had to make a stop to pick up our first born son Steven before arriving home. Upon arriving home we continued praying and thanking God for healing our newborn son, Tre'. For we already knew he was healed by Jesus' stripes, we had already decided while praying together at the hospital that we would continue on in faith and trusting in our Heavenly Father's healing and restorative power. We arrived back at the hospital the next morning to see Tre', his condition had worsened, and his abdomen was extended even more. He was visibly agitated and in extreme pain while crying almost unceasingly. It was very difficult for Beautiful and I to see our baby boy in such pain and not being able to instantly make him feel better or to provide any comfort for him.

We questioned Tre's nurse in regards to what was causing the swelling of his abdomen, she referred us to the attending ICU physician. We had missed the early morning rounds that they had made already so we had to wait for the doctor to return. We were able to see a doctor several hours later he told us that Tre's swelling could be caused by one of several different things and that they were running tests to narrow it down. We remained at the hospital till late afternoon we departed at approximately 5 PM and we arrived home just around 6 PM. We had just finished eating and were preparing to settle in for the night when the phone rang at approximately 8:30 that evening. It was a nurse from the infant intensive care unit she urgently requested that we return to the hospital as soon as possible so we could discuss their findings regarding our son's current condition.

Upon our arrival we were ushered into what appeared to be a conference room or consultation room, we were instructed to be seated and we were informed that the doctor would be joining us momentarily. In a few moments we were joined by a physician and members from a surgical team. They informed us that Tre' was suffering from Necrotizing Enterocolitis more commonly referred to as N.E.C. and that the exact cause of N.E.C. is unknown. The doctors further informed us that Necrotizing Enterocolitis is most common in premature infants that are born in the less than 34 weeks after conception and those of low birth weight, less than 5 pounds.

My wife and I of course asked what caused our son to contract this condition. The physicians informed us according to a current theory; necrotizing enterocolitis (NEC) develops when the infant suffers perinatal hypoxemia (deficient oxygenation of the blood) that results when blood from the gut is shunted (to divert blood from one part to another) to more vital organs. They stated NEC had caused a portion of his bowels to die and it was infecting his bowels as a whole and the dead portion would have to be removed. They needed to perform an exploratory surgery to discover how much of his bowels were dead; if the majority of it was dead then he would (according to the doctor's report) surely die also. That was just part of the bad report, they also stated since he was so small, sick and in such distress that the stress from the exploratory surgery could kill him.

Beautiful was visibly devastated by the doctor's report and began crying almost uncontrollably. I did my best to calm her down and to reassure her that our son would live through this. As far as I was concerned nothing had changed from the moments that my wife and I held hands while touching our son Tre' and praying to our Heavenly Father for healing and full restoration of our infant son's body. I had decided at that moment that it mattered not how bad things could appear in the natural. I refused to let outward appearances or negative doctors' reports cause me to waiver in my faith. My God is the Almighty God and He alone was in control of this situation; not the surgeons, nor the surgical team and I knew once we prayed for our son to be healed it was already done.

The doctors reiterated the possible outcomes and asked us if they had our consent to proceed with the exploratory surgery. They said they would leave us alone so we could decide how to proceed moving forward but they stated that time was of the essence, so we needed to decide quickly. I truly didn't need this time to decide anything, upon hearing their report I had already decided to go forth with the surgery and I was already sure of what the outcome would be. I did take the time given to us to call my parents and informed them of what had transpired, they immediately left their home to come and be with us.

I also took this time to strengthen my wife in her time of distress. Yes I did say her time of distress; because I had no feelings of distress at all. I was unshakable, immovable and unwavering in my faith that my Heavenly Father, the Almighty God would heal and fully restore our son. I reminded Beautiful of all the miracles our God has already bestowed upon us in our lives thus far. I also reminded her how much our Father loves us and that He promised never to leave us nor forsake us. I then proceeded to inform the surgical team of our decision to go forth with the surgery; they promptly provided us with the necessary consent forms to sign, which we did.

My parents arrived at the hospital in record time, it only took them approximately 30 minutes from the time I placed the call to them. When they joined us in the room that we were in, I had us to form a circle holding hands, so that we were touching and agreeing in prayer. In times like this it is important to know what each individual's role was? My role as the father, husband, and head of the household and spiritual covering thereof; my responsibility was and still is to lead my family through any and all situations or difficulties. For I was given the authority, grace and power to do so by my Heavenly Father and will be held accountable for my actions, as well.

Triscennea's role was the mother, wife helpmeet of the husband (the head) and caregiver for our children. My parent's role was our children's grandparents and spiritual support for us all. It was very important at this point not to have anyone else present who might have negative thoughts regarding the outcome of Tre's surgery. We all needed to be in agreement before I started praying which was also my responsibility as the head. When I began praying I didn't plead to my God to save our son. I was praying a prayer of Thanksgiving; I was thanking God for the healing and full restoration of Tre'mont. I then led us in praising my Heavenly Father for what He and He alone had already done. We then began worshiping my God, not for what He was doing or had already done. We worshiped God for who He is, "The Almighty God."

After all these things were done we waited to hear the doctor's report. My wife and my parents were crying while they sat and waited. Since I already knew what the outcome would be I was the only one with dry eyes in the room. I allowed them to occupy one side of the room as I sat on the other side alone. I felt it necessary to separate myself from everyone else because by their actions they appeared to be in a state of hopefully waiting for a positive outcome from the exploratory surgery. I, on the other hand, was in a totally different state; I was in a state of expectancy. I was waiting for the surgeon to present us with the only report he could, a positive one.

While we all were waiting I witnessed Beautiful from time to time staring at me in amazement coupled with disdain and anger because of (what she later told me) my apparent blaring unconcerned mannerism.

At this still early stage of our relationship (8 years) she often mistook my unshakable, immovable and unwavering faith in the irrefutable power of my Heavenly Father, as me being unconcerned or uncaring of present circumstances later in our relationship she came to understand and sought to have the type of faith I had.

Some of you reading this book may feel that I was incorrect in my actions by not being right by my wife's side holding her hand and reassuring her while we waited. If you all remember I already did that after we both heard from the doctors regarding Tre's condition and possibilities of what may occur if we consent to the exploratory surgery that was the correct time to reassure her and I did just that. After we all formed a circle holding hands, so that we all were touching and agreeing in prayer, that time for the need of me reassuring my wife had passed. Once we prayed, praised and worshiped my God the situation was different because prayer changes everything.

I had no choice but to separate myself from them because we were no longer in the same state of agreement. They weren't prepared in their walk of faith to follow me to the other side. They were still in the state of hoping for a favorable outcome after we had prayed, praised, and worshiped God. I had hoped that they could have joined me on the other side, a state of expectancy; but sadly enough that was not the case. Fellow believers, it will come a time when you will have to separate yourselves from the groups, even if your spouse is part of that group. It could possibly put a strain on a marriage as it temporarily did mine, but that didn't matter to me. My wife knew from the beginning that I loved her as much as a husband should love his wife; but I love my God more. She knew if I were ever placed in a situation to make a decision that would please her or make a different decision that will please my God; I will always choose to please my God. She had a choice to either accept that truth or reject it because it will never change.

After a couple hours or so, the surgeon who operated on Tre' entered the room and gave us his report. He stated first of all Tre' survived the surgery and that there was only a small section of his bowels that was dead and they removed it. He further stated that he expected Tre' to make a full recovery. I suddenly felt that the tension was released from the other side of the room and was replaced with relief, joy and celebration all of their tears stopped flowing. Their tears stopped flowing for they were tears of worry, my tears began flowing for my tears were tears of joy and thanksgiving.

As my wife and I hugged each other she asked me why was I crying now after we heard the surgeon say Tre' was fine versus before we received the news. I simply told her that I never doubted or worried about the outcome so therefore I had no tears to shed at that time. The only tears I ever had to shed were tears of joy and of Thanksgiving and that's why I was crying now. Triscennea then told me that she was so angry with me because it appeared as if I didn't care if our son lived or died. She said I acted as if I didn't hear as she heard when the doctors laid out the grim possibilities of our son surviving the surgery alone.

I assured her that there was never a point in time that I was oblivious to what the doctors were saying or to what was going on all around me. I simply told her that it didn't matter what they said because I fully and wholly trusted that my God was in control and that our son was already healed in Jesus' name. She gazed into my eyes awestruck, finding it almost impossible to believe what I had just told her. My actions that she had witnessed spoke louder than any words I could have said.

Upon arriving at the hospital I parked right at the emergency room entrance where the ambulances park when they're delivering patients in need of emergency care. I was able to secure a wheelchair and a transport person to help me get Steve out of our car and into the wheelchair so he could be transported into the emergency room. When we entered the ER we insisted on speaking with someone in authority so we could forgo the normal protocol required when first entering an ER. We felt it necessary because of Steve's current critical condition and most recent fainting episode.

We ended up speaking with the ER charge nurse (I believe that was her correct title) whom we began explaining why we came there and gave a brief history of Stevens' medical condition. The nurse upon hearing everything that we told her immediately took Steven from the waiting room to the next area beyond that where they took his vital signs. Then they removed him from the wheelchair into a bed and started an IV drip. My wife and I then proceeded to fill out the necessary paperwork so we can proceed forward. The ER was overwhelmingly crowded when we arrived there in the early afternoon and only became worse later. We were there for over 12 hours as they administered fluids to Steven and ran a battery of tests on him. It was approximately 3 AM when he was officially admitted and taken to his hospital room. Beautiful and I were extremely exhausted when we left the hospital, so we proceeded home with extreme caution. Our other two sons were asleep so we weren't able to apprise them of their brother's current situation.

Chapter 13

ANSWERING THE CALL

A multitude of people would agree that the situations that I and my family have had to deal with thus far over these two years were astronomically difficult at best. Many people would even postulate that what we were going through would be enough to drive a sane person insane or to cause a stress related illness. I would at some point in the midst of everything that had occurred and was still occurring have to concur with their hypothesis, if my family and I were facing these extremities alone. However, we didn't face any of these tumultuous occurrences or events alone; from the onset of everything we were strengthened and empowered by our Heavenly Father.

I would go as far to vehemently state that if it had not been for the Lord who was on our side sustaining and strengthening us we, surely, wouldn't have been able to make it. If we were just acting on our own limited strength and power, it would have been depleted long ago. Since our God is all-knowing and all-powerful He already knew all these things were going to come to pass and had set all the necessary provisions for us to be sustained and strengthened. For it is written in Psalms 55:22, "Cast your cares on the Lord and he will sustain you, He will never let the righteous fall." In Isaiah 46:4, "Even to your old age and gray hairs I am He; I am He who will sustain you. I have made you and I will rescue you." I feel that it is necessary to remind you that in the midst of everything that was occurring that we continued to pray, praise, and worship God.

We continued to trust that our God was more than able and would indeed deliver Steve from his false accusers and to fully heal and restore him from cancer. Although, things seemed, progressively, getting worse in the natural realm, through the grace of God I was still able to walk by faith and not by sight. I had failed to mention earlier that Beautiful had developed hypertension as a direct result from her first kidney transplant and had to take medicine for this condition. I am mentioning this fact now because several days after Steve was admitted into the hospital my wife also had to be hospitalized.

She was feeling dizzy and faint so we checked her blood pressure and it was extremely high. My wife then instructed me to call 911 for an ambulance to transport her to a hospital. I know my wife, since the birth of our first son when her lupus surfaced and she spent weeks in the hospital and has had to do so for various reasons throughout our many years together; that she hates even going to the hospital let alone being admitted to one. So when my wife instructed me to call for an ambulance because she felt something was very wrong and she needed to go to the hospital; I knew that there had to be a problem. In the past when her transplant doctors stated she needed to be hospitalized she would always try to talk her way out of it.

I had previously stated that through the course of the attacks on my family and me we continuously prayed, praised, and worshiped God. I failed to mention that I also consistently called for reinforcements during these battles and new attacks. As I attempted to trail the ambulance that was transporting Beautiful to the hospital I made two calls. The first call was to my great friend and brother in Christ, Marvin who was a minister at the time (now elder) and the second call was to Elder Roni a phenomenal sister to Beautiful and me. I apprised both of them of the current situation and we prayed together our prayers were so intensely powerful that I had to pull over to continue. I knew at the local body of Christ that I belonged to "Rhema Word Kingdom Ministries," there were platoons of prayer warriors at my disposal because prayer, praise, and worship is an intricate part of what we do there.

I was fully aware that the enemy was attempting to get me on the battlefield by myself, so that he could have the advantage over me. I thank God that He gave me the wisdom to call in reinforcements just in time before I became weakened by the new wave of attacks that he was forging against us. In fact, I called a certain number of ministers and elders so often because of the un-relenting attacks that the enemy was waging upon us, that they would in turn call Jackie at our church office who was a minister at the time (now elder) she would send the alert out to the rest of the platoon of prayer warriors. From time to time, I was unable to reach these certain individual's right away, so they suggested that I call Jackie directly. I truly thank God for Jackie because there isn't one time that I can recall that she didn't answer the phone when I needed her to touch and agree with me in prayer and to also send the alert out about the latest attack. I am so grateful to God for my Pastor, Elder Gerald L. Glasper and his wife, First Lady, and Co- Pastor Elder Toni A. Glasper; along with the many elders, ministers and members that make up our local body of Christ, Rhema Word.

We would not have made it through these unrelenting attacks without God and all the saints He had strategically placed in our lives within our Rhema Word family. I may be a bit premature in recognizing and thanking everyone because the story isn't over yet and everyone did so much more. If my memory serves me correctly, it was approximately 10:00 PM when Triscennea was taken to the hospital via ambulance. I had finished praying with Roni and Marvin so I got back on the road again. I decided to stop at a store a few blocks away from the emergency room entrance to the hospital, for I knew it would probably be a long night.

Surely, many of you remember the saying when it rains it pours. Just as I was thinking things couldn't get any worse, they did. I had made my purchase and was going to the car when my alarm control pad wouldn't disengage the alarm. It wasn't unusual for it to act up every once in a while, usually I just needed to tap it against something and it would work. Well, wouldn't you know that wasn't the case this time, I tried to make it work for about an hour, unsuccessfully. The store I was at had a night service window; its location was off the beaten path in other words it was far away from any other open establishment. I informed the cashier that I had made my purchase from what was going on with my car and that I would have to leave it there for a few moments. I told her that my wife was rushed to the hospital up the road and I will have to walk and get her key so I could move my car.

She told me she would watch my car and cautioned me to be careful in walking at this time of night down this road and that it could be very dangerous for me. With her warning in mind I began my journey to the hospital making sure I was extra sensitive of my surroundings. I finally arrived there safe and sound; then I had to locate my wife who was probably wondering where I was. I was finally directed to her bed in the ER, when I saw her, she was obviously feeling better because she was angry with me for taking so long to get to her.

I asked her how she was feeling and had her blood pressure returned to normal. She responded by saying that she felt better and that her blood pressure had returned to her normal range, which is a little higher than the average person's. Then I proceeded to explain to her what happened that caused my arrival to be delayed. I asked her for her purse which I had forgotten, we didn't bring, she only had her wallet and her medicine case. Then I remembered taking her keys out of her jacket pocket and leaving them home because I was coming and she wouldn't need them. Now, I was faced with a more serious dilemma because it was after midnight now and I needed her keys from home. I attempted to reach my sons at home but no one answered the phone, when I tried their cell phones still no answer.

My home is located in a southern suburb of Chicago very close to the state line of Indiana in fact the hospital she was transported to was just over the state line in Indiana. I also tried calling one of my youngest son's friends and received no answer. I was forced to call my parents who live in the city to ask one of them to rescue me. My mother answered the phone and I informed her of my current plight she then handed the phone to my father who said that he would come, but he needed to get dressed first and he would be there as soon as he could. In approximately an hour and a half later I was back at the hospital in my own vehicle I had to explain to Beautiful what took so long this time. The doctors decided to keep her overnight for observation and to run several tests on her.

Now I was no stranger to having my wife in the hospital and having to take care of our sons alone. I ended up arriving back home at around 3:45 AM which allowed me time for a two-hour nap before getting my sons up for summer school. As the Holy Spirit is working through me causing me to recall the accounts of my life, with crystal clarity and revelation that I didn't have while going through them; I am utterly awestruck as to how my God was able to keep me through it all. The wave after wave after wave of attacks that the enemy was hitting my family with relentlessly wasn't as effectual as it could have been or by all-natural accounts should have been.

Truly, in all honesty, I am just realizing while writing this book that my enemy, the devil devised and constructed quite an ingenious plan of attacks to destroy me and my family. A plan, that, when looked upon logically, analytically, and strategically would have had a probability success rating in the upper 90th percentile range. When my enemy devised his seemingly flawless plan to wage war on my family and I, he left out the most important factor in his equation, "The Most High God." You see everyone, when you add God into your situation, everything changes. When you take your focus off of your problems and consistently look toward the solution which is Jesus Christ your whole outlook changes.

You too will be able to go through wave after wave of attacks by our enemy seemingly effortlessly like my family and I did. I never said it was easy but it wasn't as hard as it should have been or impossible as it could have been. My God is an awesome God. He is able to do exceedingly and abundantly more than I can hope, or ask for. I had a very difficult task of telling my two younger sons that their mother was in the hospital, now. I was still very tired and weary due to the little sleep I was able to get, but my God gave me the strength to encourage and strengthen my sons after I gave them the news about their mother.

I made sure that they both got off to school on time before I totally crashed out due to physical and mental exhaustion. I awoke about 3 ½ hours later to discover several missed calls and new voicemails left for me regarding Beautiful's hospitalization. My son, Steven had become accustomed to my coming to see him early every day in the hospital, so he wondered where I was. I didn't look forward to having to tell him that his mother was in the hospital. I called Steve before calling anyone else back to update him on the most recent occurrences and to inform him that I would be coming out to see him later.

The next call I made was to my wife, Beautiful, I asked her how she was feeling and informed her that I had spoken with Steven. I was on my way to the hospital within the hour to see her. She, of course, was elated to see me and told me that she felt fine although her blood pressure was slightly higher than her norm. In the beginning of this chapter, I stated that what we were going through could cause a person to go insane or possibly cause a stress related illness. Well, it didn't cause my wife a stress related illness; however the stress did cause her pre-existing hypertension to elevate enough for her to be hospitalized. I am not questioning her faith or lack thereof; for who am I to pass judgment on the woman that I love. I just talked to our sister, Roni yesterday regarding this incident; since yesterday was July 24, 2012 which was about three years and a couple of weeks after the fact. Just to clear things up Roni isn't my wife's or my biological sister; but she is our sister through blood, through the blood of our Lord and Savior, Jesus Christ. She is just as much a sister to us or even more so, as if she were raised in the same household with my wife, or me.

Since it had been three years since this occurance I called to test her memory and to ensure my accuracy of the aforementioned events. Roni reminded me of the maternal bond between a mother and her child, which was necessary because I can't or won't pretend that I can conceive or fathom the depth of that bond. I knew that the timing of her hospitalization was terrible and was causing unwanted stress on me. Now, I had the responsibility of going to Indiana to visit my wife in the hospital ensuring that she was all right, then driving to the West side of Chicago to visit with and check on our son, Steven, ensuring that he was all right, as well. I still also had my other two sons at home to care for, needless to say, my cup was full to the brim.

Roni was great. She would visit with Triscennea while I was with Steve and was sometimes available to visit Steve while I would visit Triscennea. I am so grateful that my God sent Roni to be a true member of our family; she truly doesn't know how much she means to us. Roni, I know you're tearing up while reading this as I am while writing this. I just want you to know how much my sons and I love and appreciate you. You have been a true sister to me, as well as a true auntie to my sons and we don't know what we would've done without you. I am so grateful that I didn't have to travel between the two hospitals and care for our other two sons alone for very long. My wife was released from the hospital four days after her admission and she returned to work the following day.

At this point, I need to reiterate that I am at war with my adversary the devil and have been since I acknowledged Jesus Christ as my Lord and Savior and gave my life to him. I have always been his primary objective, he simply uses my family to get to me, to him they are simply casualties of war; a means to an end if you will. He's been watching and studying me for years learning my likes and dislikes, my strengths and weaknesses. As a true expert in the art of war he knows to constantly, consistently, test my borders or armor for a weak spot so he can gain a point of entry. He consistently attacks in waves increasing the intensity of each wave. He also always seeks an opportunity to cause disharmony or separation of the first and second in command. In this case, it is I and my wife; he knows if he causes discord it is just as effective as physically separating us.

The end result which he is looking for is for me to either fold, or collapse under the pressure, from the constant waves of increasingly intensified attacks and, or if any disharmony or separation he would cause. He also knows from his past experiences with me that this method could yield a different but equally advantageous effect on me. That alternate desired effect that he is looking for is for me to get all puffed up and full of pride. For me, pride always comes before a great fall. Steven had been in the hospital a little over two weeks when the ill effects of my pride manifested. What causes me to be so angry with myself is that I knew then just as I know now that I am most vulnerable after a great victory in battle against the devil.

I allowed the spirit of pride in and I stopped praying for me to be kept and strengthened because I felt I could handle it, just look at my most recent victory. Pride had convinced me that I could handle anything, knowing full well that I by myself can't defeat my outward enemy satan, as well as, the enemy that is in me, my sinful nature. I have and always will need my God whenever I go into battle if I want to be victorious. Since I stopped praying for myself to be kept and strengthened by God, but continued to pray for my family they were kept and strengthened. I pridefully decided that I was strong enough to take my present circumstances on by myself. My prideful thinking mirrored the insane reasoning of a madman.

My limited strength became depleted in a matter of days and I quickly became overwhelmed by all of the stress and fatigue. Instead of returning to the source of my strength and the power that had been sustaining me, which was praying, praising, and worshiping the Almighty God; I saw a means of escape through the use of drugs, yet again. I remained absent from my family for a couple of days until I came to myself. I remember leaving the establishment where I had spent the last two days, with the spirit of condemnation weighing heavily upon me. I cried aloud to God while driving away asking how anyone could forgive me for what I have just done. Just then, I looked up and saw a car turning in front of me with the vanity plates that read "Forgiven". I immediately pulled over and began to weep uncontrollably because my God answered me instantly and in spite of what I did He still had forgiven me.

Spontaneously, I phoned my wife to apologize to her for my absence and to let her know I was all right and that I was on my way home. Her initial reaction to my call was very different from what I had anticipated. When I arrived home I showered and got something to eat. I didn't want to go anywhere or see anyone because I was so ashamed of what I had done. Triscennea told me to get over myself and to get ready to go to the hospital to see our son. She then informed me of the most recent disturbing events that occurred during my absence. While I was away, exhibiting self-destructive behavior, I left my family open and unprotected from the next attack. The enemy constructively used this time of my absence to his advantage. His form of construction always has the goal of destruction.

He seeks to destroy our belief, our faith, and our trust in God's promises that He made to us.

I was informed by my wife that Steve's oncologist was pressing him to formulate a DNR (do not resuscitate) affidavit. My wife told the doctor that he would have to talk to me regarding this matter. She told him that I was out of the state and she was awaiting my return. The doctor, of course, asked her when she expected me to return, she informed him that she didn't know. I hated the fact that I had put her in a position to have to lie in regarding my absence. She really didn't exactly lie because, I was out of the state of mind that I should have been in, and she truly had no idea when I would return. In my past attempts to escape reality, the time it took for me to come to my senses would vary.

While we were traveling to the hospital to see Steve, Beautiful informed me of the event that occurred yesterday concerning the doctor and Steven. The head oncologist was making morning rounds with a group of interns as they came into my son's room he was explaining Steven's condition to them. He turned to my son and told him point blank that he was going to die from his affliction. Steve became upset and told all of them to leave his room right away. I became infuriated upon hearing what that so-called physician had said to my son. I apprehensively entered Steve's hospital room feeling even more guilty after hearing what happened in my absence. I asked him how he was doing and apologized for my inexcusable absence. He stated that he was doing all right and that he was happy that I was there now.

Reluctantly, I asked my son to tell me in great detail exactly what happened with this doctor and what was his name. He pretty much reiterated what was told to me by his mother, but he couldn't remember the doctor's name. If my memory serves me correctly the incident occurred on a Friday and I was made aware of it upon my return on Saturday. I quickly began inquiring as to the identity of the doctor who performed rounds on yesterday morning and I expressed my disdain of his unprofessional behavior which he exhibited towards my son. After several inquiries, I finally made aware of the doctor's name. I demanded to see him ASAP, but I was unable to do so because he wasn't on call during the weekend. I was forced to wait until Monday. In hindsight, it was better that I wasn't able to see the doctor on that Saturday, because I was very angry and upset with his actions. Had I seen him that day while I was still extremely angry and upset by his dealings with my son; I might have lost my composure and done something I would later regret.

On the drive home from the hospital, Triscennea made me aware that Steve already knew that I had spent some of his money that I had charge over while I was away. That news shocked and surprised me because he didn't appear to be angry or upset with me all while I was there with them. He appeared to be genuinely happy to see me and to spend time with me. When we arrived home, I called Steve and expressed my surprise that he already knew what I had done. I told him that I was so sorry and ashamed of my actions that I didn't know if he could forgive me; he promptly stated that he had already forgiven me.

Once he told me that he had already forgiven me, tears instantly welled up in my eyes and I began to weep. I told him to get some rest and that I would see him tomorrow. While I was still crying after hanging up the phone, I turned to my wife in disbelief that our son already knew what I had done and showed no anger towards me. I was so amazed and humbled by his words of forgiveness that felt so genuine, and his actions towards me were of someone who had not only forgiven, but also forgotten my trespass against him. The only emotions that my son Steven exhibited towards me were genuine love, joy, and happiness that I was there with him.

On the other hand, Beautiful's attitude shifted to the far left on me. When I first called her after being gone for days she told me to just, "Come home now, we need you." She stopped me in mid-sentence while I was expressing remorse for my actions and told me to just come home. It was at this particular time she decided to display the other emotions which she was feeling, such as anger and disappointment. My wife was wise enough to know not to show me these emotions until she got me to go where I needed to, which was to the hospital to see our son. I, on the other hand was never confused to the fact that she would be revealing her full range of emotions to me, for it was in her nature to do so. While tears were still in my eyes she let me have it full force. She began by asking me how I could leave at a time like this when Steve and her needed me the most.

Triscennea didn't even pause to wait for my response before asking me why I spent some of his money. Was it because I figured he was dying anyway and didn't need it? That last question triggered a very different emotional response from me than the first one. I actually went from being totally remorseful to being infuriated and defensive. I yelled to the top of my voice (which resembled the loud roaring of a male lion) that my son surely will not die and he would be fully healed and restored by my God. I began to verbally attack her in regards to her lack of faith during this whole ordeal. I took pleasure reminding her how slack her faith has been over these past 18 months that we have been going through.

The Holy Spirit stepped in and allowed me to feel the damage that my words were causing to the woman that I loved, so deeply, a love second only to God. Without any hesitation I stopped yelling and I grabbed Beautiful and began hugging her, oh so tenderly, and we began to cry in each other's arms. The word of God states in the book of Ephesians 4:26a, "In your anger do not sin." Also in the book of Proverbs 29:11, "A fool gives full vent to his anger, but a wise man keeps himself under control." My very wise and evil adversary, the devil who has been waging war with me for decades has learned a great deal about me through his encounters with me in battle. He has witnessed that during the points of emotional elevations is when I am most vulnerable to his attacks.

He doesn't hesitate when one of the opportunities arises; he always attempts to take full advantage of it. While I was feeling such an emotional high from the love and genuine forgiveness that my son Steven exhibited towards me, so much so, that I was in tears. He used that opportunity to spark that anger up in my wife. His goal was for her to unleash it on me at just that opportune time. If Triscennea would have done that when I first called and stated that I was on my way home or even after I had gotten there I would've been better equipped to handle it. I would have expected her to go off on me then; but he knew that so he waited for a better time to whisper in my wife's ear to unleash her anger.

I knew that the level of rage that I felt was consuming me. But, I was unable to stop it. When I took pleasure in attacking my wife regarding her lack of faith over the last 18 months that the enemy had been constantly attacking us; I knew I was assuming the role of the great accuser, satan. Although, I recognized what the enemy was doing, I still allowed this anger to have control over me and this situation was fast becoming critical. If it had not been for the Holy Spirit stepping in and intervening on my behalf allowing me to actually recognize the damage that my words were causing my wife; I don't know what would have happened. The word of God states in the book of Proverbs 18:21a, "The tongue has the power of life and death." In other words, my words (tongue) have the power to speak of life or death over any situation and in this case I was speaking death and I needed to be stopped. I am grateful that my God stopped me when He did before I caused greater damage.

The weekend was over and Monday had finally arrived; I was at the hospital to see my son earlier than usual that day. I was very eager to confront the doctor who spoke death over my son. As soon as I arrived I inquired if that doctor was in yet, I was informed that he was, so I requested to see him immediately. He had been already warned in regards to my displeasure with his actions concerning my son on the previous day. A few moments later, two doctors entered the room Steve quickly pointed out which one spoke death over him. I tactfully, yet angrily questioned the doctor concerning what he said during morning rounds this past Friday. He attempted to downplay what was said after entering my son's room. I flat out asked him if he told my son that he was going to die from this cancer. He responded no, not in those exact words. I proceeded to tell him not to even report my son's condition to him or to my wife; that he will only report to me, for I am the head of my house.

The doctor then turned towards my son when he repeated what I just said; that he is supposed to report to me regarding his condition and, me only. Steve concurred with my instructions to the doctor without hesitation he told him to speak to me and not to even consult him. Upon receiving that confirmation from my son he asked me if he could speak to me in private. I told Steve that I would be right back. The two doctors and I went into a small room down the hall located in the intensive care unit to talk. I must say as I reflect back on this that the doctor I spoke harshly to, his demeanor changed considerably after my son instructed him to speak to me and me alone. It was as if his mannerism shifted, since I want to be told alone of his condition he couldn't wait to see my reaction when he gave me his most recent report.

He told me that Steve's liver was riddled with tumors; there were some so huge that they were close to the point of bursting. He went on to say that his liver was so swollen that it was depressing his lungs and that they were at half capacity. As the one doctor talked to me the other doctor gazed at me in amazement and disbelief; because I sat there calmly receiving this report of doom and gloom, continually interacting with them without having the emotional response that they expected. They told me that there was nothing else that they could do for him. Both doctors told me that his liver would eventually shut down and because of that he would experience dementia and possibly slip into a coma before dying, or if one of the near bursting tumors were to actually burst he would die instantly.

They suggested that I allow him to come home and die with dignity. I asked them how long did I have to make a decision in regards to how we would proceed forward; he stated that they really didn't know it could be a week or a month. I could clearly see that they were both truly amazed at my lack of emotional response to this news. The doctors asked me if I wanted to see an x-ray showing his current lung capacity. I answered yes, so we left that little room to go to another room down the hall. As I walked out of the room with the doctors close behind me the entire ICU clinical staff paused and looked at me; they must have been aware of the news I had just received, because they stood in awe of my calm demeanor. Shortly after entering the room, they showed me some x-rays of Steve's lungs before the cancer moved to his liver and what they looked like presently; I could see the apparent difference they truly were at half capacity.

They kept reiterating the fact that there was nothing else that could be done as if I didn't understand what they were telling me. I decided to make it perfectly clear to them that I understood exactly what they were telling me. Due to their disbelief in my reaction to their reports, I felt it necessary to inform them that I didn't care what they told me. I fully understood it, but still didn't care because they didn't have the final word. I told the doctors that I anticipated in the beginning of my son's battle with cancer that there may be a point in time when I would hear some doctors say there is nothing else we can do. I was well prepared to hear a statement such as that, because I was never dependent on any doctor to heal and fully restore my son's health.

I was then and still am now depending on my Heavenly Father, the Almighty God to accomplish that. My God always was the only one who could fully heal and restore Steve back to perfect health. I made a decision in the very beginning after we were first informed of the presence of cancer; that I would trust God to heal my son and any report contrary to that truth from a doctor would never shake, move or cause me to lose that trust in my All Powerful God. The doctors were at a loss for words after I made myself perfectly clear to them. I then told them if we do decide to bring Steve home it wouldn't be for him to die with dignity; we would bring him home to live under the Grace of God. Before reentering Steve's room I called my churches office, and as always Jackie answered the phone. I apprised her of the current doctor's report and we immediately agreed to believe the report of the Lord that Steve was already healed by Jesus stripes, then after being in agreement, we prayed.

She told me that she would send the email out to all the ministers and elders informing them of the most recent report from the doctors. After hanging up with Jackie I returned to my son's room shortly after entering the room Marvin called me on my cell phone, asking me how Steve was doing. I told him that I had called Jackie already with an update; I spoke cryptically to him because I was not prepared to inform Steven of what the doctors told me yet. I told Marvin I was in the hospital room with my son and couldn't talk on the cell phone. Steve asked me why I hung up so abruptly with Marvin. I reminded him of the hospital rules about no cell phone usage in the patient's room; he pointed to the landline phone in his room and told me to call him back. I tried to come up with an excuse not to but, Steve insisted, so I did.

It was as if Steve knew I was trying to avoid telling anyone about what the doctors said his current condition was. I called Marvin back from Steve's hospital room phone and talked to him briefly avoiding answering any questions regarding Steve's condition. Thank God, Marvin caught on to what I was doing. Before I hung up the phone with him I told Steve that I needed to step away for a little while but I would return. I left the building but not the hospital grounds, and I found a quiet place to pray. My prayers began with Thanksgiving as they always do, for I always have so much to be thankful for. I thanked my Heavenly Father for blessing, strengthening, and keeping my family through all that we were facing. I thanked God for my increased faith so that I was able to continue to walk by faith and not by sight, effortlessly.

I asked my God to instruct me on what to do next; I already knew that my God was able to heal my son wherever he was. Steve could be healed right there in the hospital or just as easily be healed once we brought him home. My first prayer for instruction went unanswered. I knew I had to call my wife at work so I could have her meet me for lunch so I could tell her what the doctors said face-to-face. I truly dreaded making this phone call to Beautiful; for I knew I would probably have to be deceptive in order to get her to meet me for lunch. I knew that I couldn't give her any idea what I had to tell her before being in her presence.

Triscennea's faith wasn't at my level, although we both had over 20 years together experiencing personally God's miraculous power, grace, mercy, and favor ever so present and abundant in our lives. I was unable to reach her directly when I called so I left a voicemail message instructing her to call me back so we could plan to have lunch together. I then called my parents telling them what the doctors said; my father took the news devastatingly hard and my mother was upset and saddened also. I tried to console both of them by reminding them that it's not over until my God says it's over. He and He alone has the final say.

The order in which I made the phone calls regarding the doctors report may seem out of order to some people in fact I would guess most people would think I should have called my wife, Steve's mother, first. I will fervently go on record stating that my order was the correct order. The first person I needed to talk with in regards to an unfavorable doctor's report is someone who would stand and agree with me to believe in the report of the Lord and after establishing that agreement would pray with me in the manner of agreement. Jackie fit the bill perfectly and she got the word out to a multitude of other like-minded individuals to stand and pray in agreement with, the report of the Lord.

When engulfed in battle, on the battlefield every platoon member must be of one mind, everyone must share the same goal and be willing to do whatever it takes to accomplish that goal. In order to have such cohesiveness anyone who was not in total agreement must be removed or the common goal could never be accomplished. So after receiving such news I had to gather my forces together to thwart this new wave of attacks. I could not have anyone in my presence that wasn't in agreement with me, for a house divided is already defeated. I prayed a second time for instructions on how to proceed and for the second time, I received no answer. I personally felt that it would probably be better for Steven to be brought home so he could be in an environment of hope, prayer, praise, and worship. I wanted to remove him from that negative environment being surrounded by men and women of science. I knew he would be better in a faith- filled environment surrounded by those who truly loved him. Since the beginning my Heavenly Father had been in control so it was not my decision alone to make, I correctly sought divine counsel before moving forward.

As I pondered on how I was going to approach Beautiful with the unfavorable news, I decided to take a break and call Marvin back. I reached Marvin right away and asked him had he heard the doctor's report from Jackie and he had. We then immediately agreed to believe the report of the Lord that Steve was already healed by Jesus stripes and we prayed, accordingly. He asked me how Steve took the report. I informed him that I hadn't told him yet and that I was waiting to see my wife face-to-face before I tell her and then together we would tell Steve. I expressed my displeasure with having to confront my wife's unbelief with my brother in Christ, Marvin who in turn counseled me to deal with her in the spirit of patience and understanding. He reminded me that everyone doesn't have the level of faith that I have and that I must have patience; I truly received that advice from him and acted accordingly.

The next person that I called was my brother in Christ, DaShaun who just happened to be on the road traveling back home from vacationing with his family. I informed him of the doctor's report and immediately we agreed to trust in the report of the Lord and we began a prayer of Thanksgiving to our Heavenly Father. We thanked God for who He is first of all, then for all He had done and all He is going to do. We counted the healing and full restoration of Steven already done, in the mighty name of Jesus. Shortly after hanging up with DaShawn, I decided to pray for instructions on how to proceed forward for the third time. Most people I think have heard the saying the third time is a charm; well it definitely was in this case. The Holy Spirit responded to me in the voice of my wife instructing me to remove Steve from this hostile environment. Then my mind was flooded with the memory of the call of Abram (later renamed Abraham). In the book of Genesis 12:1 "The Lord told Abraham to leave his country, his people and his father's household and go to the land that he would show him."

When the Lord told Abram to leave his country He didn't tell him where he was going or what to expect when he arrived there. Abram had to trust in the Lord to guide him in his journey. The Lord did tell Abram that he would make him into a great nation and that He would bless him. Abram left as the Lord told him which required a great deal of faith on his part. The Holy Spirit brought the call of Abram to my memory because what He was instructing me to do required that I step out on faith. I was perfectly comfortable with doing that; however I was left with the task of exhibiting my faith convincingly enough to make Beautiful and Steven follow the instructions given to me by the Holy Spirit.

Beautiful called me right after I received my instructions on how to proceed, perfect timing I might add. Although I wasn't too surprised because I know I serve the One True God who was always right on time. When I answered my phone she asked me how Steve was doing, I told her he felt fine. I was not about to volunteer any other information to her until we were face-to-face. It was very close to noon when she phoned back which was right about her lunch time. I suggested that I drive to her office building and pick her up for lunch, she agreed and I was on my way. We stopped at a fast food restaurant not too far from the hospital. She, of course by now, had figured out I had something to tell her regarding our son's condition that she didn't want to hear.

The conversation began with me reminding her of how many miraculous things our Father had done for us through the 25+ years that we've been together. I reminded her of the family members whom the doctors said they were going to die and after we prayed for them we watched them recover. I also brought up her own medical history from the beginning of our relationship 27 years ago when she became pregnant with our first born, Steven, and the lupus that had laid dormant in her system until the stress of natural child birth made, it surface. Since the lupus surfaced it opened up the door to a plethora of other adverse medical situations that our God healed her from. In a time such as this, the human spirit can become weak and fatigued from battling with the enemy, and then to receive a report from the doctor stating that all is lost could be very devastating. So I felt it necessary to shabak my wife first; before giving her the doctor's report.

I informed Triscennea about my encounter with the doctor that had upset Steven and how he denied saying those exact words to our son. Then, I told her how he responded when I told him to only talk to me regarding Steve's medical condition. I conveyed how he repeated it directly in Steve's presence and how he concurred with the statement. After that had been established, the doctor appeared to be eager to give me his report. At this point Beautiful was on the edge of her seat with anticipation of what I was going to tell her. She blurted out, "Just tell me what he said!" So I told her that the doctor said that Steve's liver was riddled with tumors some of which were so large that they were at the point of bursting; if they were to burst he could die immediately. His liver was so swollen due to the many tumors that it was depressing his lungs causing them to function at half of their capacity.

While she was still crying and I was holding her I went on to tell her that they said that there was nothing more they could do for him. They suggested that we bring him home to die with dignity and when I asked how long did I have to make the decision they simply stated that I should make it as soon as possible. They, of course, couldn't say how long Steve had to live. Before she could finish asking me how Steve took the news, I told her that I wanted to inform her first then, while together, I could tell him. It took a little while for her to calm down enough for me to finish telling her exactly what happened. I reminded her that nothing had changed. From the beginning we were relying on our Heavenly Father, the Almighty God to fully heal and restore our son's health. We never placed Steven fully in the care of the doctors we were always aware that God could use the doctors and modern medicine to heal Steve if He chose to.

The restaurant we decided to get our food from had an excellent special going on at the time so they were extremely crowded. We ended up waiting just under a half hour for our order to be prepared. Just as I was bringing our food back to our vehicle Jackie from Rhema Word called to inform me that Elder Darren Hannah had already arrived at the hospital. I informed her that we weren't there at the time and that I had just told my wife the news and we were on our way back to tell Steve what the Doctor said together. I exited the parking lot, hurriedly, and headed straight back to the hospital while Beautiful was trying to reach Darren on his cell phone we wanted to stop him before he went to visit Steve because we hadn't made him aware of what was going on yet.

Since we couldn't reach Darren on his cell phone, I had my wife call Steve on his hospital room phone. He answered right away. Triscennea asked him how he was doing and told him we were on our way there to see him and we would be arriving shortly. She asked him had Darren come by there yet and he replied no, we told him if he did to have him call us right away. We both felt a great sense of relief; but we knew we still had to hurry. I then told my wife how I had prayed three times for instructions on how to proceed forward and how I received my answer on the third try. She was amazed when I told her the Holy Spirit spoke to me using her voice telling me to remove Steve from this hostile environment and to bring him home. I told her how my mind was flooded with the memory of the call of Abram (later named Abraham). How the Lord told Abram to leave his country, his people and his father's household and go to the land that he would show him.

The call of Abram was relevant to our current situation because in both instances a great deal of faith was required. Abram had to fully trust the Lord to just pick up and leave his country, his people and his father's household to go to the land that the Lord God would show him. He not only had to trust that God would direct him in the way he should go. Also that God would fulfill the promise He made to him, that He would make him into a great nation and that He would bless him. It required a great deal of faith on our behalf to remove Steven from the care of all the medical staff and medicines that were readily available at the hospital. Since our reasons for bringing Steve home was clearly contrary to the reason the doctors had suggested, we were going to follow the instructions of our Heavenly Father and bring him home to live, not die as the doctors directed.

Beautiful and I arrived at the hospital a few moments later and went directly to the ICU where Steve was and we met Elder Hannah in the hallway, just outside of our son's room. We greeted him and thanked him for coming so quickly, we asked him if he had gone into see Steve yet and he hadn't. My wife and I informed him that we hadn't told him what the latest doctor's report was as of yet. We asked Darren if he wanted to accompany us in the room as we gave Steve the report from the doctor, he said yes. As we entered the room greeting Steve, I apologize for being absent for so long, he told me it was okay he knew I was handling business.

I took a long deep breath before I began to speak. I must say, I was a bit apprehensive regarding what I had to tell him. I truly had no idea how he would receive and respond, so I prepared for the worst possible reaction he could give me. I repeated my conversation with the doctor, verbatim, to Steven from the time I first left his room with them to the time I came and told him I will be gone for a little while. Before I told him what the Holy Spirit had instructed us to do I asked him what he wanted to do, he said, without any hesitation, that he wanted to go home. I was so pleased and somewhat surprised by his reaction. He exhibited no fear, no sense of panic, and no tears at all.

Steven pretty much reacted just as I did when the doctors told me the same news. We all held hands and agreed to trust in the report of the Lord that he was already healed by Jesus stripes. Then, Elder Hannah led us in a prayer of Thanksgiving to our Heavenly Father for all that He has done and for what He was going to do. Darren had to leave shortly after we finished praying, so I excused myself from the room and walked him down to his car. My wife later told me that after we had left the room, our son proclaimed in a loud and confident voice that he was a son of the Most High God and that he would live and not die! After I walked Darren down to his vehicle and returned to Steve's room and elaborated on what I was doing all while I was gone. I told him everyone I had talked to and prayed with and I told him that I prayed to God for instructions on how to proceed. He was also surprised that when the Holy Spirit answered me after the third time praying that I heard the answer in his mother's voice telling me to remove him from this hostile environment.

My son was unfamiliar with the call of Abram when I told him I was flooded with that memory, so I explain the relevance it had to our situation and then he understood. Now since we were all in agreement to follow the instructions of the Holy Spirit to bring him home so he can live and be in a faith filled environment surrounded by those who loved him, we informed the doctors of our decision. The following day we were contacted by the hospital's hospice coordinator who in turn put us in contact with our local area hospice care organization.

Over the next few days, we worked diligently getting all the preparations in order so we could have Steven brought home to us by his birthday. His hospital bed arrived and was set up along with other machinery and medical supplies that he would need in order to be comfortable at home. The day had finally arrived. It was July 24, 2009, my eldest son Steven's 26th birthday and he was coming home under hospice care. Even though we brought him home under the care of a hospice program we still never conceded defeat, for we knew it would never be too late for our Heavenly Father to speak a word for Steven to be instantly healed and made whole again.

A plan had been formulated and was in place, I was dropped off at the hospital by my wife and I was to take the long journey home with

Steve in the back of the ambulance. I arrived at the hospital midmorning under the premise that we would be departing early that afternoon, but of course things didn't go according to schedule. Steve and I ended up waiting approximately 6 ½ hours from the time I arrived there before we were able to depart. Around 4:30 PM, in the heart of rush-hour traffic, due to our late departure time, our half an hour journey from the hospital to our home under normal conditions actually took one hour and 20 minutes. It was an extremely long and very uncomfortable trip in the very cramped area in the rear portion of the ambulance. Steve and I couldn't wait to arrive home so we could exit the vehicle.

I neglected to mention beforehand that Steve had lost his ability to stand or walk because of his extremely reduced muscle mass due to malnutrition. What we feverishly tried to prevent from happening had transpired regardless of our best efforts to stop it. I had mentioned earlier in the previous chapters that the human body will seek alternative sources for the proper amount of nutrients in order to function and survive. If a person doesn't intake enough nutrients the body will feed off the fat cells and then when they are depleted it will turn to the muscles and that's exactly what happened with Steven.

We finally arrived home just before 6 PM, the EMTs transported him up the stairs and down the hall to the room we had prepared for his arrival and placed him in his bed. I also forgot to mention because of his reduced lung capacity Steve was receiving oxygen when he was released from the hospital. So the technicians disconnected him from the oxygen tank we traveled home with and connected him to his home oxygen producing machine that we had received and set up the previous day. It was so wonderful to have our son home again with us; although his home coming was bitter sweet; not because the doctors suggested that he come home because there was nothing else they could do for him. It mattered not to us. It was because my son who had been healthy and vibrant all his life was arriving home on his 26th birthday in such a diminished capacity, although I knew this condition was only going to be temporary; it was still disheartening to see him this way.

Chapter 14

THE AFTERMATH

We were determined to celebrate our son Steven's 26th birthday and the first phase of that had been accomplished with him arriving home on his birthday. I anticipated several family members and several of his close friends to come that day. However, the number of people that showed up was extremely lower than I had expected. Steve was still very happy to be home just as we were to have him. Beautiful was on a mission seeking alternative cancer treatment methods, for we both knew that faith without works is dead. It was my pleasure, responsibility and honor to be my son's primary caregiver, a responsibility that I took very seriously. The hospice program that Steve was in provided a LPN (licensed practical nurse) to care for him two hours a day, four days a week. All the rest of the time he was under my care, since he was immobile he spent all of his time in that room.

Because I was his primary caregiver I had to be trained to take care of him properly. I was trained by the LPN who was a sweet older woman that taught me the proper procedure for changing Steve's sheets for his bed while he remained in the bed, because he couldn't move his lower extremities. She also taught me how to change his pamper and how to wash him properly. The same thing a good father does for his infant child, just as I did for Steve when he was a baby. Due to his much larger size there were some procedural tricks I had to learn to make it easier. When Steve had moved back in with us in 2008 he took his old room back which was downstairs. After he became ill, we moved him into Tre's room, our second born son. That way he would be right across the hall from us for me to be able to care for him properly.

The hospice program also provided a RN (registered nurse) visit once a week. I also had to be trained by her in caring for Steven, things like helping him to exercise his leg muscles, arms and back; which was extremely important since he was at the time bed ridden. I also learned how to properly administer his medicine and most importantly to Steve I learned the proper procedure for removing him from the bed onto his wheelchair. I needed assistance in doing so. After I was properly trained I in turn trained, my sons and nephew on how to assist me.

Steven's spirit remained uplifted despite his present circumstances. He looked forward to praying with me every morning and having me read from my Bible what the Holy Spirit had directed me to read for him. I would also read from my daily meditation book entitled "God Calling" and I have eight index cards where I have written on both sides daily reminders (affirmations) of who I am and whose I am. Triscennea's research was expansive; she was clearly a woman on a mission. My primary responsibility was to handle the day-to-day care of Steven and her job was to seek out the best alternative cancer treatments, which she did. We still had to combat Steve's malnourishment for we still needed him to be strong enough to fight this enemy invader, cancer. In order for any treatment to work he had to take in more calories.

The disease cancer always seeks to take on new territory, seeking to infect healthy cells and to make them cancerous. If Steve remained in a malnourished and weakened state it would make it too easy for the cancer to take over. We were concentrating on strengthening the healthy non-affected cells first then after effectively accomplishing that which would stop the cancer from spreading. We then would launch a concentrated attack on the cancer cells. During Beautiful's time of research she discovered several studies that affirmed that highly oxygenated cells won't turn into cancerous cells. So we sought out methods in introducing more oxygen into our son's body, his cellular system so that his healthy cells could get stronger and his unhealthy cancerous cells could be choked out with high concentrations of oxygen.

Of course, we never put all of our hopes and trust in any man-made cure not even this one. We simply went forward with doing some work on our part and trusting God to bless and direct our efforts. The most common method of delivering high concentrations of oxygen to one's system is through water. Water that had been transformed into highly oxygenated water coupled with other herbal substances that combats cancer was the formula we contrived for combating the cancer on the natural front. We never stopped fighting this war in two very distinctively different venues, on two very distinctively different fronts. The form of our defense is an offensive strategy never deviated from the beginning of this war with this enemy invader, cancer.

My family and I continued going forward every day with prayer, praise and worship to our Heavenly Father the Almighty God, trusting in Him every day and every step of the way. We had visitations and prayer weekly with the elders from my place of worship, Rhema Word Kingdom Ministries. They would pray over my son and anoint him with oil in the name of the Lord. We did just as it was written in the book of James 5:14-15. I remember a visit we had from one particular elder whom today I consider to be a great friend, and brother of Christ. I will first of all like to make a statement in the elder's defense, before making an appointment to come to my home he was made aware of the doctor's report regarding my son's condition of health. He was of course told that Steven was brought home under hospice care. With the information he was given it would cause anyone to draw the conclusion that we had brought our son home to die.

He didn't realize when he crossed the threshold entry into my home; that he was indeed entering a home full of hope, prayer, praise and worship; a home that the Holy Spirit dwelled therein. He had entered a home where its occupants walked by faith, and not by sight. With that being said when he began speaking with my son he spoke as if we had given up all hope and were believers of the doctor's report. I was somewhat preoccupied with performing some household tasks so I was only half listening to what he was saying. However when Steve looked up at me and nodded his head toward him I began to pay full attention to what he was saying to my son and I abruptly stopped him in his tracks.

I respectively, without anger or malice informed him that we believed in the report of the Lord, that Steve was already healed by Jesus stripes. I went on to tell him it mattered not to us how bad things may look in the natural we were set on a course to continue believing that our God was going to fully heal and restore Steven's health. It was imperative that we all were in agreement before entering into prayer because the only prayers going forth in my home regarding my son's condition were prayers of Thanksgiving and praise to God for what He has already done and for what He was going to do. Upon leaving, he told me that he felt blessed to come to our home because he's visited families in situations such as ours and he never knows the condition of the environment he will be entering. In short, he said he was blessed by our level of faith in God regardless of how the circumstances looked in the natural. I really didn't know how to respond to that, because I was just truly doing what came natural to me.

My son and I spent the coming weeks further solidifying and strengthening our bond with each other. I have many fond memories from those times. I watched my firstborn son grow mightily in strength, faith, and in spirit. Although his physical man deteriorated daily, his spirit man grew stronger every day. It seemed that as if a lifetime had passed from the time that I told him that I would stand in the gap for him in his relationship with our Heavenly Father, but he had to work on closing that gap himself. The son that I beheld before me was so much more spiritually mature in strength and faith than he was just a little over a year ago. The difference was so apparent, just as night is from day. I observed Steve's attitude change towards his friends and several family members who would tell him that they were coming to see him but never did, they always came up with an excuse as to why they couldn't make it. I guess most of them became tired of lying to him so they stopped answering their phone when he would call. Steve's attitude went from disappointments to acceptance after a short time he stopped calling them at all.

I had read from the Bible to him daily what God would instruct me to read. On this particular day, the Holy Spirit instructed me to read

Hebrews Chapter 13. After I read the fifth verse, the latter part of that verse reads as follows, "Because God has said, never will I leave you; never will I forsake you." I asked Steve how did he feel in regards to his so-called friends and family members abandoning him in this his moment of need. He simply looked over at me and said he was used to it now and that it no longer mattered to him. When he spoke those words to me I sensed a feeling of resolve and some sadness, also. I reminded him of what I had just read that no matter what, that our God would never leave or forsake him. I also told him that his mother and I will be here with him through it all and he can count on us.

I was saddened by and angry with Steve's friends and some family members who wouldn't come by and see him. I never called or pursued his friends to inquire why, however, I did, with certain family members. When I confronted them with the question, why? They would say they couldn't stand to see him like this. I found that to be a poor excuse because we are family and they pulled away from him when he needed them the most. Whenever, I looked at Steve back then I saw him as he had always looked healthy and well. As the Holy Spirit is bringing this back to my memory with crystal clear clarity I am remembering him in his; what was then current condition. Now, I can see that it was difficult to see him in such a malnourished state; but I still can't identify with someone not being able to withstand that level of discomfort to visit a sick, bed ridden, loved one. It was, at first very difficult for me to forgive them for their actions; but I was finally able to do just that after much prayer and meditation.

Beautiful's time off from work had ended, so she returned, reluctantly, to work. It had already been established that my job was and will be to take care of our son, Steven while he was in this state, until our God healed him. It was my duty, responsibility, and pleasure to do so, for I love all three of my sons and would gladly sacrifice anything including my life for them. Giving of my time was the least that I could do. This next event that I am going to convey to you is nothing short of a miracle. I was in my bathroom changing a light bulb that had blown; this particular light was in the ceiling in the area by the bathtub and toilet bowl. I was standing on the toilet seat; which I have done dozens of times prior to this time. This is, however, the first time that the seat I was standing on shifted just as I finished screwing in the new bulb.

Before I knew it, I was falling towards the floor in what appeared to be in slow motion. All I can remember thinking is God I can't get hurt because I need to take care of my son. I was falling on my left side preparing to brace my fall with my left elbow; at the time I weighed approximately 260 pounds, freefalling with that much force I should have easily broken my arm. Instead of arising from the bathroom floor with a broken arm; I arose with a slightly sore arm without even sporting a bruise. I couldn't afford having any impaired motor skills and especially to my upper extremities because I need the mobility in order to effectively care for Steven in his present state. To say the least I was pleasantly surprised by my falls minor effect on my body. The minor soreness that I was suffering from was still an impairment however so slightly. I knew for a fact that the results from my fall should have yielded a broken arm at least.

There is no doubt in my mind whatsoever that my Heavenly Father intervened on my behalf. Instead of falling down I actually floated down and sustained a minor injury without even a bruise as evidence of a fall. So being fully aware of the favor that my Father had already shown me; I prayed that He would remove the soreness that I was feeling. I requested to wake up the next morning fully healed and restored with no soreness. Needless to say, when I awoke the following morning I performed a full rotation of my left arm without any difficulty or even the slightest bit of soreness. Just to be perfectly clear to everyone reading this; I am in no way one of those fanatics who attempt to tie a supernatural explanation on a naturally explainable event. I have reviewed my fall several times in my mind and illustrated it with several people and we all have come to the same conclusion that my lack of injury and absence of any bruising whatsoever can't be naturally explained. I must admit I am no stranger to receiving grace, mercy, favor, love and compassion abundantly in all the days of my life thus far. I have been a witness to over a dozen miracles and the direct recipient of quite a few; however nothing like this has ever happened to me before. So I was feeling extremely blessed and highly favored at this point.

We still had the task of trying to stop Steve from losing any more weight in order for the herbal substances to work effectively. Our only problem was that it appeared that Steve's body was working against us. The more sustenance we attempted to give him the more waste he produced; it was as if it was passing directly through him. I can't remember where exactly, but my wife met someone who had faced similar difficulties when caring for a loved one with cancer. I am, of course, referring to the rapid weight loss, this person gave Triscennea the recipe for making an extremely high calorie milkshake that they said worked remarkably well. We were willing to try any reasonable idea we could find because our son was continuously losing weight, despite our best efforts.

This herbal and holistic approach we were using to combat our son's cancer wouldn't have a chance to work if he didn't receive the proper amount of nutrients to maintain and to regain the weight he had lost. Our first pressing battle was to stop the weight loss and begin the process of regaining the weight that had been lost. Steve's body had to be strong enough in order to properly defend, overcome and defeat this enemy invader, cancer. On the natural front of this battle it appeared that we were steadily losing ground, no matter how it looked I remained confident that at any moment things would turn in our favor. I knew we had to keep pressing forward faithfully and relentlessly in order to receive our breakthrough; which was always in my mind, just moments away.

Now, on the spiritual front of this battle we were steadily gaining ground. I watched with much pleasure as my son's spirit man grew stronger and stronger, day by day. Steve never complained or became angry with God over his present circumstances. Instead of blaming our Heavenly Father and withdrawing from Him; he drew closer to Him and found comfort in the word of God daily, as I would read to him. It was so amazing and inspiring to see my 26-year-old firstborn, who had been healthy all of his life; face the fact that he no longer had the ability to walk in stride with no anger or resentment. All I ever felt while being in his presence was peace; that was truly a peace that surpassed all of my understanding.

I was so grateful that I was relieved of my responsibility of standing in the gap for my son, not that I was weary from doing so. I was just so grateful that it was no longer necessary for me to do so. The gap in his relationship with our Heavenly Father had been filled in by his strengthened faith and trust in God. During these three weeks while Steven was home under hospice care he was totally dependent on me and I was happily there at his every beckon call. I didn't want my son to suffer any undue discomfort due to me being slack in my care for him. Beautiful had been back at work for approximately a week and a half when she noticed how often Steve would sometimes call me for assistance. This one time in particular she told me to stay in bed and that she would attend to our son's needs. I overheard her telling Steve to try not to call me so often because I needed my rest. I know my love meant well, because she witnessed my weariness.

When Beautiful returned to bed I didn't address what I heard her say to Steven, because I know she was acting out of love for me. I did however enter our son's room and told him whenever he needs me to call me, it didn't matter how often. I told him never to hesitate, I would sleep while he slept. Later on that same morning Steve called me into his room and told me that he really appreciated everything that I was doing for him. I told him that it was my pleasure and that it wasn't anything different from how I cared for him when he was an infant. I excused myself from his presence so that I could go in my room and cry. I didn't shed any tears of sadness only of Thanksgiving because I was so grateful to be available in this capacity for my firstborn son, my namesake who needed me to be there for him, to take care of him because he was unable to do it for himself.

The hospice nurse assigned to our son was a caring and loving woman, with whom we developed a strong relationship. There was one occasion when we had the opportunity to talk after she was finished caring for our son. She asked me if we had started making his funeral arrangements yet. I looked at her with shock and surprise that she would even ask me such a question. The Holy Spirit intervened quickly and averted my anger before it actually had a chance to develop. The Holy Spirit caused me to realize that her question was appropriate in the natural under the circumstances, since we did bring him home under hospice care.

I also had to realize up until that point we only discussed how to keep Steve comfortable by managing his pain. This was the first time the opportunity came up for me to express my true agenda for bringing my son home under hospice care. I was fully aware that the medical society, if you will, viewed Steve's case as having only one outcome, his impending demise. Since I didn't and never would put stock in the science of medicine and believe in every word written in the medical books. For I know modern medicine serves a purpose in humanity, however it is it and never will it ever be the final authority on life and or death. As I have already stated earlier, I have witnessed miraculous healings that baffled physicians, specialists, as well as, surgeons. There have been more than enough documented cases of these unexplainable miracle healings to cast a shadow of doubt on the validity of a medical doctor's terminal diagnosis.

Although everything, and I do mean everything, in the natural substantiated the doctor's prognosis of Stevens impending demise. I was still unconvinced. Every prediction that the doctors and the hospice nurse made pointed to our son's time on this earth coming to an end, was coming to pass. Yet, I still believed not in their report, I still trusted and believed in the report of the Lord that our son was already healed by Jesus stripes. I became more and more amazed by people's reaction to my unshakable, unyielding, and immovable faith. The representatives from medical science felt compelled to overtly point out Steve's present condition to me, as if they felt I was in denial. I must reiterate that walking by faith and not by sight in no way means that I was in denial about hearing or understanding what I was told or by somehow ignoring the physical manifestations that had come to pass.

If anything, walking by faith and not by sight did the exact opposite. I had crystal clear clarity of everything that was said to me and everything that was presently coming to pass in the natural. I simply didn't care about everything that I was seeing. I remained so focused on Christ and the promises of my Heavenly Father that none of those things mattered to me. I still knew, trusted and believed that all it would take is a single word from my God to heal our son. Every day that I awakened I knew that this could be the day that Steven would be healed and made whole again by a single word from my God. I was living in a state of expectancy on a daily basis. I wish I could fully explain the peace that I had while staying focused on the Lord who was the only one with the solution. I was fully aware of the problems but staying focused on them would not profit me at all. I am not aware if anyone who is reading this book has ever had the true experience of walking by faith and not by sight, if you haven't, I have to tell you, it changes you forever.

I informed the nurse that we didn't bring my son home under hospice care so that he could die with dignity we brought him home because medical science had given up on him; they stated that they had done all that they could humanly possibly do from a medical standpoint. The medical books that they base their prognosis on were the facts that they practiced medicine from. We on the other hand live our lives according to the truths contained within the pages of the Bible (The Sword of the Spirit). Because of Beautiful's medical condition (hypertension) we have always had a blood pressure cuff in our household. She would take her blood pressure ever so often, whenever she felt amiss. We began doing the same for Steven when we discovered that our machine came up with different results from what his nurse's more advanced apparatus did; we decided to upgrade to the same machine.

The doctors gave us some predictions of how Steve's behavior would become when the time would be drawing nearer to his physical demise. They said since his liver wasn't functioning fully that he would begin suffering memory loss and confusion, because his brain would cease to operate correctly. We were told that he would start sleeping more and it would become harder to wake him. They had also informed us that his heart rate would elevate because it would have to work harder to pump his blood through his system. After I had been properly trained in the removal and transportation of Steven from his bedroom he requested to be moved daily which I enjoyed doing. But I needed assistance in doing so. Steve never gave up on living; in fact, while he was bedridden he ordered a new laptop and purchased a new radio for his truck as well as having his brakes done. He surprised his mother by giving her his current laptop, which of course, was fully functional. Our son even went online and ordered an upgrade for his cell phone and had it mailed to the house.

A few days after he set up his laptop and was becoming acclimated with his new phone's many different functions, Steve attempted to show me one of the high tech functions that required a pass code to be entered first. I became alarmed when he exhibited some confusion when attempting to enter the correct number sequence. I instantly remembered the doctors predictions concerning what Steve's condition would be like towards the end. Over the next couple of days he began spending more time asleep than awake. It became progressively more difficult to wake him up during this period of time. When we were successful in waking him; he awoke in a dazed and confused state. We were very concerned so we called his nurse and asked her to come by to check on him. We were constantly checking his blood pressure which was extremely elevated each time.

The nurse finally arrived, it seemed like we were waiting forever for her to come when, in actuality, it took her a little over an hour to arrive. Upon her arrival she immediately examined Steven taking his vital signs and so forth. After her examination was complete she looked at me and my wife, with tears in her eyes, saying that we should be preparing ourselves for our son's demise. Beautiful and I looked at each other, she had begun tearing up, and I smiled then we turned back to the nurse and I said it wasn't time for our son to go, yet. We told her that we were going to call the ambulance to come and get our son. She then informed us that we had to sign a form ending our hospice care agreement, first. I informed her that she needed to hurry up and get it because I wasn't going to wait too long for any legal documentation to be signed before I would call to have my son cared for.

She provided me with the necessary documentation needed to end our hospice agreement, after a brief overview of what it entailed I signed it. My wife was on the phone calling for an ambulance to come and transport Steve to the nearest hospital. An ambulance arrived very quickly after the initial call was made, approximately 15 minutes later they had arrived. Steve's hospice nurse was very helpful with conveying the necessary information to the EMT that had arrived at our home. We provided them with a brief history of our son's condition and informed them why they were called regarding his current condition. They took his vital signs which were still very elevated; then they connected him to their portable oxygen tank and finish preparing him for transport. Beautiful decided to ride in the back of the ambulance with our son, as they transported him to the hospital and I followed behind them in our car. The nearest hospital was in the state of Indiana which was less than 10 minutes away.

Chapter 15

THE AWAKENING

We arrived at the hospital approximately 7 minutes later; Steven was still in a disoriented state. An ER nurse immediately took blood from him to see what his vital levels were. He was also connected to several devices to monitor his pulse, blood pressure, oxygen saturation level and heart rate. They ordered several different tests for Steve, one in particular, was a CAT scan so they can see if the cancer had moved to his brain or not. I, of course, accompanied my son to the place where the tests would be done. Steven's liver wasn't even functioning at half capacity because it was riddled with so many tumors. He had retained an abundant amount of fluid in his body, primarily in his abdomen, which made it hard and very painful to move him.

Steven needed to be moved from the bed he had been transported in to the table of the CT scan machine. He was being somewhat uncooperative because of the pain he was experiencing from being moved. I was assisting the technician in moving when he moaned loudly from the pain; I explained to him what the tests were for and how important it was. He was still in a dazed state but responded to me from a state of clarity saying, "Dad it doesn't matter." The technician looked at me very strangely after Steve made that statement. I asked the technician why was he looking at me like that, he explained his surprised look was because he didn't realize that I was his father.

The technician and I were finally able to move him on to the table for the CAT scan. The scanning process only took approximately 15 to 20 minutes. We decided that it would be easier and safer if we left him on the table until the transport person arrived to assist in moving him back onto the bed. We had to wait approximately a half hour for someone from the Transportation Department to come. When he did arrive we were able to move Steve with ease. Triscennea was eagerly awaiting our return, in the emergency room. We ended up spending approximately 6 hours in the ER before he was moved to a room in the intensive care unit. We remained with him as they got him situated in his room. We left shortly afterwards, because we were simply exhausted and had to go home to care for our other two sons. The next day we returned to the hospital to see Steve and find out how he was doing, medically. Upon arriving to his room we met his nurse who introduced herself as soon as she saw us. We immediately asked her how he was doing and if an attending physician was available for us to talk with.

When we interacted with our son he still wasn't quite himself, although he was able to hold a conversation with us. He spoke with a very soft methodical voice. Steve was well aware of his mother's lowered immune system so when he had to cough, he asked his mother to step away from him. I remember it was so funny because when he covered his mouth he let out a very soft almost silent little cough. Beautiful chuckled when she heard his cough and told him that she didn't have to move for such a little cough. One of the attending physicians came to his room shortly thereafter. We stepped out to speak with him. He informed us that Steven's lactate or lactose level was extremely high and that he was extremely malnourished. The doctor expressed confusion over the information contained in Steve's chart he saw that he was under hospice care so he asked us what happened and why was he here.

At that point we explained to the physician that contrary to popular belief by the medical community that we had been dealing with; we weren't convinced that Steve's death due to cancer was an impending fact. Yes, we brought him home under hospice care but that in no way was a confirmation that we had conformed to the beliefs of the doctors. Our reasoning for bringing him home under this type of care was for him to be comfortable as we waited for him to be healed. We were not waiting for him to die. During the course of this battle there had never been or will ever be a time that we would concede defeat in the face of this enemy invader, cancer. I remained fully aware throughout this whole ordeal that this battle was being fought on two uniquely different plains of existence, the natural and the spiritual plain. I know that my nemesis the devil was using cancer to attack us in the natural while still attacking us in the spiritual realm.

We explained to the doctor that we had sought alternative methods for combating our son's affliction. Since all conventional methods had failed we decided on a holistic and herbal treatment for our son and that the probable reason why there were such high levels of dairy byproducts in his system was due to the high calorie protein shakes that he was ingesting to combat his malnutrition. So the doctor simply asked us what we expected them to do for him in his present condition. We stated whatever you can humanly possibly do for him. This had already reached the point that I was prepared for it to reach; a point that medically and humanly there was nothing more that can be done for him in regards to curing him. We had reached the end of our ability to affect a viable cure for him all that remains now was a supernatural cure that could only be done by my Heavenly Father, "The All Mighty God," and I was very comfortable with that.

What the doctors, non-believers and even some believers couldn't understand was that I was in a totally different state than most people would be in under the same circumstances. I was in a state of expectancy. From the very moment I awakened every morning till the time that I laid down to rest, I was expecting my God to speak one word and heal my son. I am recording these events some years after they occurred and I can't help but to remember how much peace I had during this time, it truly surpassed all understanding. Just thinking about how easy it was to walk by faith and not by sight, truly blows me away. I was able to do so by keeping my focus on Jesus Christ, the solution; not the problem, cancer.

I am not and will never claim to be a holier than thou follower of Jesus Christ. I wouldn't dare make that preposterous claim; nor would I ever insult your intelligence with such a claim, especially with what you've read about me so far. I have read the word of God, gone to Sunday worship and attended Wednesday Bible study, on a regular basis. I have heard sermons preached on spiritual warfare and had previously been made aware of how to engage in battle with my adversary, satan. This, however, was the longest most grueling battle that I had ever had to fight thus far. I must say that when this battle started back in 2008 and is still raging on even now in 2012. I have experienced many victories and suffered many losses and setbacks; but it has truly allowed me to see where I am in my walk of faith with the Lord my God.

I have grown, and am still growing and getting stronger, with every attack of the enemy. I foolishly thought when I started writing this book last year that things would get easier. I don't know what I was thinking especially since I have been learning more and more about the strategies of my enemy. I guess I was hoping that my Heavenly Father would get him off me while I completed this assignment that He gave me, only to hear Him remind me that His grace is sufficient. The physicians and medical team at this hospital took a more humanistic approach in caring for our son, Steven. They inserted a feeding tube into him to combat his malnutrition. He was only there for a short time, less than a week when his condition deteriorated rapidly. His oxygen saturation level had become very low so they increased the level of oxygen he was receiving.

In a matter of days, after arriving at this hospital Steven had become unresponsive to external stimulus, he had stopped blinking his eyes one day when I came to visit. Regardless of what the doctors were telling me I knew he could hear me so I kept talking to him, reading to him from my daily meditation book, "God Calling," from my book "God's promises for your every need" and of course from my Bible. In the intensive care unit that he was in there were specific visiting hours. My aunt, Carolyn who has worked second shift hours as long as I can remember, would visit Steve most every morning unless she had other pressing business to attend to. From time to time our visitations would overlap and I would see her in person. Mostly, I could just see the evidence of her presence daily she would anoint Steve with holy oil from head to toe every time she visited him.

I love my auntie Carolyn so much. She has such a kind and giving heart. When she was made aware that Steven was in the hospital not too far from where we both lived she took it upon herself to be there for him every single morning that she could possibly be there, before going to work. I really enjoyed the times when our visits would overlap which wasn't often. There was one time that our visits overlapped, that I was particularly glad that they had. I was engaged in a conversation with a doctor that was a specialist in infectious diseases. There were only four of us in the room at the time, Steven, the doctor, my aunt Carolyn and myself. The doctor was trying to convince me that my son couldn't be healed and that he would surely die soon.

Immediately, I told him that my son would be healed and made whole again by my God. He excitedly asked me (while raising his voice considerably) then why did my God give him cancer. I stated emphatically that He didn't; but He will heal him from this cancer. He became even more infuriated and began to raise his voice even more stating that it wasn't possible for him to be healed. I told him very calmly that He will surely heal my son and that I had witnessed God's healing power before. You see the doctor simply based his claim on the outcome of Steven's condition on what he learned from his medical books. I was stating the truth from what I have witnessed prior and what the word of God (the Bible) has told me; that my son Steven was already healed by Jesus' stripes.

I have prayed for people that the doctors have sent to hospice facilities to die and have witnessed them being healed and coming home. All the miracles I have been a witness to with Triscennea's medical history alone was more than enough to convince me of my God's healing and miracle working power. So as I stood before this doctor with my sword (Bible) in hand; I was able to tell him with all certainty and confidence that I believed the report contained within the pages of this book verses my sons medical chart that he held in his hands. Even though he was so angry and was still yelling at me I remained calm. I calmly told him that at this point in time we should agree to disagree; because there was nothing I could tell him to convince him of my God's healing power and that he would never convince me to believe a lie.

When I told Beautiful what had occurred she became instantly upset, she thought that I should have reported him. I simply told her that that wasn't necessary because he didn't upset me. Actually, his lack of faith saddened me, for he couldn't take my peace because he didn't give it to me. I began to print out Scriptures regarding healing in bold extra-large print and displayed them at the foot and head of my son's bed. I, also, posted them in other key areas around his room. Our sister elder Roni provided us with a radio/CD player so that songs of praise and worship would fill the atmosphere of Steve's room. Roni also brought us a magnetic banner in the shape of a fish which read "Covered by the Blood of Jesus" and on one end of it read Ephesians 1:7; which we hung above the entrance to his room.

It was imperative to make sure that the atmosphere of Steve's room was condusive for the presence of the Holy Spirit; which I truly believed had been accomplished. I know that we were possibly reaching the most critical point in this battle and it was not a time to waiver in our faith just because of how things appeared in the natural. There had begun a noticeable change in the atmosphere whenever we entered the IC unit where Steven was. I don't know if it was because I always entered full of joy and cheerfully spoke to everyone I encountered. The staff would look at me as if I were speaking in a foreign language before responding back to me. The Holy Spirit just right now at this very moment informed me that I was acting and speaking as a foreigner to them. Many of them were for the first time encountering a true representative of the Kingdom of the Almighty God.

In the unit in which they worked there were many terminally ill patients and the friends and family that arrived to visit them came up with the absence of joy, cheer and hope. When I entered the place the atmosphere shifted. I caused disruption and confusion to the people that were there. For they, unknowingly, became witnesses to a servant of God who trusted him wholly and was able to walk by faith, and not by sight. I was only able to do that by keeping my focus on Jesus Christ, the Author and the Finisher of my faith. Steven started developing infection after infection it seemed as if as soon as he was getting over one, another would arise. Our home phone line in our bedroom was located on my wife's side of the bed and she would physically shudder whenever she saw the name of the hospital on the caller ID. There was one particular morning the hospital called between 2 and 3 AM. Beautiful woke me up so I could answer the phone.

A nurse informed me that Steve had taken a turn for the worse and we needed to get down there as soon as possible. I told her we were on our way. My wife asked me what was going on and I told her we needed to get to the hospital right away, she told me whenever the phone rings and it's the hospital calling she becomes a nervous wreck. I told her calmly and with all certainty that our son was going to be all right, we just needed to go there right now. The hospital was only approximately 7 to 10 minutes away from our home; so actually it took longer for us to prepare to go than it actually took to travel there. I would consistently fill the atmosphere in our car with songs of praise and worship. My wife, Beautiful started to look at me as if I was a foreigner also. She asked me that morning how can I continue to be so upbeat in the midst of everything that was transpiring. I simply asked her why wasn't she, since we both know our Heavenly Father was in control of Steve's destiny and all He had to do is speak a word and our son would be healed and made whole again. I reminded her that I wasn't just praying and hoping he would heal Steve, I am praying and expecting God to heal and make our son whole again. I made a conscious effort not to become angry with her over her apparent disbelief; but it became increasingly harder especially when I felt we were standing at the brink of victory.

I wanted and expected my wife, my love, the mother of our sons, the woman who had been by my side for 27 years thus far through thick and thin; a woman that had been a witness with me and a recipient of our God's miraculous healing power to stand strong in faith with me. The Holy Spirit dealt with me immediately, instructed me not to speak harshly to her or to be disappointed in her lack of faith. The Holy Spirit reminded me of my role as the head and spiritual covering for my family and that my level of faith was more than enough to see my family through this to the very end. My role with her was to strengthen, comfort, and to lead her, by example.

When we arrived they had just finished connecting Steve to a ventilator machine to assist him in breathing. They showed us the monitor that displayed the amount of breathes Steve is taking on his own and the amount that the machine was doing. At present Steven was breathing more on his own, but needed assistance from the machine. They of course reminded us of how sick he was and asked us was there a DNR (do not resuscitate) order on file; we told them no. They asked us if we wanted to put one in place at this present time, we of course declined and stated that we would honor his wishes to do everything humanly possible to keep him alive. The doctor also had to prescribe our son a medicine that increased his blood pressure because it was low.

We went home a little later that morning after Steve appeared to be stable. The correct term that they used for him was critical but stable. At this point, we were both physically and mentally exhausted, when we arrived back home. A few days had passed since the last incident and he remained in a critical but stable condition. I remember being in Steve's hospital room, it was on a Wednesday. Triscennea and I were in the room alone with Steve as we watched his vital signs start falling; his nurse came in and asked us what we wanted to do, in other words did we want to just let him go. Beautiful looked over at me and asked should we just do nothing and let him go. I stated that we should honor his wishes and do everything we could humanly possibly do to save his vessel on this earth.

Upon hearing our wishes the nurse activated a code blue alert; which in short means that a life-threatening event was occurring and we were instructed to leave the room. I didn't want to go far away from his room, so we were just a few yards away at the nurse's station where I could still see them working on him. I am unaware of what the hospital's procedure is in cases like this; while the code blue team was working to revive my son who had flat lined, the chaplain came over to stand with us and someone from the hospital security was in a triangular position between us and my son's room. My wife's back was turned towards Steve's room as she faced me in a distraught state and the chaplain was facing me also, seemingly trying to block my line of sight to Steve's room.

The chaplain stood there silently as I prayed with and ministered to my wife. I continually watched them trying to get my sons heart back to a sinus rhythm. They were working on him very aggressively as I continued to calmly minister and reassure my wife that our son was in the hands of our Heavenly Father and that he was going to be all right. The chaplain kept his eye on me as I ministered to my wife and then turns around to see what I was looking at when he turned back to me he had a look of amazement in his eyes. This instance brought something back to my memory. I remember reading a book and it showed two pictures, the first picture was one of a forest full of trees and everything was perfectly still and the other picture showed a tree with a bird in it and in the background there was a raging waterfall. The author posed the question; which picture is a true depiction of peace. There were several of us in a class setting and our instructor asked us to answer that question.

I purposely waited to hear the answers from several of my classmates before I raised my hand to give mine. Everyone who answered before me chose the picture of the forest because there was inactivity and peace. I raised my hand and chose the other picture because it was a more honest and true depiction of how life really is. You see although there was a raging waterfall in the midst; peace was still present by the tree with the bird. Honestly, how often in life will everything be perfectly still and quiet, clearly, not often enough. I felt then as I still feel today that my peace isn't commensurate to any external situation. In other words in real life something is always going to be happening, be it good or bad. I just refuse to let those things dictate whether I will be happy or sad. In short, just because a tumultuous event is occurring in my line of sight involving someone that I love and in the natural doesn't look good at all, doesn't mean that I can't still have peace. What you must understand is that I was fully aware of what was going on, I even had a bird's eye view of it; but my mind and my focus was on Jesus Christ and He kept me in perfect peace in the midst of it all.

The look of amazement that the chaplain gave me wouldn't have surprised me at all if it would have come from a lay person. However, because of his position as an ordained minister, and a man of God, I didn't expect a look of disbelief and amazement from him regarding my reaction or lack thereof to what was happening with my son. Sometimes, I am too critical of the individuals who have been called to ministry, seeing that I too have been called. In his defense, he had no idea of the depth of my relationship with my Heavenly Father, nor could he have known the journey that I and my family had been partaking in over the last 19 months. I must admit that my genuine calm and peaceful demeanor would take anyone by surprise. Even as I am reviewing the scene that was transpiring before me in my memory; I am truly amazed at how God kept me so calm and at peace with what I was witnessing.

The cold blue team worked on Steven for an hour or so until they were able to get him stabilized they also drained all of the excess fluid that was built up in his abdomen which was an excessive amount. We were informed by the doctors and other medical staff members that the next few hours were very critical and that he probably wouldn't make it through the night. They asked us if we were spending the night so they could tell us where on the floor we could wait and slumber until morning. I informed them that we wouldn't be spending the night because it was Wednesday and our church has Bible study on Wednesdays, which we attend regularly and that we would be attending tonight, as usual.

The nurse I was talking with looked at me with surprise and disbelief after I told her we wouldn't be spending the night. I, also, noticed to my surprise a very similar look coming from Beautiful. I knew my God didn't need me present to keep and heal my son and I trusted my God fully and wholly. My wife asked me was I sure that we should leave in light of what we were just told by the doctor. I reminded her that our God was in control and that He didn't need us here to keep our son. I went on to tell her that if she wanted to stay then that is what she should do; but I wasn't. For me, nothing had changed my God was still in control, Steve is in His hands and tonight is Wednesday in which I am accustomed to attending Bible study and that's where I was going with or without her.

Triscennea became very upset with me because she was afraid that if we left, our son could die and we wouldn't be here with him. I was very close to losing my patience with her apparent disbelief, but I heard the Holy Spirit's voice reminding me to patiently deal with her and to lead her by example. In order for me to lead her she must be willing to follow. I knew I had put her in a difficult position because she wasn't emotionally strong enough to stay at the hospital without me. She displayed such a feeling of panic when I said that I was going with or without her. Even though her faith wasn't strong enough for her to leave willingly; her fear was too strong for her to stay there alone.

I didn't realize then that this was a monumentally defining moment in my walk of faith with God. I suppose I didn't realize it then because to me it was a no-brainer and I was so focused on Jesus Christ that it didn't really matter what the situation looked like or what the doctors said. I proceeded forward without any doubts, fears or worries concerning my son making it through the night. I knew that he would with or without us being in attendance. We arrived at our church Rhema Word Kingdom Ministries towards the end of the praise and worship portion of Bible study. Normally, during the critical situation my son was going through, I would have called my church to inform them so we could be in agreement and prayer. There truly wasn't time to do that this time because the event transpired very quickly and I had my wife to minister to at the time. No one at Rhema Word was aware of what had just occured before our arrival there.

I knew it wouldn't have made a difference in the outcome of my son making it through the night if we stayed or left. I, also, knew by us leaving it would make a definitive statement to the medical staff at the hospital, to our enemy, satan and to our Heavenly Father, The Almighty God, that we trusted Him fully and wholly. I felt it was more important to be in the presence of the Lord with a host of fellow believers giving glory to the one True God whose only begotten son is Jesus Christ. Although, our Pastor Gerald L. Glasper and everyone else didn't know what was going on presently with our family at the time, God knew. Odinarily after we all partook in praise and worship, we immediately proceed with the reading of God's word from the Bible. On this particular night, we didn't my pastor called my wife, myself, and another member from Rhema Word up to the front of the church. He instructed the congregation to extend their hands towards us as they prayed for us, and our family members that were ill.

He then anointed all of us that were called up to the front, individually, with blessed oil as he himself prayed for our strength and the healing of our loved ones. Then, he instructed the entire congregation to encircle us and touch and agree with us in prayer for the healing of our family members. Lastly, our Pastor instructed everyone, individually, to touch and agree with us giving us a word of prayer and or encouragement as they went back to their seats. It is just wonderful how my God gives me exactly what I need when I need it. We went to church that night to attend Bible study, as usual, which consist of prayer, praise, and worship, the reading and teaching of the word of God. What we received was prayer, praise and worship and was anointed with blessed oil, prayed over by our pastor and the entire church. There is great power in the individual prayers of a believer who has been saved and even greater power when a host of saved believers touch and agree in prayer.

Had we stayed at the hospital that night we would have clearly displayed a lack of faith, trust and belief in my Heavenly Father's ability to keep our son without us being present; as if our presence truly was needed in order for God to keep him. Had we stayed we would have missed the glory of God going forth through our local Body of Christ, Rhema Word. We would have missed the magnificent blessings that we received that night in the house of the Lord. My God doesn't play favorites with his children, in other words, He doesn't love one more than the other. He loves us all the same. However, as children of God we can't all receive the same favor from Him we have to have faith in order to please God and it's our faith that activates the power of God in our lives.

The Kingdom of God does not operate as this world does. There is a common phrase going forth in the world today, "seeing is believing." The people of God already know or should already know that's not how it works. If you have a kingdom mindset; we believe first without seeing. We speak those things that aren't, as though they already are. If you are a born again, true believer in God and you're not experiencing God's power manifesting in your life, check your level of faith. For it is written in the book of Matthew 17:20b, "I tell you the truth, if you have faith as small as a mustard seed, you can say to this mountain, move from here to there and it will move. Nothing will be impossible for you."

If after you have checked your level of faith and realize that you want more; all you need do is honestly pray to God for the increase in your measure of faith. Now, you have to be ready, and be in a state of expectancy for God to provide you with the opportunity to work out your faith. It is time for we Christians to realize that God has already given us a full measure of faith; we just have to use it more and more each day. The opportunity to work out your faith more than likely won't occur like you think it will. God will create or allow a situation or circumstance to occur for you to have the opportunity to stretch your faith. I wish not to scare anyone, but, I would like you to be aware of what could possibly happen. After praying for more faith you could have your hours cut down from full time to part time or lose your job, altogether. That gives you an opportunity to either panic or hate that you ever said that prayer or you could trust God to provide a way for you, regardless of your present situation.

The first thought of many believers would be that this is an attack from the enemy. We may think that the devil somehow heard us pray to God for more faith so now he's attacking us because he doesn't want that for us. That would be a logical assumption if an individual truly believed that they were providing for themselves alone. I will tell you the truth; my God can provide for you if you don't have a job. I am speaking as a true witness because He is providing for me, presently, while I am doing this work (writing this book) that He instructed me to do. Now I have been actively looking for a job, to no avail. My God has even instructed me to stop saying that I am unemployed, when asked what I do for a living I am to say that I am a writer. I must say it was a little uncomfortable to say at first, however, it is the truth.

If you have a job, it is because it's in God's plan, if you don't its God's plan. Because, I know I have applied for jobs that I should have gotten but didn't. Oh, did I mention that I have been praying to God to provide me with the opportunity for my faith to be stretched, also. As I have already stated, He won't necessarily, do it in the way I think He should. Man's ways are not like God's ways; I had to learn this truth earlier on in my walk of faith with God. Today, is Thursday, November 29, 2012, which is one day before my 47th birthday. I received a call today in regards to a position I had applied for in a company, I was informed that they wanted me to start training Monday morning. Earlier, I explained that I have been actively seeking work to no avail and I have applied for positions that I should have gotten but didn't. Well, this position in particular, after I applied I knew I should get because there was a great need for new hires. However, so were some of the other positions that I didn't get. I had applied online and because of the great need I expected to be called within days of the completion of my application, but that's not what happened. A week had passed by and, I forgot about it and continued on with my employment search.

Just before the end of the second week after applying, I received a call on a Friday afternoon regarding scheduling an interview for Monday afternoon. The exact time was scheduled and I was informed of what information I needed to provide at the time of the interview. I prayed to my Heavenly Father pertaining to this position because I had been down this road before. He told me that this position will provide me with the opportunity to minister to people and I will be hired. I, of course, was really happy to hear that; even though the other positions, I had applied for and didn't receive, paid more but didn't afford me the opportunity to minister to people. My ideal job is not measured on any pay scale, but on the opportunity to earn a living and make my God's presence known on the earth. This position will provide just what I have been lacking, financially, but the benefit to be able to do the will of my Father, is priceless.

I love my God so much!!! He always provides me with a confirmation of what He tells me. I attended Sunday worship as I usually do every Sunday and received the confirmation through the anointed man of God my pastor Gerald L. Glasper. He was preaching and the title for his teaching was "God is about to change everything." The teaching in whole was so relevant to me, one statement stood out more than everything else. In the midst of his preaching he stated that I had been applying for job after job and they have been saying no, well now they're going to say yes because God is about to change everything. I truly don't know who else that was for; but I knew it was for me.

We left Bible study and went straight home. We had prepared ourselves for bed then called the hospital to check on our son's condition. We were informed by his nurse that he was critical but stable as I already knew he would be. Beautiful and I got up the next morning and went to the hospital to visit Steve when we arrived there his condition was the same as the night before critical, but stable. Over the next few days we continued to visit our son as usual on one of our visits we saw and conversed with one of Steve's doctors. He asked us about the incident that had occurred a few days ago when the code blue team was called in to resuscitate our son. He began telling us that Steve won't be recovering from this and that he had no brain activity. I disagreed, because he consistently shows sign of recognition of my presence in the room with him.

The doctor believed I was just imagining that he acknowledged my presence and he went forth attempting to prove his point. He began by loudly calling out Steve's name to him, as he continued to do so he pressed on his distended abdomen and squeezed his swollen legs with no response from him. After he felt he successfully proved his point he stated that we just witnessed no response from him and that our son was a vegetable with no brain activity, and no chance of recovery. Triscennea became infuriated by his statements and actions. She told him he was enjoying telling us that our son was as good as dead right now and she asked him if he had any children. He responded yes. She went on to ask him how he would feel if a doctor was to tell him the same thing about his child and appeared to enjoy doing so. He vehemently denied taking any pleasure in conveying such news to us and apologized if we took it that way. I told the doctor that I understood that he was just trying to reinforce what he was stating to us regarding our son's condition and his prognosis by showing us that he didn't respond to any physical stimulus.

I already knew that we were baffling the doctor by continually exhibiting hope in what he and the medical community considered a hopeless situation. I simply stated to him that our son wanted everything humanly possible to be done to save his life here on earth and that we were going to honor his wishes. I chose not to get into a lengthy discussion with him regarding my faith in God's healing and restorative power, because my wife was with me and was already upset with him. I felt that it would cause more harm than good at this particular point in time. The doctor left us alone in the room with our son, directly, after the end of our conversation with him. I began to calm down and reassure my wife that it is never too late; for we have God on our side and He is in control. I reminded her at any point in time, all our Heavenly Father need do is speak a word and our son will be healed and made whole again.

During this period of time in my walk with God, He primarily spoke to me through dreams and visions. I would share my dreams regarding Steve with Beautiful in the attempt to reinforce that God was getting ready to heal him. At this time, I will share two particular dreams and my interpretations of them both. The first dream was in what appeared to be a workplace cafeteria or lunch room type setting. I had already sat down and was about to start eating my lunch when I saw Steve enter into the dining area with his tray of food. I remember becoming so excited to see him and being amazed at how good he looked. I, immediately, stood up and called out his name so he could come and join me for lunch. I told him that he looked great and that I was so happy to see him with his weight back and to see him walking around again. I asked him how he was doing. He stated that he was doing great and feeling great, as well. I was so elated to see my son healed and made whole again. I asked him when did this happen, but, when he answered his speech was garbled so much so that I couldn't understand him. I told him that I couldn't understand him and asked him to repeat his answer, when he repeated I heard the same garbled response.

Steve's lunch break was apparently over and he told me he had to get back to work and that we would talk later. During our time together as we conversed, I had no problem understanding every word that proceeded out of his mouth, except when I posed the question of when he got healed. I awoke from my dream feeling encouraged and excited to tell my wife about it so she could be encouraged, as well. My interpretation of the dream was that Steve would soon be healed and would remain with us so he could share his testimony with countless other people. When I shared the accounts of my dream with Beautiful her interpretation was very different from mine. Upon me finishing the accounts of my dream and giving her my conclusion of what the dream meant, she looked at me strangely as if I was incorrect.

She told me, with all certainty, that I had misinterpreted the dream, and then began to prove her conclusion. Beautiful reminded me of when

I asked Steve when did he get healed that his speech was garbled and I couldn't understand him; but I could understand everything else he had said. I concluded that to mean that God did not want me to know a head of time when he would be healing Steven. Triscennea went on to tell me that she believed the dream was reinforcing the fact that our son would be healed; but that his healing would not occur here. The revelation she received from my dream was that I couldn't understand him when he told me when he got healed because he received a perfect healing upon entering heaven and that's where I was when I saw him. I, of course, refused to agree with her so we decided to agree to disagree.

The second dream had a totally different setting. The dream took place at Steve's old high school here in Dolton. We were there attending a parent- teacher conference, the high school is very large and confusing to get around if you don't know your way. In the middle of the building there is a rectangular courtyard which is an outside, open-space which is used as a shortcut by the students and the faculty to exit one side of the building to get to the other side, quickly. This courtyard is the location where my dream took place. In my dream, the sun was shining brightly and it was unseasonably warm for the time of year that it was. The school had tables set up in the area so that parents could receive their children's report cards and class schedules. There were several tables set up (alphabetically) according to the letter of the last name of the students such as one table was labeled A-E another F-J and so on.

Triscennea, Steven, and I stood in the line for the table labeled F-J which was extremely long as were the other lines. I remember looking up at the sky and commenting on how blue and clear it was, there was hardly a cloud in the sky. All of a sudden an extremely loud siren began to wail, it was our village tornado warning signal. Immediately after the warning siren began, the sky grew dark, the winds began to blow fiercely and powerfully. We were all informed of the impending danger that was coming; a tornado had touched down near us and was heading our way. We were instructed over the schools public announcement system to come into the building through the door we were closest to.

There were at least 150-200 parents and students in the courtyard, not including, the school faculty and volunteers. Everyone began to scramble for the doors nearest to them, it was utter chaos. My family and I remained calm in the midst of this chaos all around us. We were walking together towards the nearest door to us. Everyone else had made it in by this time and we were less than 100 feet from the door when Steven turned around and began walking towards the middle of the courtyard. I instructed my wife to go inside the building as I followed our son. He was looking up as he was walking, so I did as well; it was raining horizontally with the wind still blowing fiercely the sky was a strange orange color. As we both were looking upwards and walking towards the middle of the courtyard; we gazed upon an ominous black storm cloud with lightning coming from it. We stood there together watching as this treacherous cloud passed over our heads without causing us any harm. After this ominous black cloud had passed, the sky returned blue and the sun began to shine again just as before.

When I awoke from this dream, I was very excited about the events that had transpired in it. Although, Beautiful disagreed with my interpretation of my last dream I was yet still excited to tell her about this one. As far as I was concerned this dream further supported my revelation of our son being healed and made whole again here on this earth. My interpretation of this most recent dream was that even though this deadly storm had entered our lives with the capability to cause great destruction and even death, it would not do so. In real life, this storm (cancer) appeared all of the sudden with such force and power; it turned our sunny, warm days to dark and rainy days. The winds of change blew fiercely and powerfully, and we were warned of the impending danger of the destructive force of it.

I was totally convinced just as in the dream this storm (cancer) would pass by us with its capability to cause massive destruction and even death; that it wouldn't. I believed, just as in the dream, when the storm came in and changed the atmosphere totally but after it passed everything was restored back to the way it was originally. The first chance that I had, I excitedly shared my dream, along with my interpretation of it with my wife, Triscennea. She quietly and attentively listened not saying a word until I was finished. Then, I asked her was she now convinced that our firstborn Steven would be healed and made whole again here on this earth. She responded by restating what she believed the first dream meant, when I couldn't understand Steve's answer for when he was healed. She was still convinced if our God was going to heal him here on earth He would've done it already. Beautiful supported her conclusion with the statement that it is well beyond the point for God to show that it could only be by His power that Steve would be healed.

At this point in time my wife and I decided to agree, to disagree as to not cause any strife in our relationship. We both did agree that our Heavenly Father has the power to heal our son and that He would. We just disagreed on where the healing would occur. On August 31, 2009; which fell on a Monday that year I read from my daily devotional just as I did every day. This particular day the title was Pray and Deny, and it referenced the book of Matthew 17:21, "Howbeit this kind goeth not out but by prayer and fasting." Instantly, I knew that's what I needed to do, so, I began fasting. I had already been praying all along the way. During our weekly Wednesday night Bible Study on September 2, 2009 our pastor taught on prayer and fasting. I never was one to believe in coincidences, I didn't tell anyone about my fasting other than my wife. Pastor Glasper made a statement that you can pray and fast until you pass out; but if you don't know what God's Will is you could be doing it in vain.

His words cut me deeply. I was convinced that I knew what God's will was for my son from my interpretations of the dreams He had given me. I truly never considered the possibility that I could have misinterpreted my dreams so that they would line up with what I wanted the most; which was for my son to be healed, made whole again and remain here on this earth with me. That Wednesday's Bible study marks one week exactly after Steve had to be resuscitated and the doctors believed he wouldn't make it through the night. Which, of course, he did. The medical staff had been informing us all week that they have been struggling to keep Steve's pulse and blood pressure regulated. In order to keep him regulated they had to add two more medications in addition to what they were already giving him. Our son's condition was no longer critical but stable; he was now critical and deteriorating. The doctors said his heart was working so hard to keep him alive that soon it would give out.

Triscennea and I had talked with Roni early Thursday afternoon and she informed us of a story she read about on the Internet regarding a terminally ill young man who was miraculously healed after having a visitation from Jesus. I am unable to recall the specifics of the accounts of that young man's healing; but what was most important that it came after he had a personal visitation from Jesus. After Roni told us about this story we all agreed that that is exactly what Steven needed a visitation from Jesus. Later that afternoon we were informed that they were quickly reaching the maximum dosage of the three medications that they were administering to our son and when that occurs there was truly nothing more they could do; which really didn't matter because my God still has the final say. As I am writing this book the Holy Spirit is allowing me to relive each situation as if it were currently happening to me presently. I find this blessing to sometimes be wonderful and terrible at the same time. I am able to recall my memory of these events with crystal clarity. I can actually see myself being unshaken, unmovable and steadfast in my walk of faith each instance.

The difference now being I am intensely feeling emotions that I didn't feel as I was going through the actual events. It's as if God shielded me from them while I was keeping my focus and sight on only Jesus Christ. I must reiterate at no point was I ever in denial about what was going on in the natural with the condition of my son, I simply held on to the truth. The simple truth of the matter was that I believe in and serve a Supernatural God who is all powerful. We were called by a medical staff member from the intensive care unit where Steven was, they informed us that they were about to reach the maximum dosage that they can give him and that the medicines were no longer effectively working. My wife's sister and nephew were visiting our home when we received the call so they came to the hospital with us.

I then called our sister in Christ Roni to update her on what was said and she informed me that she would meet us there. We were all in the room when Roni arrived we visited Steven for a little while before the nurses had to do a shift change and perform some type of medical procedure on Steven; so they asked us to leave the room for a while. My wife was in a state of distress trying to deal with our sons deteriorating medical condition. We all waited in the waiting area down the Hall from the ICU. Roni and I were concerned with the amount of distress Beautiful was exhibiting so we talked and prayed to God concerning Steven's present condition.

Shortly thereafter a nurse came to the waiting area to inform us that we could return to the room. My wife immediately stated that she couldn't take being in that room anymore it was stressing her out too much. So only myself and Roni went back to see Steve, we were excited about telling him the story of the young man that was healed after a personal visitation from Jesus. When we arrived back at Steve's room Roni began to speak in his ear telling him about the young man's miraculous healing and that he too needed a visitation from Jesus so he could be healed. I was standing back a few feet as I noticed the more Roni talked about and prayed for a visitation from Christ; Steve's vital signs started to decrease slowly at first then more rapidly.

I remember as I was witnessing what was occurring all I could think of was to tell Steve that we meant for Jesus to come here to him not for him to go there to Jesus. Then all of a sudden a peace came over me, truly a peace that surpassed my understanding and I went over to my son and told him to do whatever Jesus tells him to do. When the nurses saw Steve's vitals began to crash they had us leave the room. Roni and I were about to wait just outside the room by the nurses station, just as Triscennea and I did a week ago, but they informed us that we couldn't wait there we were instructed to go back to the waiting area down the hall. As we were walking away, a code blue was announced over the intercom system

I knew when Beautiful heard the code blue call she would instantly know it was regarding Steven. When Roni and I arrived back at the waiting area it was as if she was expecting to see us. She began crying after she asked us was that code for our son, and we confirmed her that it was. I lovingly held my wife tightly while rocking back and forth assuring her that everything would be all right. We all held hands and Roni led us in prayer; after all was calm we sat peacefully down and waited. It seemed as if we were waiting for ever to hear back from the medical staff. After approximately 20 minutes or so we saw a priest walking down the hall towards the ICU. Upon seeing him Triscennea said that he was here for our son. Shortly after seeing the priest they came to tell us that Steve didn't make it. He had passed. A doctor walked with us back to the room where Steve's earthly remains were, and just outside of his room stood the priest we had seen a few moments ago.

The priest entered the room with us offering his condolences and offering to perform the last rites for our son which we declined and asked to be left alone with our son's remains. Our sister, Roni thought that meant for her to leave also. Of course, it didn't we wanted just our family in the room as she clearly qualified as such. Beautiful held one of our son's hands as I held the other and she laid her head on his chest and openly wept. I stood there pondering on the fact that I had already planned a course of action if this very thing were to happen. As I had stated earlier on in this book that if Steven were to fall asleep (passed from this earth realm) that I would pray to my Heavenly Father in the Mighty name of Jesus to wake him back up.

The time had come for me to enact my course of action, but I didn't. I was reminded by the Holy Spirit of the peace I had felt earlier when Steve's vital signs began to crash and that I had released my son to go to Christ. Only then, after I had finished my thoughts that I was able to begin to weep, as well. Some time had passed then my wife lifted her head from our son's chest and Roni leaned over and asked Steve "What's Heaven like?" We all laughed then cried tears of joy. It was so remarkable how Roni's question instantly changed the atmosphere from sadness and despair to joy because we knew Steve had already accepted Jesus Christ as his Lord and Savior; because of this fact, we all knew that he was in heaven right now.

Now it was time for some phone calls to be made. Roni called our pastor, Gerald L. Glasper and our friend, as well as, Brother Marvin, to inform them of our son's passing. My wife called her parents and her brothers to inform them. I called my parents also to inform them. Beautiful and I dreaded going home having to tell our two remaining sons,

Tre'mont and Centarious, that their big brother had passed. It seemed like it took forever for us to leave the hospital that night after Steve's passing. Our sister, Roni remained with us through it all as she had been since the very beginning. We were instructed to go to the administration office of the hospital's morgue so we could receive a contact name and number for whomever we chose to prepare our son's remains for his homegoing celebration and burial.

Just in case everyone didn't notice I am very careful not to use the term that our son died, although, that is an accepted term used by the world we live in. Our son, Steven had accepted Jesus Christ as his Lord and Savior so he indeed is not dead; he is surely alive with Jesus Christ. I use the term that he passed because that's exactly what he did; he passed from this earthly realm of existence to his new home in the heavenly realm to be with our Lord and Savior, Jesus Christ. My parents were at home when I called to inform them of Steve's passing, for they had already visited him earlier, before our visit. My mom told me that they would leave right away to go to our house so they could be with our son's. Dad had also been busy making phone calls, he had informed several of his brothers and sisters of Steven's passing.

When Triscennea, her sister, nephew, Roni, and I arrived back to my house my parents were already there along with other family members. I remember all the anxiety I was feeling prior to informing my remaining two sons that their brother had passed; it was the worst feeling I had ever felt in my life, thus far. I think part of what made it so hard was that I had convinced them that not only was our God able, but that He would heal Steve so that he'll be here with us. I had been sharing my dreams and my interpretations of them with my son's and they were strengthened by them, as was I. I never exhibited any doubt to my family, despite all the negative circumstances that were occurring that Steven would be healed by our Heavenly Father and would remain with us.

I, most of all, was concerned that their faith would be shattered because of my leading. I wanted only my wife present when I broke the news to our remaining sons. I made sure we were all in close proximity of each other when I told them; after I was able to get the words out of my mouth Tre' began to yell out as if he were in agonizing pain, Centarious cried out in disbelief stating that I said that he would be all right. At that moment, we all hugged and cried together. Centarious broke away from our group hug first stating that he had to go. He said he needed to take a walk. I tried to stop him but decided to let him go. Tre'mont fed off of his brother's emotions and began to yell out loudly in pain from the loss of his big brother.

Several of my uncles, aunties and cousins began arriving from my mother and father's side of the family offering their condolences. We received a call from our pastor who prayed with us over the phone and encouraged us, during this our time of bereavement. My brother from Rhema Word, Marvin, as well as, his wife Carolyn arrived to our home. Marvin had also been a constant visitor and a source of strength for me and my family. When I saw Marvin and we embraced I experienced a greater emotional release; I cried the most and the loudest while hugging this man that I consider a brother. I remember crying out in a loud voice "My son is gone man, he's gone." It was such a powerful release of emotions that it literally left me weak; Marvin continued to hug and cry with me until I got it all out.

I told him how much I loved and appreciated him and truly thanked God for him. I went on to tell him that that was the most that I cried and the greatest release of emotions that I had all night. I reminded him of the promise I made to him in Steve's hospital room while he was yet still in a coma that I would accompany him in going to the highways and byways to compel people to come to Jesus Christ. More and more family members began arriving so I thanked Marvin and Carolyn for coming by and for being so supportive during this time. Marvin and Carolyn left and my immediate family and I were surrounded by a multitude of other family members. Dad suggested that we go out to purchase some food for we hadn't eaten dinner, yet. If my memory serves me correctly, he bought a large amount of chicken with several side orders for whoever might be hungry.

Centarious arrived back at home surrounded by his friends and girlfriend for the added support that he needed from his peer group, along with his cousin. He informed me of something that happened that was very strange; he said he had received a text message from Steve's phone, it was all numeric. I asked to see it; but he said it freaked him out and he deleted it accidentally. I immediately went into the house, upstairs to my room to verify that his phone was still turned off, and in the place where I had it, and it was. We talked about how strange that was and impossible because I had his phone and it was off. Centarious then decided to share a conversation that he had with Steve prior to him passing. He reminded me of the circumstances surrounding that encounter so I remembered the day that it occurred.

When Steven first came home under hospice care, I was his primary caregiver. One afternoon, when I was in the room with him, Centarious sent me a text asking me if I needed any help with anything. There is usually a signature option on most phones when you send a text message to my surprise he changed his signature to, "Steve stay alive." I showed this to Steve, he then asked me to go and bring his little brother to him; so I did and then left them alone to talk. I had never asked either of them about their conversation at that time because it was private and it was between two of my son's. I honored their privacy and never even thought of it again. Well, this was the night that I found out what they conversed about. Steve asked him what was up with his text signature "Steve stay alive," Centarious, of course, told him that he wanted, as we all did, for him to live through this.

Steven told him that he would be okay with either outcome, if God allowed him to live he would be happy, or if God were to call him home he would still be happy. He told him either way would be fine with him and that he shouldn't worry because he was going to be all right. I was so surprised to hear that this conversation had transpired between the two of them and I was also a little hurt because he didn't share his feelings with me. I couldn't understand it at first because I was the one with him the most, day in and day out, caring for his needs since he arrived back home on July 24, 2009, his 26th birthday. I had figured since I was the closest one to him during this time frame that if he would share those feelings with anyone he would share them with me first.

I shared my feelings of hurt and disappointment with my wife, Beautiful. Her being the wise and loving mate that she was; she explained to me why he couldn't share those feelings with me. It was because I wasn't able to accept anything but him being fully healed, restored, and remaining here with us. I rejected any possibility of his healing occurring any other way; although, I was aware of my Heavenly Father granting individuals a perfect healing by bringing them home to be with Him in Heaven. Beautiful made me realize that I put our son, Steven, in a situation that he couldn't be totally open and honest with me regarding his feelings. I was totally focused on Jesus Christ and what I wanted; I made the mistake of not seeking what my God's will was regarding my son.

I can't exactly remember how long everyone who had come to offer their condolences and support stayed. If I were to guess, I would say we were surrounded by friends and family members for at least four hours or so. In about an hour or so after that, after everyone else's emotions had settled down and the acceptance of Steve's passing had taken root; Triscennea, Tre'mont and Centarious all laid down and went to sleep. The whole house was finally quiet and still except, for me. I remember being angry and very upset with my wife for sleeping so peacefully. I wanted to just shake her, angrily, to wake her up and ask her how she can sleep at a time like this; our eldest son was gone. I was so distraught and angry with my Heavenly Father for not saving my son like I knew He could and would.

Even though I wanted to disturb my wife's peaceful sleep, I couldn't bring myself to do so. It seemed like all of the sudden I found myself out of my bedroom, out of the house and outside in my driveway crying out loud asking my God why He had done this. I felt that I had done everything according to His word and that He failed to deliver on His promises. I prayed every day most of the time for my son's healing, the Elders from my church Rhema Word Kingdom Ministries also came and prayed with and over my son and anointed him with oil. I led my family in believing God for this miracle healing; stressing that not only that our God could do this easily; but that He was going to at any time. It would never be a time that it would be too late for His Power to be activated.

My God had strengthened me so much during the course of this battle and enabled me to truly experience walking by faith and not by sight. I peacefully, yet powerfully, stood up to the doctors when they said it was hopeless and that my God couldn't save my son. I stood on my God's word and his promises despite how horrific things appeared to be in the natural. It appeared despite of all this, all the things He had shown me in my dreams and visions; that He failed to deliver in the end. I would just like to remind everyone that I was at no time operating by my own strength, it was plain and simply my God that was strengthening me through all of this. It was my Heavenly Father that was giving me peace in the midst of turmoil, He, and He alone was working in and through me; that's why I was so confused about how He could do all these things and not come through at the end.

My God made it so easy for me to stand throughout this long and drawn out battle. There was not even a moment when I was in a state of denial about what was occurring in the natural right before my eyes. I knew without a shadow of a doubt that my God was and still is greater than any circumstance, sickness or anything that I may be faced with. Standing in the middle of my driveway looking up into the sky I loudly cried out, "My God, my God why hast thou forsaken me?" Why have you made me look like a fool in the faces of my enemies, as I stood on Your word and Your promises? How could you do this to me Your good and faithful servant? Was there anything that I have left undone in your eyesight Father?

I went on and on like this for hours without receiving an answer from my Heavenly Father. I just stated that I received no answer, when the truth of the matter is, that I didn't bother to listen for an answer. I never took the time to reflect back on the answers that He had already revealed to me through my Pastor about the importance of knowing what God's will is, and through my wife, Beautiful who told me that I was misinterpreting the meanings of my dreams. I would love to be able to tell you that, yes, I was angry but I sinned not, that I made it through this horrific night unscathed. The truth of the matter is that I allowed myself to be consumed by anger, the feelings of betrayal and the excruciating pain that I felt over the passing of my son, Steven.

It is very difficult for me to reflect back on certain instances during this time of my life especially when I fall. But it is important for you to know no matter how many times I had fallen my Heavenly Father never turned His back on me and He has always forgiven me. I felt so overwhelmed I didn't run to God because I was angry with him, I sought a means of escape; so I returned to my familiar means of escapism through the use of drugs and alcohol. Being selfish and self-centered caused me to abandon my wife, when she needed me the most. Our sister, Roni came to the rescue she was there with Triscennea searching for funeral homes to prepare our son's body, and to find a grave yard for a final resting place for his earthly remains. When I returned home that night, broken and full of guilt, my wife welcomed me back with open and loving arms to embrace me.

Triscennea forgave me instantly and told me that I can't do that again. She expressed how lost she felt and that if it had not been for Roni she didn't know what she would've done. She went on to tell me how Roni spent the whole day with her going from funeral home to funeral home to acquire the best deal and that they even found the cemetery. Roni has truly been a Godsend to our family. Beautiful and I thanked our Heavenly Father for sending her to us to be a true part of our family. The following day, Roni came over so that we could finalize our contractual agreements with the funeral home and cemetery. She was, of course, concerned about my state of well-being, as any sister would be. I expressed to Roni all the anger I felt towards God for calling our son home. I told her how I felt betrayed and made a fool of in the faces of my enemies; while I stood on God's word and His promises. She just quietly and lovingly listened to me go on and on. When I had finished she stated that it was okay to be angry with God and that I should ask Him to remove this anger from me.

This, of course, made no sense to me. I asked her how am I going to ask God to remove this anger that I am feeling, when it is He, that I am angry with. She told me that none of this has taken our Heavenly Father by surprise, He already knew that I would be angry with Him. Roni told me to just ask and, she knows for a fact, that He'll do it, when I am ready.

Well, I was in no way near being ready to let go of this anger just yet; but I still listened to what she had to say. Later on that night while my wife and I were preparing for bed I decided to share with her the turmoil I was going through the night before; I informed her how distraught I felt and how angry I was with her for being able to sleep so peacefully after our son's passing. I told her that I was so angry that I wanted to angrily shake her and wake her up to ask how you can sleep at this time, our son is gone.

She explained to me how much of a nervous wreck she was through these last few weeks of Steve's time here on earth. Beautiful stated that she could have never made it through this if it were not for me strengthening her and exhibiting such calm and peace, through it all. She stated that when he finally passed that she felt a peace and sense of relief come over her. Now that it was finally over, and that's why she was able to sleep. Beautiful told me that prior to Steven's passing that that was my time to be strong; to be the one that our family leaned on and drew strength from. She told me that now I can lean on her and draw strength from her. She assured me that it was okay to feel weak and to be an emotional wreck. My wife said that she had been strengthened by our Heavenly Father to carry me for a little while and that it was okay to experience all the emotions of grief.

It was so amazing hearing those words coming out of Triscennea's mouth; especially after the emotional state that she had been in over the past several weeks. This little woman, Beautiful, my wife, was exhibiting such strength and resolve that I knew it was our God at work in her. Over the next couple of days, I was just that, an emotional wreck. I found myself crying every time that I talked about Steven's passing, uncontrollably. I also was still holding on to the anger I felt towards my Heavenly Father. This was such a monumental turn of events for me, I now was the weak an emotional wreck; but my pride and stubbornness wouldn't allow me to ask God to remove this anger and heaviness from me. I allowed this to go on for several days until I was fully sick and tired of all the heaviness that I felt in my heart and the anger towards my Father in Heaven. I earnestly prayed to God to remove this sadness and anger from me because I had all that I could bare and it instantaneously, went away.

It was as if a 3000 pound weight had been lifted off of me, it was as if I had been walking around in a place of darkness where there was no hope, only despair. My God was just waiting on me to ask Him. He lifted the weight from me and shined this heavenly light upon me, so that I was no longer in darkness. My God strengthen me so much instantly that I was ready to assume my lead role again as the head of my family. Triscennea and I knew we wanted our pastor Gerald L. Glasper to perform our son Steven's Home Going Ceremony; but if he were unable then only one other man would do and that was our Youth Pastor, Shawn Aldridge. We were informed that Shawn definitely wouldn't be able to do it and we had planned for Steven's home going to be held on a Friday or Saturday. We were also informed that our pastor was leaving to go on vacation that Thursday so we had to get things together for a Wednesday ceremony, we just needed it to get our Pastor on board.

When we informed Roni of our dilemma and how no one else would do, if it wasn't Pastor Glasper or youth Pastor Shawn Aldridge. We needed to meet with him right away because our time was running short to get everything together. Roni seemed a little apprehensive in approaching pastor Glasper regarding our desire for him to perform our son's Eulogy for his Home Going Celebration. Beautiful being the bold outspoken little woman that she was stated that everyone acted as if they were afraid to talk to Pastor Glasper. She said she wasn't so we had to set a meeting with him which should have taken place Sunday, September 6, 2009, prior to the beginning of worship. For whatever reason, Pastor did not arrive early enough for us to meet before our worship service; Pastor Glasper informed us that he would meet with us afterwards then he suggested that we stayed for worship.

We hadn't intended on staying for worship, in fact, our son's Tre'mont and Centarious were at home awaiting our return so we could shop for their suits. No one else, that we encountered that Sunday, expected us to stay for worship. I decided to go home and get our remaining son's and bring them back to Rhema Word Kingdom Ministries for Sunday worship. Beautiful and I could have just stayed but I felt that it was important that my whole family be present. I called home, before leaving church, so that they would be ready to come out as soon as I arrived home. They, of course, questioned why were our plans changed and that they were tired and didn't feel like attending Worship today. Their feelings regarding this matter were of no consequence because I had spoken and all they were required to do was to obey without question.

My sons were ready and came out upon my arrival; we made it back, just in time, and was seated in a different area than usual. We were seated in about the fourth row middle section of the church, a place we as a family never set before. We enjoyed, as usual, a wonderful Sunday worship service. When the time came for announcements to be made, our family was spoken of as he had us stand and stated that the congregation should pray that we be strengthened in our time of bereavement due to the passing of our eldest son, Steven. He also made mention of how great it was to see us here as a family after so recently suffering the passing of our child.

Pastor Glasper also announced that the Home Going Service would be held here at Rhema Word this Wednesday at 10 AM and urged, for those that could; be in attendance. My wife and I thought it strange for him to first of all commend our presence here today when he himself suggested that we stayed. We later came to the realization that he did only suggest that we stay and meet with him afterwards, he didn't require it. It was still our choice and we obviously had chosen well. When I think back on our bold request of our Pastor to alter his schedule at a few days' notice as we weren't even active members, in other words we hadn't joined a ministry so that we could serve in the Body of Christ. With that being the case, all the different ministries tirelessly made themselves available to us during our most critical time of need. I am not aware of any other church under the same circumstances that would go so far out of their way in service of a family like Rhema Word Kingdom Ministries did for us. I am forever grateful to my Rhema Word family, for doing so.

After our Sunday worship service was over we met with Pastor Glasper. Beautiful in her boldness, started off by stating that we had to have him officiate over our son's home going ceremony and if that were totally impossible; that Pastor Shawn Aldridge would do. She also told him that many Elders seemed afraid to approach him and she told them that she would because she wasn't afraid of him. He responded with a smile and told us of his plans to start his vacation this Thursday and that he had to pray to God about it before giving us an answer as to whether or not he would be able to do it.

At the time we fully didn't understand why he was unable to give us an answer right away; but we of course accepted and respected what he told us and awaited an answer from him. We were made aware of our Pastor's decision either late Monday evening or early Tuesday morning, I can't remember which. We were also told that we needed to present an order of service right away, in which we were required to provide several lines of data, and Pastor would do the rest. For whatever reason, Beautiful and I always did conduct ourselves with boldness and a sense of entitlement since the very beginning of our union as husband and wife. As I think back on when we first joined Rhema Word in 2005 we attended regularly for a little over six months, or so, and were seriously considering joining.

We had been attending several churches throughout many years but never finding the right one to join. We both took commitment very seriously just as we did with our commitment to God and each other. That is the reason we were slow to commit, for when we do it's for a lifetime. We requested to have a meeting with Pastor Glasper. We stated that the purpose for the meeting was because we were considering joining but we needed to ask him some questions first regarding the church's doctrinal beliefs and practices. At length we discussed our walk with the Lord and where our journey had taken us, how long we had been searching for a church home. We discussed our former belief system and how God had been revealing the truth to us about how we used to pray and that what we believed was convoluted. The more we searched for the truth the more God revealed to us. I choose here not to get into the specifics of what our questions were; but I will say that our Pastor backed his answers to our questions with Scripture, so there was no confusion. He didn't answer us simply with what he felt; he answered us with what was written, the simple unadulterated truth. We decided to join as a family that upcoming Sunday.

We were pressed for time as we worked diligently to get everything in place for Steven's Home Going Celebration. I wanted to make sure that it was a celebration of his life, not the mourning of his passing. I selected a song by Donald Lawrence "I'm Healed," to be played and requested Anthony Scott, an awesome man of God, to dance to it which he agreed to do. So many friends and family members wanted to participate in this celebration of Steve's life. Our friend and neighbor, from directly across the street from our home, Debra Frazier's daughter; also a friend of Steve's, T'kumah Sadeek (Candice) offered to sing. Keith Austin, a childhood friend of Beautiful and I; who is a talented musician and songwriter offered to play. It was so amazing how much grace, mercy, favor, love and compassion was shown to us by our Heavenly Father, allowing us to get everything organized together in a matter of days, at such short notice. It was nothing short of a miracle how our God had placed everything and everyone that we needed at our disposal. Our church was just about filled to capacity on a Wednesday morning for Steven's Home Going Celebration. I never wanted a funeral for my son, that type of service signifies a sad occasion, it marks the death of a loved one; so it would've of been inappropriate. My son Steven isn't dead; he's alive with Christ in heaven because he accepted Jesus Christ as his Lord and Savior.

There were so many members of our Rhema Word family in attendance. So many of them were there in the capacity of service; which ranged from our Pastor, ministers, elders, praise team (singers and dancers), sound ministry (which I am now a part of), trustees and ushers just to name a few. They all gave of themselves, made a sacrifice to be in attendance at such short notice. I am forever grateful to them for showing us so much love and support in our time of need. During the awake portion of the service I saw so many faces that I didn't recognize a lot of them females. It was later made known to me that they were past coworkers of Steven's when he worked as a transporter and later was promoted to transporter supervisor at a local hospital. He held this job and he attended DeVry University full time pursuing his degree in Electronics and Computer Technology.

I anticipated that there would be sadness and crying occurring during this awake portion of the celebration I was just surprised at how many of the people I saw weeping uncontrollably that I didn't know. Everything was going well and pretty much according to plan and schedule. When it came time for remarks that's when things became somewhat awkward. The first woman that Steven ever loved came up to speak as she talked of their past love and stated that they were planning to rekindle that love when he got better. Another young lady got up to speak and she stated that she was his current girlfriend and spoke of how Steve loved her and her children and was assuming the role of their father.

I had already decided that I was going to speak after everyone else was done with their remarks. I felt that the remarks had gotten to be totally inappropriate, so I knew that I had to get up and speak before the young lady who was in a relationship with my son between the times that the two who had already spoken, decided to speak, also. I truly can't recall everything that I said while I was up there, other than that Steven so wanted to be married and he wanted to have children, but he didn't and God obviously had different plans for him. I also reminded everyone that we were gathered to celebrate Steven's life not to mourn his passing. Although he only had 26 years to live here on this earth he accomplished much and lived his life here to the fullest. I requested that everyone stop being so sad and to join me in celebrating my son, Steven's life; which is worth celebrating. Steven enjoyed his life here and had no fear in leaving this place to go to his true home in heaven.

My Pastor gave an excellent eulogy. At one point, he referenced a statement written concerning Steven in the obituary. The statement itself was simply that Steven loved the Lord. This statement had stood out to Pastor Glasper because as he stated you don't see that written about many young men and women in an obituary, these days. He then began to recall when he visited Steven in the hospital and he expounded on his countenance. Pastor stated that many times when he makes hospital visits that some people would be very fearful and even angry concerning their condition and current situation. He stated that that wasn't the case when he entered into our son, Steven's, room; he was neither fearful nor angry.

With the exception of when Steven was first informed alone, that he had cancer he has never since that moment exhibited any form of fear or anger, regarding his situation. He had matured and grown so much in faith during this last year it was utterly amazing. He had learned to trust God with everything regarding himself, including his life, so he had no reason to fear or be angry. Steven came to trust God fully and wholly and that He had his best interest at heart. He came to believe that all things were working together for his good according to God's plan for his life. He had already given his life to Christ. In doing so, he knew that he would partake in the glory and the suffering of Jesus, a true disciple of Christ can't have one without the other.

Chapter 16

GOING FORTH

I met with my Pastor sometime later; I am unable to recall the purpose of the meeting. He repeated something that he had said to me at Steven's burial of his earthly remains. He stated that I had done everything right and reminded me that I still have two sons left that needed me to lead them by example. Pastor Glasper posed a question to me. He asked me if I was presented with the same opportunity to minister to someone in the same situation as Steven, knowing what the outcome may be. Would I be able to do the exact same thing with that person? That was such a powerful question and I was unable to answer him right away.

That question caused me to ponder for a few days before I was able to come up with the answer, which was yes. I knew I could do it again even better than before because, I will be taking into consideration of what my God's will may be for that person. That would be the only difference; my actions would still mirror what I did with my son. When my Pastor asked me that question I had no idea that I would have the same opportunity in a little over a month from when he posed that question to me. My uncle, Willie, had been battling with cancer for a while; in addition to previously receiving a quadruple bypass surgery.

My uncle's condition took a turn for the worst and he was hospitalized. Upon receiving this news, I received the revelation that the opportunity that my pastor spoke of had come and it was time for me to go to work. My first course of action was to find out if my uncle had accepted Jesus

Christ as his Lord and Savior. Upon my first hospital visit, with Willie I asked him was he saved. He asked me what I meant. I asked him had he verbally out loud accepted Jesus Christ as his Lord and Savior. He said he had not. I asked him if he believed that Jesus Christ is the only begotten son of God, and is God. I asked if he believed that Jesus died on the cross for his sins, and the sins of the whole world? That in three days he rose again and ascended to heaven and is seated at the right hand of the Father. I also asked him if he believed that he is a sinner and that he is in need of a Savior? I asked him if he would give his life to Jesus Christ and accept him as his Lord and Savior? His answers to all of these questions were yes. I then had him repeat his confession of faith after me; which entailed him basically repeating out loud everything that he just told me that he believed. I informed him; after we had finished that he was now saved.

My visits with my uncle Willie entailed me reading the word of God to him, repeating the lessons that my pastor taught me in Bible Study, and sharing the word that was given to me on Sunday. I continued to pray with him, for him, and anointed his head with blessed oil. Upon one of my visits with him I recall asking him if he believed that God has the power to heal him? He responded, "Yes, Stevie, because I believe in you, you have been through so much and you're still standing." I, immediately, corrected him by saying, "Don't believe in me, believe in who sent me; The Almighty God." He said that he did. I was, later, informed that his cancer had spread from his lungs to his brain and that there was nothing more they could do for him other than keep him comfortable.

My uncle had a DNR (do not resuscitate) order placed in his medical file. Sometime had gone by since I had visited my uncle Willie. I was informed that his health was deteriorating rapidly. I remember entering his room and one of my aunts was the only one there with him. After speaking to her, I asked how he was doing? She stated that he had been in and out of consciousness and when he was conscious he was really incoherent. Willie must have heard my voice because he opened his eyes and held my hand. He looked directly at me and excitingly said, "Stevie I made it, I made it Stevie," and then he slipped back into an incoherent trance like- state. To my knowledge, that was the most he had spoken in several days, as well as, being the most coherent.

When he spoke those words, "Stevie, I made it!" It actually sent a chill through my whole body and after he said it he went back to an unconscious state, like nothing had happened. I prayed to my Heavenly Father for a revelation of what my uncle meant when he said that he made it. But, I received no answer. The next time I saw my uncle, Willie, I was with my father, his brother Henry. He had been transferred to a hospice ward connected to the hospital where he had been admitted. There were no monitors connected to him to show his blood pressure, heart rate, pulse, etc. From what I was told, my uncle, Willie was at peace with whatever was going to happen next.

We arrived there to find several of his brothers, sisters and other family members already present. We all were told that he could pass in a matter of days, or even hours, that's why everyone gathered to be at his bedside. We all had taken our semi private time with Willie and all of us totaling about a dozen stood around talking amongst ourselves. Willie was in an incoherent state, mostly unconscious, all while we were there. All the signs indicated that his demise was imminent and, possibly, very soon.

I am never one to trust in any doctor's report; because I knew that all my God had to do was speak a word and my uncle would be healed and made whole again. Before most of us were ready to go, someone suggested that we have a group prayer and they also suggested that I lead us in prayer. I of course, being the praying man that I am, would never turn down an invitation to lead believers in prayer. I was praying in the Spirit. I can't exactly remember everything that, I said except that my God is all powerful, and that it would never be too late for him to heal Willie. I remember hearing myself state that we will have God's answer to our prayers concerning Willie tonight. I will state with all certainty that statement didn't come from me; it came through me.

My father and I had parked close to where my aunt, Carolyn (his sister) was parked. After we left the facility, together, we all stood in the parking lot and talked for a while. I always look forward to and enjoy talking with

Carolyn; she has such a spirit of peace and genuine concern for other people. I truly love and appreciate her for being there for my son, Steven during the last weeks of his time here on this earth. I would occasionally bump into her at Steven's bedside. I would always see the evidence that she had been there, by the blessed oil that she would anoint Steven with.

My auntie, Carolyn, is known for her loving-kindness and genuine concern for other people's well-being, especially her family. I never asked her to be there with my son or to do the things that she did. Just being there with me in Steven's room as I had the verbal confrontation with one of the specialist, assigned to Steve's care, was comforting to me. Carolyn is always eager to care for someone in need; she doesn't wait for, or even need to be asked. All she needs to know is that someone is in need, and she's there. She has been there for her mother and she was living with her until she was no longer able to provide her with all the care she required; but faithfully spent time with her at the nursing home that she was in. She also cared for her brother (my uncle) Willie; moving him in with her, and taking time off from work to care for him. I am truly grateful for, and thank my Heavenly Father, for my auntie Carolyn, and I love her very much.

Later on that evening, I received a call from my father stating that my uncle Willie had passed some hours after we had left. I received a chill throughout my whole body as I recalled the Holy Spirit speaking through me stating that whatever was going to happen was going to happen tonight. That night, I also received my answer as to what my uncle meant when he said "Stevie, I made it." Willie had seen heaven and knew that he was going to enter soon. He was so excited because he had seen the Glory of God, and he knew his ties to this earthly realm would soon be severed.

I experienced a great sense of joy in the fact that my uncle was saved, at peace and had received a glimpse of heaven knowing he would be entering there soon. My role in Willie's last weeks of his life here, however small it was, I know it was ordained by He who sent me, the Almighty God. I was glad that I had the opportunity again, as I did with my son, Steven, to pray with, pray for, and minister to a loved one in their time of need before leaving this earth. Beautiful and I had talked about what had transpired during my last visit with my uncle Willie. I had told her how surprised I was that the family had requested that I lead them in prayer. We further discussed how I was praying in the spirit. Also, how I heard myself say that we all will know what will happen regarding Willie being healed and fully recovering or receiving a perfect healing and going home to heaven tonight.

When I received a call from my father informing me of Willie's passing I received a second chill through my whole body again when I told Beautiful the news. She told me that it was good that I made myself available to God to be used in this manner again. I agreed with her 100%; but I also hoped that this wouldn't be my only ministry; to minister to people who are about to leave this earthly realm. If this was indeed my calling, I, of course, would accept it because all I want to do in this life is to serve my God any way He sees fit for me to serve Him. My God has a way of calling me to do a work for Him when I don't necessarily feel that I am ready or even capable of accomplishing it. I am fully aware that my God would never set me up for failure. Whenever He gives me a work to do he has already given me the ability and the resources to complete the work, successfully.

When given an assignment to do by God my responsibility is to faithfully make myself available to be used, so I can complete the work. It truly never has anything to do with my personal abilities. A perfect example of this truth is me writing this book. Truly, all I am doing is making myself available to be used by the Holy Spirit, who is directing my every stroke of the pen.

Chapter 17

THE CALL TO MINISTRY

The first man that I, instantly, bonded with when I first started coming to Rhema Word Kingdom Ministries was DaShaun Blankenship, he was a minister then, now Elder and always my brother. Since I met him DaShaun has been there for me in very critical and pivotal points in my walk with God. It was only fitting that my God used him to give me that nudge that I needed to answer my call to ministry. I was having a conversation with him one day when he began encouraging me, by stating how much I have grown and progressed in my walk of faith with God. He went on to say, that the way I talk today is so much different than I did when he first met me.

DaShaun told me that I should stop wasting time. The Pastor was beginning a new M.I.T. (ministers in training) class and that I need to set up a time to talk to him in about being in that class. He said, he knew that I was already aware of the calling all my life and that it was time to proceed. My brother had the ability to see the potential in people even when that particular person didn't, and also could motivate a person into action. I did just what he suggested that I should do. I first talked it over with my wife, my number one fan, and motivator; she, of course, agreed. So only after making a decision to move forward I called Jackie to make an appointment to see Pastor Glasper regarding joining the M.I.T. class.

Surprisingly, I was able to procure an appointment to see my Pastor within days after expressing my interest to Jackie in joining the MIT class. I must admit, I was feeling somewhat apprehensive regarding my upcoming meeting with Pastor Glasper. I had no idea what questions he would ask me, let alone what my answers would be. I had mentioned earlier on that I am very analytical in my thought processes, as many of you know in order to analyze you must have a sufficient amount of data (information) which in this case I didn't.

The day had come for my meeting with the Pastor. He was very personable when greeting me as I entered his office. He verified with me my purpose for wanting to meet with him and he asked me what made me think that I was called to be a minister? I hesitated, momentarily, before answering him; I then stated that as long as I can remember all I have ever wanted to do was to serve my God any way that He saw fit. I told him that long ago a young lady who was a direct report of mine asked me what I truly desired to do with my life. I was hesitant in answering her, so she coaxed me on and I had given her the same answer. The only reason why I was so hesitant was because I knew my lifestyle was truly not in line with my desire to serve God.

I have come a long way since then, so I can now express my desire to serve God without hesitation. Pastor looked me in my eyes and told me that I really didn't answer his question. He said I failed to tell him how I felt that I was called to minister to the people of God. He went on to say that answering a call to be a minister is nothing to take lightly. It is a difficult assignment. He told me that he would allow me to sit in on the class and he instructed me to pray to God for a Scripture regarding my call to ministry. I was instructed to tell him the scripture after God gives it to me. Pastor Glasper told me that it's imperative for God to give that Scripture because when things get rough, and they will. I will even get to a point when I would question if I was really called to do this; that's when I can refer back to the Scripture that was given to me.

I started attending the class that following Monday. I was so eager to learn from this man of God because he met and exceeded my expectations of how I felt a Pastor should be. Beautiful and I searched for many, many years and attended a multitude of churches before finding a Pastor with such an anointing on his life, such as Pastor Gerald L. Glasper. He was all that I was told he was by his big brother, Jimmy, and just as he said; that if my family and I attended Rhema Word Kingdom Ministries we would join. Since I was given the opportunity to learn from such a man, I wasn't about to waste it; I sat front and center so I wouldn't miss out on anything he had to say. I was pleasantly surprised to learn that he truly has a sense of humor, even though he was very strict and serious in training future ministers and leaders. He had a true anointing for preaching, teaching, and ministering the Word of God in such a way that a person can easily understand.

He made sure that we understood that being called to ministry wasn't easy. It would be hard work and that the people that we minister to won't always be appreciative or be receptive when we minister God's Word to them. He stated that there would be times when we would get frustrated, make mistakes and even doubt that we were called by God to minister to His people. That's why it was imperative that we receive a Scripture from the Lord regarding our call to ministry. I remember sitting in class one Monday evening in my usual seat that was always available front row center. I was utterly amazed at his ability to divide the word of God and explain it to us with such ease. I thought to myself that I wanted to be just like him. Pastor abruptly stopped in mid-sentence of what he was teaching and said, "No you don't, you don't want to be just like me, I am not the mark that you want to reach." He went on to say that we all should strive to be like Jesus Christ for that's who he is working to be like.

I, literally, stopped breathing for a few moments when this man addressed my thoughts, just as I thought them. I had already had several experiences with Pastor when he revealed some things about me that he couldn't know unless the Holy Spirit had revealed it to him. This time it was instantaneous so it literally blew my mind. Pastor Glasper told us that we may want the same anointing that he has on his life and the ability to divide the word of God like he does and to hear from God as he does, but we must know that it cost him something. He said we should always be careful when asking for the same anointing that someone else has because we have no idea what that person had to go through before receiving it.

He was open and kind enough to share some of the things he had to go through to get to where he is now in his walk with God. We were cautioned not to always be so quick to blame the enemy for all of our trials, tribulations and adversities we may face as we move forward in our ministry. It could well be God, giving us the opportunity to stretch our faith, increase our patience, perseverance, and to prove how much we truly desire to serve Him despite the difficulties we are facing, at the present time. I continued coming to class, regularly, and I also kept praying daily for God to give me my Scripture for my call to ministry. I was fervently praying daily without receiving an answer for three weeks, yet, I continued. I knew in my heart, that I was called to minister to the people of God, so I was confused when God wouldn't give me my Scripture, right away.

I didn't understand then, but I know now that God wanted me to show how much I wanted to serve Him and that I would keep seeking an answer from Him no matter how long it would take. It was truly my time to diligently chase after Him just as He had chased after me for all those years. My Heavenly Father has shown me so much grace, mercy, favor, love and compassion despite the fact that I continued to run from my calling and practiced all manners of foolish behavior. My God was patient with me and in hot pursuit of me for many, many years; so me waiting a few weeks, or so, for the Scripture for my calling to ministry was truly nothing in comparison. Three and a half weeks had passed before God gave me my Scripture, and I was blown away by it. I asked God was I hearing correctly from Him. He confirmed with me that I was; because it was such a powerful Scripture to me I prayed for a fuller revelation as to its meaning. You see God sees me for who I truly am, all I can see is all that I had done throughout my whole life.

For as long as I can remember all I ever wanted to do was to serve my God any way He saw fit. I still don't have a preference as to how I wanted to serve God. I do, however, have a divine must to serve Him. I have always loved God more than anyone or anything else and my first heart's desire is to be used by Him any way that He desires. I leave it all up to my creator as to how I serve Him, because only he knows my purpose so to me any specific idea desire or preference is futile. Because, I, the creation can't tell the Creator what I was created for, only He knows. Purposely, I have neglected to provide you, the reader, with my Scripture because it's for me. I did share it with my wife, Triscennea and she was taken aback by what Scripture God had given me, also. I do read from a study Bible that actually breaks down and explains the meaning of certain verses of Scripture. My particular study Bible did choose to expound on the meaning of my Scripture verse; so I received a better understanding of it.

When I first met with my Pastor he told me to tell him what Scripture God gave me as soon as I received it? I must be honest; I was hesitant to share it with him right away; even though I asked God to confirm that I was hearing correctly from him. I still didn't trust me. I knew, for a fact, that the Holy Spirit talks to my Pastor directly, instantaneously even, so when I tell him what God gave me he would know right away if God truly gave me that to me or not. An additional two weeks had passed and I was still attending class regularly, without sharing the Scripture I had been given with my Pastor. I had, however, written it down on an index card and had been reading it out loud daily. When the third week had arrived, I had the card with me and I was instructed by the Holy Spirit to give it to him. That night, right after class had ended, I reminded pastor Glasper that he told me to tell him the Scripture that I was given by the Lord, and then I handed him the card.

Pastor smiled at me when I handed him the card saying "Oh this is it? You wrote it down." I watched him closely. Holding my breath in anticipation as he read the card, after he finished reading it, he tilted his head to the left and said, "Yes, this is it!" I, immediately, exhaled with a sigh of relief. The fact was that because of the weight of the Scripture had that I was given I found it hard to believe that it was truly for me until I received confirmation from this mighty man of God. As the class went on, week after week, I was totally amazed by all the teachings and revelations I was receiving from this anointed man of God. The more he taught me the more I wanted to be like Jesus and the more that I learned that I truly wasn't like Christ. The more knowledge and understanding that I received in class the more I realized that a great work had to be done in me so that I could even slightly resemble Jesus.

There is a popular saying with the people from my generation, "When you know better, you should do better." Well, now, that I began to know better, the better that I knew that I couldn't do better, at least not by my own strength and power. I received the revelation that only by divine guidance, intervention, faith, perseverance and the death of my flesh can this be accomplished. I needed God to, literally, make me all over again. I learned just because I am saved and have the desire to be more like Christ it just doesn't happen; it required a great work to be done in me. My time in the MIT class was an awesomely powerful, yet humbling experience. I learned so much more about God's love for us and His nature. In doing so, I received a better revelation of how far apart is man's ways from God's ways and a truer appreciation of that truth. Before attending this class, I thought that I had a better understanding of my Heavenly Father's nature, depth and extent of His love for His creation. I quickly learned that my methodology and ideology was miniscule at best.

The fact, of the matter, is that I truly never thought that I could fathom the depth and the width of God's love for us; but I did (before this class) think that I could somewhat imagine it. Week after week, went on and I was pretty much undone after each class. I was, indeed, so pleased that I had finally stopped running from my God and had truly made a beginning on answering His call on my life and yet realizing how much I need to learn and how far I had come and how far I had yet to go. My class had a set scheduled time to begin and to end; however, we rarely ever ended at the appointed time. I remember one evening Pastor ended the class early; which really meant he ended class around its appointed end time. I was standing outside having a conversation with one of my classmates, my brother in Christ, Joshua Carey another anointed brother in Christ.

I can't exactly recall the particulars of our conversation except that it had to do with the awesome training we were receiving and how powerful the teachings were to us. I was facing him in a south easterly position when while we were talking I witnessed a light traveling in the sky from the East to the West. It was traveling in a straight line at first until it started to descend at a 90° angle and touched down in an empty field across the street. It appeared to me that a star had fallen from the sky. After it had fallen to the ground, I asked Josh did he see it. He told me not at first, not until he looked at my facial expression as I watched the event occur, then he turned to look.

I asked Josh had he ever witnessed anything like that before and he replied no, then I said me neither. As I think back on that event I cannot fully understand why neither of us went across the street to examine what indeed had landed in that barren field. By nature, I have an inquisitive and analytical mind so it would have been only a natural reaction for me to go and investigate the landing site. Instead, Josh and I briefly discussed what we had seen and soon afterwards parted in our separate ways. That very same night I went home and told Beautiful what we had witnessed and she was amazed because she had never seen such a thing as that before. I did pray to God to give me the meaning of what I had been a witness to. I didn't receive any revelation regarding the meaning of the event I had witnessed. I excitedly continued to attend class even though many times I felt a sense of inadequacy due to everyone else's knowledge of Scriptures in comparison to my own. I, also, couldn't help but notice that everyone there served on a ministry except me. Many times, I felt out of place, like I didn't even belong there; but yet, I still sat front row center.

My desire to serve my God and to answer his call far outweighed all of those feelings. A week or so had passed and I still didn't receive any revelation on what Josh and I had witnessed falling from the sky. Also, there had not been a news report regarding this event. I soon afterwards stopped praying for the meaning of what we had witnessed. However, I am glad that I didn't witness this event alone. Beautiful was still struggling reconciling with Steven's passing. She hadn't forgiven herself for the time when our relationship with him was estranged for a little over a year. I reminded her that Steven loved us both very much and that he had moved past that before he left this earth. Triscennea felt that since I practically spent every day, mostly all day with him during his last six months or so on earth, that I was afforded the opportunity to fully reconcile my relationship with him. She stated that she didn't have the quality time with him that I did and that there was still so much, not said and undone, between them.

We were introduced to a card game named Phase 10 by some friends from Rhema Word; which we enjoyed playing very much. On Saturday night, October 9, 2010, we invited Corey my brother-in-law over to play Phase 10 he arrived accompanied by a female acquaintance, our good friend Robin was already at our home so we played for hours that night. We were drinking Moscato Wine that night enjoying the game and each other's company. I remember Beautiful complaining of having a headache that night; she also was acting a little peculiar that night, as well. My wife was never one to keep driving at someone; that's my behavioral characteristic, not hers. That night she kept driving persistently at Corey to come to Rhema Word one Sunday; telling him that he would love it and even if he didn't join, he needed to find a church home. He replied that he would come one day, she suggested for him to come (at that time) tomorrow. I could see that her persistence was beginning to bug him, so I asked her to stop badgering him and reminding her that she was acting more like me with her tenacity then herself.

I had to tell her to stop asking him, that he already told you that he would come one Sunday. She wanted to know, specifically when; that was the answer she was looking for and Corey was unwilling to give her a set date. Even though, his big sister was beginning to agitate him, he remained cool and continued to beat us in Phase 10.

We awoke the next morning; which was Sunday, October 10, 2010 and we departed from our home to go to Rhema Word Kingdom Ministries. Everything started off normally accept when they asked if anyone was visiting us or anyone who was not a member to stand. They instructed the members (as they do every Sunday) to greet our guest and welcome them to our church. As a family we never made a practice of walking around the church to meet and greet the visitors, only if they were in direct proximity of us would we do so. This particular Sunday Beautiful left her seat and went around meeting and greeting our guests; which was totally out of character for her. I even watched her go up to our Pastor, Gerald L. Glasper and Co-Pastor Tony A. Glasper and give them a hug. She also greeted our sister, Roni, with an, extensively long hug; which I found very peculiar at the time. When she returned back to her seat I asked her what was that all about; she replied that she just had felt like it, no particular reason.

When we returned home she began preparing our Sunday dinner; which was always much more extravagant than all the other meals that she prepared during the week. I remember coming into the kitchen to see if she needed help with anything and she brought up some concerns about some things that I needed to do in the future for myself. I did think it was a bit strange that she was concerned about my future, not our future. She was stressing something that I needed to do for myself going forward. As I reflect back on these occurrences that I have just mentioned and what I will be talking about next; I realized that we truly were in two entirely different places. For instance, after our son, Steven passed and we paid off his truck I chose to have vanity plates that read, "OUR SON 1." It was then, and still is, very important to me that I proclaim our son's victory over satan, cancer, and suffering. My wife had purchased another vehicle and also ordered vanity plates that referenced our son Steven, as well. Hers read, "MIS U SG2" and they arrived that Saturday, October 9, 2010.

It was a holiday weekend for us because the next day, Monday was Columbus Day and the business' that employed us recognized that particular holiday so we were both off of work. Robin called us and asked if we would come over for an impromptu barbecue she was having. We didn't even finish cooking our meal; we immediately left to go over to Robin's house. When we arrived, it was already dark and only a few people were there, just family, in which we fitted into perfectly since we've been friends for 20+ years. We were having a good time enjoying each other's company and eating barbecue. I remember having a conversation with Craig (Robin's oldest son) about love and marriage. Craig was in his early 30s at the time and was on his second marriage; he felt that he got married too young. I began to share some of Beautiful's and my history of how young we were when we got together and I informed him that we got married at the age of 22 years old. I told him that there was no such thing as a fairytale marriage. You know, when they lived happily, together, ever after. I informed him that that wasn't reality the reality of marriage is that you have to work at it, make sacrifices and changes for the good of your marriage.

The conversation that Craig and I had brought back so many memories of the love I shared with Triscennea; I became very sentimental. I stood before everyone there that night and professed my undying love for my wife. I told them that a priest that I was working for at the time asked me when I was 18 years old did I love Triscennea and I answered, "Yes!" He then asked me if I could imagine living my life without her and I answered, "No!" I then, openly, confessed to everyone that night that I still can't imagine living my life without her and this is after being together for 28 years and being married for 22 of those wonderful years.

Chapter 18

A Defining Experience

Robin and Craig were sitting on the stairs of her front porch; Triscennea and I were sitting on chairs, directly in front, facing them. Robin was complaining of how Craig was expressing concerns of her dating some guy and wanted more information on him. He stated that he loved his mother and that his concerns were valid. We watched them go back and forth in their conversation for a while until Beautiful interrupted by stating, "At least you still have your son." I already knew that my wife was having a hard time accepting our son, Steven's passing; it had only been a year and a month since it had occurred. That night, and at that instance, I saw a deeper sense of sadness over the loss of our son in my wife than ever before. Shortly thereafter, we said our goodbyes to everyone and started on our journey home. It was well after midnight when we left Robin's and arrived home. We took a bath and went directly to bed. Often times we would have an extensive conversation in bed before going to sleep, no matter how tired we may be; however this particular night we didn't.

When we awoke the next morning Monday, October 11, 2010, I decided that I would cook us breakfast. I got up and performed my normal regiment, got dressed and went directly into the kitchen. I remember being so happy that we were off of work together and I was looking forward to spending some quality time with my wife. I had started setting everything out preparing to cook, then I went back into the bedroom where Triscennea was still lying in the bed. I asked her if she wanted sausage or bacon with her breakfast; she requested sausage. I went back into the kitchen and started frying the sausage when I was almost finished, I was interrupted by a strange hee-haw sound. I thought it was my sons goofing around so I yelled for them to stop, but the noise continued. I turned the stove off and decided to go and investigate the origin of the strange loud sound that I continued to hear.

All of a sudden, I remembered that my youngest son Centarious had left home already to go to a friend's house, so it couldn't be my two sons making this noise. I rushed towards the bedroom stopping at the bathroom to find Beautiful on the floor making this strange noise as she was breathing. At this point, my breathing stopped and my heart dropped as I dropped to my knees to turn beautiful over only to see her eyes rolled back into a blank stare. I yelled for Tre'mont to come and help me try to get his mother up from the bathroom floor, as I also tried to get her to regain consciousness. It seemed surreal, I was in a state of panic; I instantly flashed back to when Steve fell out in the same bathroom, the year before.

When my attempts failed to wake her up, I had Tre' call Centarious to tell him what was going on so that he could come back home. While Tre' was talking to his brother on his phone, I was calling 911 from the house phone requesting that an ambulance be sent to our home. Centarious called me on our house phone because he couldn't understand what Tre' was trying to say. I informed him that his mother passed out in the bathroom and I am unable to wake her or to get her up and I needed him to come home right now.

I remember asking God what was happening? Why was this happening? Tre' and I were finally able to get her up after I had him call Centarious so that he could come home. We were walking with one of her arms around his shoulders and the other around mine; in the midst of us carrying her to the couch in the living room she regained consciousness. Gently we laid her down on the couch. We heard the sirens from the ambulance arriving so I told Tre' to go downstairs and let them in. Triscennea asked, why was an ambulance here? I then informed her that she had passed out in the bathroom. She replied, "No I didn't!" I asked her how she got from the bathroom to the couch in the front room, she stated that she had walked.

It felt like I was in the twilight zone because that's exactly verbatim what Steven had said to me just last year. Tre' had let the EMTs in and I called for them to come upstairs where we were. Beautiful began, to adamantly profess, that she felt fine and that she didn't know why they were called. I convinced her to at least let them take her vital signs. As they were taking her blood pressure she looked at me as she touched her temples with her right hand and said "Aaawww I have a headache," then she immediately lost consciousness and started making that strange noise again while she was breathing.

My heart dropped again as I told the EMTs that that was the sound she was making when I found her passed out on the bathroom floor. I asked them why she was making that sound; but they could give me no answer. I gave them the pertinent information on my wife and they prepared her for transport. Centarious arrived home as they were bringing her downstairs and out of the house. They told me what hospital they were taking her to as they were placing her in the ambulance. Centarious was still standing by the door with Tre' and his friends as he yelled out, "Oh my God, no first my brother, now my mother!" As he started to openly cry uncontrollably. I went back over to my sons to comfort them with a hug and told them that everything would be all right.

I was unable to show them that I, too, was in a state of shock and was truly concerned about what the outcome would be. My God calmed me down so that I was able to calmly speak words of reassurance and comfort to my son's. Centarious verbalized what he was feeling; Tre' however was excited and scared but was nonverbal at the time. The similarities between what had just happened with Beautiful and what had occurred with Steven just a year before was to glaring to ignore. I refused to let that be the focal point of my thoughts at the time. The ambulance had left, approximately, 10 minutes or so before I did, due to my conversation with my son's.

The hospital where they took my wife was about 10 to 12 minutes away from our home. I pulled over, three or four blocks, before reaching the hospital to call Roni to inform her of what was happening. We immediately prayed for Triscennea's healing and full recovery. She then told me that she would contact the other elders and ministers along with our Pastor. My faculties were intact enough for me to continue my drive to the hospital's emergency entrance. By this time 20 or so minutes had passed since they had left my home with Beautiful. There was some difficulty at first in finding her location even though I informed them what ambulance company had brought her there and approximately when she should have arrived.

A sense of frustration and panic began to set in as I waited for what seemed like hours to find out where she was and for me to see her. In actuality it only took five minutes or so; but since I was so stressed, concerned and angry because I wasn't ushered in immediately it seemed like a lifetime of waiting. I had her insurance information and her tote bag sealed with her prescription medication bottles. The ER attending physician asked me questions regarding her medical history; which I was able to answer with accurate details. They brought up when she was brought their last year when her blood pressure was extremely elevated due to the stress of our son being hospitalized.

The doctor started asking me a line of questions such as, "Has she been taking her medications regularly as they were prescribed?" I informed the doctor that she had been taking a large regimen of medications for over 20 years and that she is very disciplined in doing so. He asked me has she been overly depressed lately. I began to understand where his line of questioning was going, so I cut to the chase. I asked the doctor was he asking me if my wife was suicidal. If maybe she tried to kill herself with an overdose. He reluctantly answered, "Could it be possible?" Because right now he couldn't explain the state she was now in medically. I replied vehemently no! That was not possible, my wife would never or could ever try to take her own life.

I told him that he could definitely abandon that line of thinking and concentrate on finding out what's causing my wife's current condition. He attempted to explain to me why he had to ask. I interrupted him by stating that it doesn't matter and that he should just move on; because of what he asked me was not only an impossibility but an absurdity as well. They continued to run tests, draw blood and monitor her vital signs, as well. I called my parents as well as Beautiful's parents to apprise them of what was going on.

They performed a CAT scan of Beautiful's head and found that she had several ruptured blood vessels in her brain. The doctors also told me that they were ill-equipped to handle a trauma like this and that she needed to be airlifted to another hospital, immediately. Pastor Glasper arrived shortly after I received that devastating news. Upon his arrival, I was in an emotionally distraught state; I was crying uncontrollably and was barely able to communicate to him what the doctors said about my wife's condition. Pastor stood on one side of Beautiful as I stood on the other, he prayed with me and over my wife.

Usually the presence of my Pastor and his prayers would bring me to a place of peace; however this time it didn't, and he saw that. In seeing that I was still very distraught; he told me just what I needed to hear to usher me into a place of peace. He stayed for a short while after I had calmed down. He asked me if my sons and I needed anything, and reminded me that I would not go through this alone. An individual from the ER medical staff informed me that they had room for her at a certain hospital. The only problem with their choice was that wasn't her hospital. I wanted her to go where she had been a patient for over 20 years; the place that she had both of her kidney transplants, where they were familiar with her medical history.

The doctor was getting frustrated with my being adamant that she be transferred to the hospital of my choice; which was only a few blocks away from where they chose for her to go. My unyielding behavior soon took root and they began to investigate the possibility of Triscennea being admitted where I wanted her to be. An hour or so had passed before they returned to me with the news that she would be admitted to the hospital of my choosing. I am finding it immeasurably difficult to fully express how and what I was feeling at this present time. I must first state, that my faith and trust in my Heavenly Father was still as strong as ever. This time, however, I knew from what I had learned in the case of Steven, that I had to consider what my God's Will was in this case, not just what I wanted the outcome to be.

In facing this current medical crisis concerning my wife, I began to encourage myself by thinking of all that our God had brought us through over the past years. I thought of all the medical challenges that we had faced together over the past 28 years and how our God showed Himself strongly in defeating every sickness that tried to overtake my wife, Beautiful. I recalled how my God enabled me to walk by faith and not by sight, as long as I kept my focus on Jesus Christ. I, also, recalled the peace that He had given me throughout the many challenges and bad doctor reports we received regarding Steven's condition. I chose then, as I choose now, not to believe or have faith in the report of the doctors; I choose to believe in the report of the Lord that my wife is already healed and made whole again by Jesus' stripes.

Because I am a born again Christian, a man of faith and a true follower of my Lord and Savior Jesus Christ; I can proclaim victory over this sickness in the Mighty Name of Jesus. I was actually upset with myself over my initial response to the situation; because I have seen my God perform miracles all my life and have been a direct witness to them. The Holy Spirit reminded me that there is no condemnation for those that are in Christ Jesus. He reminded me that I am still a fallible creature, an emotional being and that I have the propensity to have doubt even if just for a moment. I have always held myself to a higher standard than I do for everyone else, because of all the grace, mercy, favor, love and compassion my Heavenly Father has shown me all the days of my life.

All I really needed to do is remember that the enemy wants me to be in a state of self-condemnation; in doing so my focus is off of Jesus Christ who is the source of my strength. I will always be the first to admit if at any point in time I chose to face these difficulties all by myself; I would surely be defeated. It is only when my eyes and my focus are set on Jesus that I surely come out victorious. I departed from the hospital as they prepared my wife for transport. The drive home was very difficult but I needed to check on my sons and let them know what was going on with their mother. I came home assuring them that their mother is in God's mighty hands, and that He would take care of her. I knew it was important for them to know that she had been transferred from the hospital that she was taken to since that was the very same hospital in which their brother Steven had passed away.

As the head and spiritual covering for my household it is very important that I set the correct tone; which is one of faith in the Almighty God and that He is in control of this situation. I explained to them that our God is more than able to heal their mother and that He would. All we need do is trust and believe in His healing and restorative power. We prayed together as a family in faith for Triscennea's healing and full restoration, and then I left to be with my wife. I had already informed my parents and my parents-in- law that Beautiful was being airlifted to her hospital, in the city. I, also, called Roni, Marvin, and DaShaun to inform them of the transfer.

Today, is Tuesday, July 30, 2013; which would've been Beautiful's and my 25th wedding anniversary. I must admit that I find it challenging to write and relive this portion of my life on this particular day. As I have previously stated, the Holy Spirit brings these moments back to my memory with crystal clarity and I experience all the emotions along with it and in some cases more vividly than I did originally.

When I arrived at the hospital where my wife was taken, I promptly sought her location. They were, at the time of my arrival, running some tests on her so I had to wait to see her. A room in intensive care was designated for her, after they completed the tests I went there to see her. Beautiful was still in a coma and they had shaved a large portion of her hair, and drilled a hole in her skull to relieve some of the pressure off of her brain. It was very difficult, to say the least, to see my best friend, my second love in this life (the first being my Heavenly Father); my wife and the mother of my children in this condition. I greeted her with a kiss on her lips and told her that I loved her. I know, I stated that she was still in a coma; nevertheless I knew that she could feel my presence when I entered the room. She could still hear my voice and feel my kiss; even though she was unable to respond. A short time had passed before her doctor entered the room. I introduced myself to him stating that I was Triscennea's husband and I asked him what her current condition was. He began by stating that my wife was very sick and that a brain aneurysm was the cause of her passing out and slipping into a coma.

The doctor explained that the aneurysm in her brain did not burst, for if it had she would have died, instantly. It did however, rupture and began to bleed, profusely. He said that her brain was swollen and that's why they drilled a hole in her skull to relieve some of the pressure. The doctor went on to say, that they needed to repair the rupture but he also believed that she had more ruptures than the initial one that brought her there. Upon hearing this news, all I could think was, I know that my God would never have me face more than I could bare. I did however, feel that I was being brought to the brink of all I could physically, emotionally, and spiritually handle.

It had only been a short span of time since my family and I faced the whole ordeal of my eldest son being placed in jail and charged with murder. Everything that we had to go through to get him released on bail, preparing for his trial, then the following year him being diagnosed with cancer. Then facing that battle, as well as, battling for his freedom. I witnessed my son change from a healthy, vibrant, young man who had his whole life ahead of him, with a bright future. In an instant, everything changed. He was placed in jail, charged with murder (when it was clearly self-defense) not only was his future in jeopardy, but his freedom, as well. And as if that wasn't enough the following year being diagnosed with cancer so he was fighting for his very life, as well, as his freedom.

Then, I realized that I was no longer focusing on the solution, which is, Jesus Christ. I had allowed my mind to focus on and relive the past difficulties that I had already faced and, through Christ Jesus, had came through victoriously. I did choose to remember how I was able to confront those challenges with a peace that surpassed all understanding; a peace that no one or nothing in this world could have given me for that peace came only from the Lord. Yet, another opportunity had arisen for me to place my trust in the doctor's report or the report of the Lord; I did then and will always choose to have faith in the report of the Lord. I treated this situation no differently than the situation with my son, Steven. I called upon the elders of my church to come and pray over her and anoint her with oil in the name of the Lord, Jesus.

Some may ask how I could believe in the same manner for knowing that after doing all this that my son, Steven passed away. I believed that my God could and would heal and fully restore my son. In no way, shape, form or fashion did my God fail me; He just decided to give Steven a perfect healing; which was His right and decision to make. Yes, Steven is my son but first and foremost he's God's son, too. If you noticed I am not referring to him in the past tense because he is not dead he is alive with Christ. I trust in the Will of my Heavenly Father fully and whole heartedly; for you see, He knew Steven's end before his beginning. I am referring to when his time on this earth would end before it even began. I have had people say to me that it was so unfair for him to have to go through all that suffering the last two years of his life. When that statement was first said to me the only way I could respond was that it was God's Will.

It wasn't until several more people had made that same statement to me that my Heavenly Father gave me revelation on why it had to happen that way. We all have a designated date and time to be born into this world and a designated date and time to exit this world. My God knew, of course, that Steve's time here was coming near to an end. Steven had turned away from his mother and me; he also had begun to turn away from God. My God in His infinite wisdom had to sit him down; so he allowed him to be falsely accused and placed in jail for murder. He was now away from the world that he knew where he had begun to think that he was in control of his own destiny.

He was charged with murder in a state where they don't give bail for anyone charged with murder. Steven was placed in a position where he had nowhere else to turn but to the one who has all power, the Almighty God. So he began his journey to increasing his faith and total dependency on God for only God could save him now. He finally realized that by himself he was powerless. As I have already stated previously in the earlier chapters of this book that my God made a way out of no way, and my son was freed on bail. Not only was he freed on bail, but was able to reside with us outside of the state where he was charged with murder and was able to procure a position with an excellent company within three weeks of being released.

He was also allowed to leave this state for the job training that he needed for his new position; our God is an awesome God.

I had been ministering to Steven on God's faithfulness to us and instructing him to continue to close the gap in his relationship with our Heavenly Father. I constantly reminded him how our God made a way out of no way and that God didn't set him free for him to be imprisoned later; that's just not in His nature. The following year after Steven was released from jail on bail and after he and I were laid off from our job in the same week; I began going to the doctor with him regarding the lump on his neck that was later diagnosed as cancer. We, as a family of believers in the Almighty God and members of the Body of Christ (church) were faced with yet another challenge even before the first one was resolved. My faith in God did not waiver due to this new development; I saw it as another opportunity for my God to show just how mighty He is. I witnessed my son's physical man deteriorate before my eyes rapidly, but I also witnessed his spirit man grow stronger and mightier, day by day.

Steven witnessed his friends and some family members turn their back on him. He finally got a revelation of how true and deep his mother's and my love was for him. He came to realize that no matter how many people left him or turned their backs on him that God will always be there for him; that He would never leave him nor forsake him. My God used all these situations to prepare my son and His son, Steven to come home to heaven, victoriously. Steven did go home in victory for he overcame everything that the enemy threw at him. Being jailed, the sickness of cancer, being abandoned by his friends and some family; I proclaim Steven's victory through Jesus Christ!!!

That's how and why I can treat this situation and confront these difficulties in the same manner, as before. I remained at the hospital with my wife for several hours into the night. I was, of course, concerned about my son's and their mental state so I constantly checked on them via telephone. It was after midnight and Triscennea's condition was listed as stable, but critical. With a great deal of reluctance, I kissed my wife good night, told her that I loved her and that I would return tomorrow. I was at that time working for a school bus company so the next morning I went to work. When I was first hired, I was given a route of a woman who was out on medical leave due to a brain aneurysm. I was informed that she was back at work doing well; so I sought her out so I could hear her story of victory over her condition.

Let me start off by saying, that it truly didn't matter even if no one previously had survived a brain aneurysm that began bleeding; because Beautiful would be the first. However, since there was a survivor in the midst I wanted to hear about her ordeal. The Holy Spirit led me to her and we talked. She stated that she really didn't share her story with many people; but since my wife was going through this ordeal she decided to talk to me a total stranger. My God is a provider, that's all I was thinking, as this woman opened up to me. She informed me that her situation was different, because they caught hers in time; in other words, before it ruptured and began to bleed. She stated that they found more than one so they operated on her and repaired them all. Today, she was doing well and stated that she was truly blessed that they found them in time. I was glad to hear her victorious testimony; although her situation was very different from Beautiful's.

Yes, I stated that I went to work the next day; even though, my wife was in the hospital with the doctor telling me that she was very sick. I was able to go to work and effectively perform my duties not because I didn't love my wife, or care if she survived or not. I was able to go to work loving my wife and leaving her in the care of my Father in Heaven, "The Almighty God," who didn't need me present in order for Him to heal her. I can't even begin to tell everyone how God honors and loves our true displays of faith. Believe me when I tell you that I was at ease going to work and while I was at work no one knew or could tell that I was going through any difficulties. Those that I did inform were amazed at my calm and cheerful demeanor. I came to work just as grateful and cheerful as I always did.

That's why it was so important for me to do that self-check on myself when I realized that my focus was off of Jesus, the author and finisher of my faith, my source of strength, power and the solution to all of life's problems. For I remember the only way that I was able to walk by faith and not by sight was by keeping all of my focus on Jesus Christ. The day was Tuesday, October 12, 2010 after coming from work and returning home to cook and care for my son's; I returned to the hospital to be with Beautiful. I can't even begin to verbalize the love I have for my Rhema Word Kingdom Ministries Family. I was joined that evening by three elders, friends, brother and sisters from Rhema Word Roni, Marrlla, and Marvin.

I am so grateful to God for them being there that evening with me, praying with me, supporting me; taking time out of their lives to spend time with me during my family's time of need. They stayed with me for hours, their presence made a world of difference to me. The doctor came out with the results from the scan that they had performed on Triscennea, he stated that there were three additional bleeds other than the one that brought her there. I informed the doctor that he could speak freely because every one that was present was part of my family. He showed us what they would use to repair the ruptured blood vessels in her brain and informed us of how dangerous this operation would be. He asked me if I wanted him to perform this procedure and he confirmed that I understood that she possibly wouldn't make it through. But, it was all that they were able to try because it was imperative that they stop the bleeding.

The doctor offered me the opportunity to think about it; but informed me that they should start as soon as they possibly could. I told him without hesitation to perform the procedure, he told me that they would as soon as I signed off on it officially; but they would immediately start preparing her for the surgery. He stated that the surgery would take several hours. Just as with my son Steven's case my faith isn't in the doctors or even the surgeons hands; my trust and my faith is in my God who is and always will be in control. I didn't need time to think about what the possible outcome would be on the operating table; all I needed to know is that they had a course of action that they could take. For I, already knew that faith without works is dead. I had to put action behind my faith. In other words, as long as there was something that they could do I will allow them to, and trust my God for the outcome.

Marvin, Roni and Marrlla prayed with me and stayed with me for the duration of the surgery which actually took approximately four hours.

Their presence and prayers were a source of comfort to me, in which, I truly needed at a time like this. The surgeon finally came out to inform us that the surgery was a success, and that she was recovering. He told us that the next 24 hours or so were very crucial and continued to remind us that she was very sick. We all gathered around and sent up a prayer of praise and thanksgiving to our Heavenly Father for all that he had done and for all that He was going to do.

Shortly after receiving the good news, everyone else departed, I remained until I could see my wife. An hour or so later, she was back in her room and I was instructed that I could see her. I talked to her for a while informing her of the surgery that was performed on her and letting her know who was there with me praying for her. I of course reminded her how much I loved her and told her that I and our boys are praying for her speedy recovery so she can return home to us. Before departing from the presence of my wife I prayed over her and anointed her with blessed oil. I remembered all the obstacles and medical difficulties that we had faced together during the course of our lives, which began at the tender age of 16. By the age of 17, we had our first son Steven and she became very ill shortly thereafter and was diagnosed with Lupus. I prayed, fervently, for her then and through the course of our lives and I saw our God work miracles on our behalf time and time again; I simply saw this as another opportunity for God to show up and show his might and power in this situation. as well. I departed shortly thereafter and went home to be with our son's.

The day is Wednesday, October 13, 2010 I awoke that morning preparing myself for work. I had already left the house and was on my way to work when I received a phone call from the hospital stating that Beautiful's condition had taken a turn for the worse. I immediately called my supervisor to inform her of what was going on and that I wouldn't be in to work today. The school bus company that I worked for had its base of operation that I was assigned to was only 15 minutes away from my home. I stopped back home letting my sons know that I had gotten a call from the hospital regarding their mother so I wasn't going to work today and that I was now going to the hospital.

It was imperative that I kept my sons informed of what was going on. It was equally important that they see my reaction to any adverse news that I received regarding their mother's condition. As the head and spiritual covering for my household I set the tone, and that tone was calm and faithfilled. I could have just called them while I was enroute but I knew that that could have had a negative impact on their minds, emotions, faith and spirit. I knew that it was important for them to be informed of each event as it unfolded so that they would have an opportunity for their faith to be increased, I wouldn't suggest that parents do this with smaller, younger children. My sons were older and had just previously faced difficulties with their brother's fight with cancer. I did it then in the case of their older brother so I will continue on in this fashion with their mother.

I arrived at the hospital and was informed by the doctor that Beautiful had developed an extremely bad infection. He again informed me that my wife was very, very sick and they didn't know when or if she would come out of the coma or if she would how much irreparable brain damage had occurred due to the aneurysms and the swelling of her brain. He informed me that they were treating the infection with a regiment of antibiotics and that she had a high fever due to the infection. The doctor stated that her body had undergone a massive amount of stress over the past few days and that the prognosis for any recovery from this was dismal, at best.

I was unaffected by his unfavorable prognosis, for my faith is in the great physician, Jesus Christ. I knew that the doctors were only human with limitations in what they can accomplish, medically. That's why my focus was on and remained on the solution Jesus Christ who still is the Author and the Finisher of my Faith. I called my church office to inform Jackie of what was going on. I gave her the report from the doctor and we immediately agreed together to trust the report of the Lord.

My position as a school bus driver was part-time; my day consisted of a morning run and an afternoon run. It was getting close to the noon hour so I decided to go back to base and make my afterschool run. I figured I would come back afterwards, so I kissed and told her where I was going and that I would return. I was able to leave her presence easily because I had already given this situation over to my God and I knew that my presence wasn't necessary or required for Him to perform a miracle on Beautiful's behalf. I arrived back to my employer's base of operation and was told by my supervisor to go and be with my wife. She couldn't believe that I came to work in the first place with my wife being so ill. I informed her that there was nothing more that I could do than what I have already done; which was entrusting the healing of my wife into my God's All Mighty Hands. She told me that I couldn't work, and to go and be with Triscennea.

Since I was told that I couldn't work, as well as, being instructed upon my leaving, not to come in tomorrow either and to keep her apprised of my wife's condition. I know it must've been difficult if not impossible for her mind to process how I had such a calm demeanor. As I think back on her reactions to my calm state, perhaps, she believed that I was in shock or denial and that the realization of what was going on might hit me later while I was driving a bus load of children. The reactions that people were having to my response to the situation continued to surprise me. I couldn't understand why my demeanor seemed so foreign to them. Their reasoning led them to believe that I was either in denial or in a form of shock, or something.

I couldn't make them understand that I was fully aware of the severity of what was going on, medically, with Beautiful in this natural realm; and that I never fully relied on the doctors abilities to do anything other than be used by my God to help my wife. As I am recording these events along with my feelings as well as my reactions to them; I now with the help of the Holy Spirit I can see how my faith baffled and confused most people. I was, however, surprised at the reactions of some believers who couldn't understand how I was able to stand so strongly in the face of these difficulties. What they didn't know; but now do know thanks to my Heavenly Father instructing me to write this book and me making myself available to be used by the Holy Spirit to write it, that I am no stranger to witnessing my God consistently make a way out of no way.

If I ever had the slightest bit of doubt, all I ever had to do was to look at all that my God had brought us through. I know that my God is unchanging, in other words He is the same God now as He was during all the other many situations that Beautiful and I faced and He performed miracle after miracle on our behalf. Since God did it back then I had no doubt that he would do it again. When I arrived back at the hospital and went to see Triscennea, I was greeted by an Elder from my church that was already there. The nursing staff was preparing to perform a shift change and to do some sort of procedure on my wife so we left the room. The Elder then informed me that several other ministers and elders were there as well, they were allowed to convene in a small conference room on the floor since it was so many of them.

I was so grateful, and pleasantly surprised, to see those all gathered in response to my family's need of support and prayer. Everyone greeted me individually with a hug and words of support and encouragement; then we all prayed in Jesus's name for Beautiful's healing and full recovery. My Rhema Word Family never ceases to amaze me in regards to them exhibiting their love and support for members and families. It was even more surprising to me since I had just returned in 2008 when the ordeal began with my son, Steven and we were just attending church not actually serving in a ministry.

Elder Beverly Covington was one of the Elders that was present. Elder Covington is a mighty woman of God that I love; and am so grateful to my God for placing her in my family's life. She pulled me aside to express her concern about how I was holding up in the face of everything that was going on. I emphatically told her that I was good and was being strengthened fully by my Heavenly Father. This wise and wonderful woman of God told me that she expressed her concerns regarding me to the others and they felt that they were unfounded. She told me that I have appeared to be holding up strongly on the outside, and then she asked me how I was really doing on the inside. I informed her that I was doing well inside also on the outside, and I thanked her for her concern. She told me to re-examine myself and assured me that I didn't need to keep up an exterior of strength all the time and that it was all right to be weakened in a time such as this.

At that time I was unaware of the fact that she had prior knowledge of my past, told to her in confidence by my wife. Her being the upright woman of God that she is wouldn't allow her to betray such a confidence. I truly had no doubt despite what the doctor's report of Beautiful's condition was; that my God could and would heal her as He did so many times before. Although after talking with Beverly, I found myself thinking how grateful I was that I at least had 28 years of love and 22 of those years being married to my best friend. At the time, I was confused as to why those thoughts even entered my mind so I quickly dismissed them.

The doctor who specialized in infectious diseases told me that they were losing their battle with the infection that my wife had and that it didn't look good. I asked all of the appropriate questions regarding other medicines and or alternative treatment options that were available. I was informed that they would continue to do their best and I was again told that she was very, very sick. I believe they kept informing me of how sick she was expecting a different reaction from me in which they would never receive. What the doctors couldn't understand was the more they told me how powerfully sick Beautiful was the more I thought of how Mighty and All-Powerful my God is. I remained steadfast, unmovable and unshakable in my faith in the Great Physician, Jesus Christ.

The way I was able to handle all that was going on may have seemed unnatural to many of the people that I encountered; however to me it was a natural and normal response. I couldn't understand how people who believed in God and who are saved could lose faith or have doubts when it seemed as though everything around them was falling apart. I had to pause after writing that last sentence because I realized how that may sound to many people. What I can say is, if you choose to focus on all the problems or situations that you are facing, rather than the solution, Jesus Christ as I was doing then you probably would become overwhelmed, dismayed and find your faith lacking.

The best way that I can explain this is that we all have freedom of choice. We can either choose to focus on problems, difficulties and situations that are obviously too great for us to handle, or simply choose to focus on the solution, Jesus Christ. All that I can tell you, without a shadow of a doubt, is that it works for me. I made everyone who was there aware of what the doctor said that my wife's condition was and told them that I would continue to believe in the report of the Lord, that she is already healed by Jesus's stripes. Those that remained, prayed with me and we all touched and agreed that my wife would be healed. Then they left. I left sometime later after spending some quality time alone in prayer with my wife, Beautiful.

Today, is Thursday, October 14, 2010; I arose early in the morning and traveled to the hospital to be with my wife. I arrived there at about 9 AM and I was greeted by many ministers and elders from my church, which I considered all family. There were so many present that we just about filled the whole waiting room on the ICU floor. My parents also joined me there a short while later, and they were pleasantly surprised to see all the people who had come. We all couldn't come to the room at the same time so they rotated in shifts; I, of course, being present always. I am finding it difficult and next to impossible to remember every specific detail that occurred during that morning, so please bear with me. I had failed to mention that Beautiful had been placed on life support because she was unable to breathe on her own the previous day.

While my father, mother and I were in the room with Triscennea her oxygen saturation level began to steadily decline and her heart rate and pulse became erratic. We were asked to leave the room as they attempted to stabilize her. The time was somewhere between 12:00 noon and 12:30 PM. My Pastor Gerald L. Glasper had arrived and I met him in the hallway by the waiting room where everyone was gathered. I told him what the doctors had told me, that her demise was imminent, and could occur within the hour. I expressed to my pastor that I was still holding on to my faith that God could and still would heal my wife, despite what the doctors said.

Upon hearing what I told him, he immediately called for all of his Elders and Ministers to gather in the hallway. After they were gathered, we began to proceed down the hall to Beautiful's room; our procession was interrupted by a doctor coming towards us. The doctor looked astonished to see all of us coming in the direction of her room. He paused for a moment and told me she had already passed. We continued to proceed to

Triscennea's room because we still knew that it wasn't too late for God to perform a miracle.

The room that she was in had beds for two other patients with the individual spaces being separated by a curtain. I walked to the right side of her bed which was at her left and my Pastor was at her other side. The doctor informed us that we had to leave because they had just brought in another patient and needed the space and privacy to settle them in. I, of course, ignored his request and didn't even acknowledge that he had spoken. Everyone else had left except Pastor and I, who responded to his request stating that I was the husband and could he stay. Regardless, to whatever his response was, I wasn't going to leave my wife's side and neither did my pastor.

Earlier in this book while we faced Steven's battle with cancer; I stated that I would never falter in my faith of God's healing and restorative power. Even if he were to fall asleep (passed from this world) I would simply pray for God to wake him back up. Well, as I stated I, didn't because while his vital signs began to crash I felt a peace that surpassed all understanding and I was able to let him go. This was not my initial response to the passing of Beautiful. My pastor was holding my wife's hand on one side of the bed praying and I was holding her other hand praying. I started off by telling God okay everyone else is gone except for Pastor and I, Lord you can wake her backup now. I continued praying in this manner professing my faith in my God's power to awake those who have fallen asleep and reminding him of all the times that he had healed her in the past, it seemed like I went on and on for hours in this manner never shedding a tear waiting and fully expecting my God to honor my request.

I could feel my pastor's eyes gazing at me after the true time span of a little over five minutes. It took me that long to realize that it was His will that she come home to Him. It was only after that, that I began to weep profusely placing my head on her chest for a while; then, finally, kissing her goodbye. My pastor allowed me time for my initial grieving then he ministered to me and prayed with me over my wife. It seemed so surreal to me that I was facing a magnanimous loss again in such a short span of time. I still know, as a matter of truth, that if it were God's will he could've brought her back. I wasn't angry because with the passing of my son, Steven, I truly learned, believed, and accepted God's sovereignty; that He and He alone has the right to do whatsoever He wills.

I collected myself, physically, and emotionally, before leaving her empty vessel in that room. I realized that I had to go home to tell my son's Tre'mont and Centarious that their mother had passed away. I so dreaded the thought of me presenting them with this devastatingly tragic news and having to witness their reaction. My loss and my son's loss were, of course, different albeit was the same person. When Steven passed I mourned the loss of my firstborn son, my namesake, the first product; if you will, of the love that Triscennea and I shared. Tre'mont and Centarious mourned the loss of their big brother, a young man that they looked up to and wanted to model their lives after.

With the loss of Triscennea (Beautiful), I mourned the passing of my wife, best friend in this world, only true friend. A woman that I grew up with learned and shared everything with. Mother of my children, my greatest supporter spiritually as well as emotionally and finally a wonderful human being that helped to make me whole. With the passing of Triscennea, my sons had to suffer the loss of their mother, nurturer, the soft and tender touch of a mother's love, their biggest cheerleader and mediator between them and me.

Although, we lost the same persons their roles and values in our lives were uniquely different. I simply couldn't know what it's like to lose my big brother because he's still present in my life; just as I can't begin to fathom what it's like to suffer the loss of a mother, because, thanks be to God, she also is still present in my life. Tre'mont and Centarious can't even begin to comprehend the losses that I had to face simply because they've never been married or have had any children.

As I walked with Pastor down the hallway back to the waiting room where the majority of everyone who had come was; I felt as if I was completely numb. It felt as if I was an actor in a movie with one tragedy occurring after another or a nightmare that just keeps getting worse and never ending. At that point in time, I truly wasn't able to fully process everything that had unfolded and was still unfolding. I thought first about controlling the flow of information that my sons may receive. So I grabbed their cousin (my nephew) who was present at the time, and told him not to call my sons with this tragic news.

Emotionally, I was numb, so when I was greeted by the many that were in the hallway they witnessed no outpouring of tears or emotions from me. I received their individual hugs, condolences and words of encouragement from them. I was then led into the waiting room where we all gathered for prayer. Since everyone present there were born-again Christians and true followers of our Lord and Savior, Jesus Christ the prayers that went forth reflected that fact. The hour of grieving was upon me and my family; but joy will come in the morning. We had just suffered another great loss in my family but we knew that absence from the body meant present with our Lord.

My son, Steven and my wife, Triscennea had accepted Jesus Christ as their Lord and Savior; there was no doubt that they were reunited together in heaven with our Lord. With that being said, we only need to mourn the loss of their presence here with us, because they are not dead they are alive with Jesus Christ and we will see them again. Triscennea's mother, brother, and sister were present and, of course, took the passing of Beautiful devastatingly hard. Jackie, my mother-in-law and Corey, my brother-in-law were very concerned with my emotional state, especially concerning me driving myself home to break the news to my son's. I conveyed to them that I was all right to drive but my father came with me, per my mother's request. We did, however, drive home in the style of a convoy with everyone that was leaving following behind me.

My memories of the following events are relatively vague and patchy at best; however I will give as much detail as I can remember. We all arrived at my home from what seemed to have been my longest drive in this life. I was so full of anxiety while I was walking to my door, so much so that it was truly very difficult to see straight. Upon entering my home, I called for my sons to come downstairs in our family room. I had them stand in front of me, side-by-side, as I placed my arms around them. I told them that their mother had passed, and then I pulled them close to me tightly for a group hug. We all wept openly and loudly, this sense of loss was so deeply painful for each of us; my sons losing their mother and me losing the love of my life, my wife.

While I was embracing my sons, crying for a moment, I felt that my reason and purpose for living and going forward left when Beautiful did. I have always said and told my wife and sons that I love them as much as I was supposed to; but I love my God more, that is still true today. That being said, I still for a moment had lost my will and desire to live. I quickly had to compose myself, and began consoling my sons over the loss of their mother. As we still were embracing each other I lead us in prayer, first of all thanking God for the time we had with Triscennea, as well as, Steven and giving glory to God that they were now reunited together in heaven and that we will one day see them again.

Soon after, I let them go my mother and other members of my family took my son's aside to talk to and console them. I truly hated the way I felt when I let go and fully embraced the passing of Beautiful from this world. I had never experienced such feelings of doom and gloom regarding my life, and my future life without her. I came to a full realization that I had actually spent more of my life with her than without her. We were together for 28 years and we were only 44 years old, so only 16 years of our lives were spent separately. I truly couldn't remember how my life used to be without her and I was unable to visualize living my life without her now.

So many of my family members came to be there with us, and I am including my Rhema Word Family because they truly are family in every sense of the word. My father suggested that we go out and purchase some food for all that were gathered. We decided that chicken would be the best universal choice; because just about everyone likes chicken. It is very difficult for me to remember specific events chronologically or otherwise; which baffles me because I am such a detail oriented individual. With the passing of my son, Steven I was able to recall the events in chronological order as they occurred. I was even able to recall some details that I had forgotten about with crystal clear clarity with the help of the Holy Spirit; but with Beautiful's passing I am unable to do so.

I am aware that men of science, such as psychiatrists and psychologists, suggest that our minds will block out extremely traumatic events from our memory. The only conclusion that I can postulate is that my memory loss is due to the fact that because it was so traumatic the only way I could function was not to fully process the events as they were occurring. It is impossible for a person to fully grasp the sense of loss of a spouse unless it has happened to them. I must factor in the length of time we were together, as well as, being married. We grew up together; we shared the transition from adolescence to adulthood together, as well as, the birth of all our children together. We experienced a multitude of trials, tribulations, triumphs, and glory together. We experienced our God moving mountains from our path and were witnesses, as well as, recipients of a multitude of miracles.

We had experienced so many victories together with our God being the tie that held our marriage together. I felt that no sickness, disease, demon on earth, or devil in hell could prevail over us; because, God was truly with us and for us. The thought of Beautiful not being here to share my life with was a reality that I refused to process. It was impossible for me to envision any future without my wife being by my side. We shared such a magnificently rare union because of the age that we started, and the adversities we faced together, the miracles that we directly received and the strong and mighty presence of our Heavenly Father in our lives.

Everyone eventually left my home except for my nephew who spent the night to support his cousins. I was still so numb, but I knew I had to lead my son's by example through this tragedy. I used the term tragedy loosely because on one hand not having Beautiful's presence here with us is a tragic loss; but the realization of where she is now is a triumphant victory for she is now in the presence of God in heaven. I was able to function because I kept my focus on where she had transitioned to, not where she transitioned from. I could have nothing but joy when I thought about my wife, Beautiful, in heaven in the presence of our Heavenly Father and reunited with our son, Steven, who she so desperately missed.

Sometime during the early morning hour, when it was still yet dark, I was able to fall asleep. I awoke around noon hoping that the experiences of the previous day were only part of a nightmare; but they weren't, sadly to say this was truly my present reality. My mother called, shortly after I had awakened to see how I was holding up and to remind me that we had to start making arrangements for Beautiful. She knew full well that I wouldn't be feeling like doing anything this day, and she also knew that she had to push me into going forth with making the arrangements. With motherly love and some stern insistence, she reminded me that we had to have Beautiful's remains moved from the hospital's morgue so that it could be processed for her homegoing and burial, asap.

We decided that we would use the same funeral home that we used for Steven last year. This is the same establishment that both my parent's families have used for the past thirty some years. I must sadly say, that the memory of making such arrangements were still fresh in my mind. I wanted to accommodate as many of family and friends who wanted to pay their last respects by attending her homegoing as I possibly could. I was asked which day I would like to have it on that following Friday, October 22, 2010 or Saturday. I was informed with the choice of Saturday we had time constraints because they close the cemetery earlier and that it would be more expensive. Of course, the cost didn't matter, we just had to be punctual regarding her homegoing service.

I had to have my Pastor, Gerald L. Glasper, eulogize my wife in my mind no one else could do it, he, of course agreed. The order of service almost mirrored Steven's exactly from the previous year except for some different songs that I had picked out specifically with her in mind, which were her favorites. The love, caring, and genuine thoughtfulness of our Rhema Word Family truly blessed us that entire week. A group of members came by every day bringing us food (good food) and staying to pray with us, encouraged us and truly, uplifted us during this, our time of bereavement.

When planning Triscennea's homegoing service, my primary focus was to make it a celebration of her transition to heaven and to celebrate her life spent here on earth. I have attended fifty or so funerals in my lifetime thus far; and they were conducted as a time of sadness, that's exactly what I equate the term funeral with, as a time of weeping and sadness. Steven and Triscennea didn't have funerals, they had homegoing celebrations. Even though the presence of sadness was there; but it wasn't as prevalent as the tone I set, a time of celebration for their work here was completed, accomplished and they received their reward, Heaven.

So many of my brothers and sisters in Christ of Rhema Word sacrificed time from their lives and busy schedules to work all week in helping with this homegoing celebration, so that it would be successful. They even planned the repast that was held at the church, prepared all the food, I mean, good food and served my family, as well. I didn't have to lift a finger except to hold a fork to eat. I could never repay them for all that they had done for me and my sons and they would never allow me to even try, because they are every bit of my family and that's what family does.

First lady, Co-Pastor, Toni A. Glasper came to me stating that now was the time for me to stay very prayerful, because it is finished. She stated that she knew I had stayed very busy with preparing for this moment and I had so many people around me all week and now the phone calls and visits will soon cease and I will be left to face the reality that my wife is gone. I will now have to go through the full grieving process.

Chapter 19

A PATH LEADING
THROUGH DESTRUCTION

I must admit that, I had no idea of the journey that I was soon to partake in, a journey leading through hell and destruction. The Lord my God brought me through that day of closure, I even found myself consoling and encouraging others that day; all the while being unaware of the hell that I would soon be going through. Somehow, I fell asleep that night. I said somehow because the numbness had started wearing off and my present reality had started beginning to set in. I still wasn't angry with God, as I was right after Steven had passed; because I learned of and embraced my God's Sovereignty. The truth of the matter is that Steven and Triscennea belonged to God and He had the right to call them home when He chose to.

The next morning was Sunday, so I woke my sons up so we could attend a worship service at Rhema Word. We all in some small part of our minds wanted to stay home and, sadly, embrace our new reality. I definitely couldn't forsake the assembly of the people of God on this day of worship so we all went to church. My father and mother were in attendance also; we met them there. Dad's birthday was October 17, that previous Sunday; he decided to take us all out to eat to celebrate after church was over. My cousin, Shirley, met us at the restaurant to join in on the celebration.

I was so glad that my father had taken us out to eat. Besides the fact that I enjoyed celebrating his day of birth and another year of having him here with us; it also took my mind off of my new reality that I was beginning to accept. Later on that night, instead of staying prayerful and asking God to see me through these feelings of hurt, anguish, despair and loneliness. I decided to wallow in them. I cried so much that I thought I would become dehydrated, instead of drinking water as I should have; I decided that alcohol might somehow ease my pain and suffering, at least for a little while.

I need to say, that getting drunk didn't help me at all; in fact, it made everything worse. I began feeling a greater sense of depression, and even hopelessness. When I looked at the bed we both shared; it felt as if the walls began to close in on me, it became hard for me to catch my breath and I began feeling dizzy. The more I tried to get my breathing back in order the worse all the symptoms that I was feeling became and I began to panic. All I could think was that I needed to leave. When I stepped outside the feeling of panic slowly slipped away and, surprisingly, I felt stone cold sober. I stayed outside for an hour or so trying not to focus on what had just happened. My mind began to be flooded with past memories of the 28 years that I had with Beautiful. The memories went back to our beginning friendship, then fast forwarding a couple of months to when I first told her that I loved her.

The floodgates that had opened, releasing all of these memories to me, at first brought me peace and comfort. I know a great number of you reading this have heard the saying that even too much of a good thing can be bad for you. Well, I would have to agree with that saying in this case, because I was being bombarded with memory after memory and I became overwhelmed. All of these past memories coming at me, one after another, I was unable to gain control of this procession. I needed it to stop, so I screamed out loud in agony "STOP!" then it, finally, did. When it had stopped, a great feeling of depression, loneliness, hopelessness and anger came over me.

At first, I was experiencing each of these emotions equally; however, in my case, whenever anger enters the equation it usually becomes the dominant emotion. This case, sadly to say, was no different. I was infuriated that all of these memories came up not because they were bad memories.

But because I realized that there wouldn't be any new ones added. It was over, Beautiful was no more. I would have liked to be able to say at that moment I fell to my knees and asked God to help me through this; but I can't. I am capable of doing some horribly stupid things when I allow anger to be a dominant force within me. My God is always present and that night was no different. I know today that his arms were open and extended towards me awaiting me to come to him, but I did not.

God loves all of us in this world so much, that while we were yet sinners He gave us His only begotten son, Jesus Christ, to die on the cross for our sins so that we could be reconciled back to Him. Our Heavenly Father did this in spite of the fact that we hadn't recognized that we were in fact sinners, or even knew that we were in need of a Savior. My God would never force me or any of us to love Him, that's why He gave us free will. I would like everyone reading this book for just a moment to close your eyes and picture the Almighty God as He truly is, a loving Father waiting with open arms to embrace you. He is waiting patiently for you to receive the gift of salvation by accepting His only begotten son, Jesus Christ, as your Lord and Savior.

Salvation is a gift because we are incapable of earning it. We have all sinned and fallen short of the glory of God. "The wages (the payment) of sin is death. But the gift of God is eternal life through Jesus Christ, our Lord." Romans 6:23. Anger is a God-given emotion. It is not evil nor is being angry an act of evil or sin. For it states in the book of Ephesians 4:26 "Be ye angry and sin not: let not the sun go down upon your wrath." God is telling us here that it's all right to be angry but we shouldn't allow that anger to lead us into sinning, and we shouldn't go to sleep angry.

It was no surprise to my God that as time went on, that I would become angry at the fact that Beautiful was no longer with me, or that I would turn the focus of my wrath upon Him. I will reiterate that I had the right to be experiencing the emotion of anger, but I had no right to allow my anger to lead me into sin. I knew that one of the battlefields that the enemy chooses to wage war with me is in my mind. He bombarded me with those memories in hopes that I would become overwhelmed, angry and it would lead me to sin. My anger, that I allowed to fester, grew stronger and stronger coupled with feelings of sadness, regrets, and hopelessness. I was no longer satisfied with being right outside of my house; because when I looked upon it I no longer saw it as a home because my wife Beautiful was gone.

I told my son's Tre'mont and Centarious that I would be back. All of these emotions began consuming me, with anger being the dominant one. I drove around for hours crying, incessantly, and then I chose a means of escape, drugs. That was the only thing that I could think of that would take my mind off of everything else. For whenever I began to use drugs that always became my primary focus. Nothing else mattered and I felt nothing as long as I continued to use. There is power in the name of Jesus, I knew then just as I still know today; had I called upon the name of Jesus all of that would have ceased. I refused to call upon the name that has all power because I was angry with my Heavenly Father for placing me in the state that I was in. He had taken my Beautiful One away from me.

It came to be that I was at a point that I didn't know how to live without her. I didn't know if I could; I just knew that I didn't want to. I found the pain and all of the other emotions were too enormous to bear, so I chose not to feel anything, just the effects of the drugs that I was using. Whenever I tried to lie down to sleep, my mind would be flooded with her image and memories of her so I decided not to try anymore. I continued on with the drugs and alcohol. The only way I got any rest was when my body would shut down and I would pass out.

This horrible cycle of events went on, and on, and on, it was as if I were in the twilight zone, or something. Whenever I would regain consciousness after passing out time and time again; I would open my eyes hoping to see Beautiful's face and hearing her voice because it was just a terrible nightmare. Each time, I awoke I was slapped in the face with the reality that she was gone and I was, yet again, consumed by those emotions. I felt as if I was losing my mind, it was as if I was losing my grip on reality.

My birthday was coming up in about three weeks and I couldn't bear spending it alone without my wife. I was constantly reminded by the enemy that I wasn't married anymore; because my God had taken my wife from me. He kept reminding me because I was constantly turning down sexual advances from many of the women that I encountered. The men that I was around also tried, time and time again, to connect me with women to have sex with. I finally accepted the fact that I was no longer married and had no wife to be faithful to. I became so angry that my God had called Beautiful home and left me here alone; that I decided to get back at Him.

For my birthday celebration; which began two weeks before my actual birthday, I decided to sin by taking part in debauchery, lust, drunkenness, orgies, and carousing. My act of rebellious behavior went on for days, ever increasing because with every act it became harder to satisfy my fleshly desires. Several days had passed of me sinning in this manner when finally I called for it to cease. I didn't cease this behavior because I could no longer take it; I ceased because no matter how much I increased I was no longer able to satisfy my flesh. I had partaken in acts that I had fantasized about many times; but knew I could never do because they were extremely lewd acts.

The feeling of shame came upon me because I had crossed that boundary I said that I would never cross. The feeling of shame didn't last very long. Eventually, my flesh rose up and demanded satisfaction. My man of flesh was so much more powerful than my spirit man due to malnourishment. I was powerless to refuse the demand. Since increasing in numbers was no longer able to satisfy my flesh; I decreased to the one individual that could, no matter what state I was in. I clung to this one not out of love, but out of an extreme case of lust. This went on for some time.

I soon began to feel terrible about my connection to this woman and cried out to my Heavenly Father, for forgiveness for what I was doing and to help me bring it to an end. Although, I hadn't even attempted to talk to God for over a month; He answered me by declaring that it soon would end and that I would write about it. Somewhat to my surprise, my Heavenly Father answered my cry straightway. I always knew that God loved me, for I am His son and He always was there to answer my cry for forgiveness and help. I was somewhat surprised this time, because I purposely put a lot of planning and thought into the sins I would commit to get back at Him out of anger.

I wept tears of joy because I knew at that very moment that He had already forgiven me and was patiently waiting to hear from me. Despite my acts of wrath and rebellion towards Him. I was stunned for a moment that He said I would write about it. There was a sense of relief for I knew if He would have me record these events that I wouldn't only get through them; but I would, successfully, get through them. My God then brought back to my memory when He told me that I had at least three books in me, just about 30 years ago. I, of course, had forgotten all about that, because I knew then, as well as now, that I didn't possess the capability to complete such a task. What I was now sure of was that I would be writing about what I had been going through, because God had appointed me to do so. I, by His Power, would become capable of completing this task.

It would be a logical assumption that I ceased all of those actions and returned to the source of my pain and dismay to face it head on. But, I didn't. I had been disconnected from my source of strength, Jesus Christ for such a long time that my Spirit Man was in such a weakened state that he was easily overpowered by my flesh, so I continued. The intensity of pleasure and satisfaction had become amplified after I had cried out to my Heavenly Father. My thoughts of facing my new reality and finally allowing the grieving process to begin, became overwhelming for me. I became satiated by these newfound feelings of pleasure so much so that I thought of nothing else.

I, no longer thought of facing my pain while, allowing it to have its time, to get past it. Not when I was fully entrenched with so much pleasure and satisfaction. The enemy was aware that I had opened up the lines of communication with my God and for the moment had successfully stopped me from moving forward. My actions in this case somewhat mirrored the actions of the younger son in the parable that Jesus told regarding a man who had two sons found in the book of Luke 15:11-24. I, too, after squandering all that I had saved for a while, was near starving because I was given no food to eat. I, then, thought of my Heavenly Father who always provided for me and my family through His endless resources.

I took the focus off of me and my pain. I thought of how I had abandoned my sons when they needed me the most; it was for a while as if they had lost both of their parents. Once again, I cried out to my Heavenly Father asking Him "When would this end?" He simply replied when I stop. Upon hearing God's answer, I prayed for the strength to end this hell that I was in and I was instantly strengthened, and I returned home. I was welcomed back home by my sons with open arms and tears of joy. I knew a process of rebuilding had to take place and I knew it wouldn't be easy. The first major step had been taken; I was back where I belonged. During the first days, all I did was eat, rest and prayed to my Father in Heaven.

My prayers were that of thanksgiving, thanking Him for protecting me, seeing me through this horrible time and strengthening me to come back. I thanked my God for never turning His back on me; even though I turned my back on Him. I also, thanked my God for keeping my sons safe when I was in no condition to do so. All while I was away, I never once dreamed of Beautiful; because I never slept I would go on and on until my body shut down and I passed out. I became ready with the help of my Heavenly Father, who strengthened me to finally face my feelings of pain, remorse, loneliness and to start my process of grieving.

I knew that I had to go through the process without the use of any mood altering chemicals. By my own strength and power I knew that I would fail miserably; so I looked towards Jesus Christ to see me through all of these emotions that I had so desperately avoided before. After I became stronger, physically, my grieving process began. I allowed myself to miss her, to feel the sense of loss, disparity and anger, without sinning this time. The process of getting my house back in order had begun. I was met with resentment and anger from my sons, due to my absence. They had to deal with their emotions, as well, so I prayed for us all that we would have the patience with each other to see us through.

My methodology in dealing with my sons had to alter sharply for I had to become both mother and father to them now. Just thinking about going through this transition overwhelmed me from time to time; so I was constantly in prayer asking my God for strength, guidance, and patience. It was as if I had to relearn my parenting skills, all over again, so that I could add a mother's perspective in all of my actions and decisions regarding them. I have always believed and still adamantly believe that children should be raised in a two parent household. Thank God that my sons are older; however due to the back to back traumatic experiences, that we all have had to face they are in dire need of a mother's love and care. I was unable to become what they needed overnight, so I thanked God for blessing them with surrogates.

My sons were being raised by a loving mother and father that were in a covenant relationship with Jesus Christ, as well as, each other. We truly had a three-quarter strand marriage; for we wouldn't have lasted 22 years being married if Jesus Christ wasn't in our relationship. Beautiful and I also truly loved each other. I won't say we had a perfect marriage, especially me spending time running from my Heavenly Father's call upon my life. This caused her and our children great pain and suffering. The fact still remains, despite all the adversities we were faced with as husband and wife we were still in love with each other and remained married. Since there is no such thing as a perfect marriage what ours lacked in certain areas it abounded in others. It is because Jesus Christ was prevalent in our marriage that made it successful.

Emotions were extremely heightened in my household due to all of these factors. Had I tried to face all of these things at once without my Heavenly Father; I would have become totally perplexed and overwhelmed. Dealing with the restructuring of my household was a full-time job in itself; but coupled with me finally facing that Beautiful was gone I was working overtime. I stated before that I hadn't dreamed of my wife since she had passed; well, that finally changed. I found myself dreaming of her whenever I fell asleep. Beforehand, I had stated that too much of a good thing can be bad for us; well these dreams started off great, but soon brought me into a state of confusion.

No matter how I try to be positive, concerning my new reality, or to get used to my new normal; I hated it and tried to find reasons not to accept it. I overly enjoyed spending time with Triscennea again and again even though it was only in my dreams. I had reached a point that I preferred sleeping over being awake. When I was awake she wasn't here sharing my life and loving me; but in my dreams everything was as I thought it should be. Yet again, I took my focus off of my source of strength, Jesus Christ and quickly fell into a state of deep depression. I began sleeping more and more because in my dreams I found happiness; I was reunited with my wife, Beautiful. It had gotten so bad that I actually began to question which state was reality.

Somehow I tried to convince myself that I was really awake when I was with my wife; that was real and my existing in this world without her was a dream. In actuality it was a terrible nightmare. My rationalization for my confusion was simple; I knew that my Heavenly Father loved me too much to allow me to go through this pain from the loss of Beautiful for no apparent reason. I became a nervous wreck trying to convince myself every time I would awaken to the reality that Triscennea was gone; that this was just a nightmare, because the truth was too painful to bear. So I would spend as little time awake as I possibly could, just performing the bare necessities like showering, drinking water, and eating a little food.

A deep depression had come over me, for I was able to sleep more and more hours. It mattered not how many hours that I had just slept, be it 8, 10 or 12 I still awoke feeling extremely tired. This went on for just over a month, and I felt as though I was going crazy. I tried over and over again to convince myself that my perception of reality was flipped upside down. No matter what my mind was trying to convince my heart to believe; my Spirit Man kept revealing the truth to my heart even though it was extremely painful to face. These struggles that I was facing were revealed to me, even though, as I write this down it sounds insane. As I look back on these courses of events; I had to have suffered a psychotic break, because I found it difficult if not impossible to distinguish fantasy from reality. I actually spent my time awake trying to convince myself that this is the time when I am in fact, asleep. Believing true reality only came after I laid down, closed my eyes and I was there with Beautiful.

Tre'mont my oldest living son remained faithful in going to worship service pretty much every week. Centarious my youngest son wasn't as faithful, but still attended. I on the other hand, hadn't started back yet. My sons would come home from Sunday Worship Service stating that so many people were asking about me and inquiring as to when I planned to return. The guilt and shame that I felt from my reaction after Triscennea's homegoing celebration was weighing heavily upon me. I know, for a fact, that my Rhema Word family members, that were closest to me, knew what I had done and I simply didn't know if I could or ever would be able to face them again.

I know that I didn't react perfectly after my eldest son, Steven's passing; but only a few were aware of those wrongful acts. I was nearly finished with my M.I.T (Ministers in Training) classes; the last time I attended was right after my wife's passing. Pride played a huge role in my difficulty in returning, for I was commended by so many of my classmates, ministers, and elders regarding the outward strength that I had exhibited. As I have stated before, that I hold myself to a higher standard of conduct than I do most other people. I was just recently praying to my God about this very thing; I asked Him was I being conceited by doing so? Did I secretly think that I am better than everyone else?

The answer I received was somewhat surprisingly simplistic. My Heavenly Father knows my heart better than I ever could, or will. I was told that there is nothing wrong with me setting a higher standard for myself for it is good to set goals for myself, goals that I have to truly strive to achieve. He revealed to me that I think lowlier and meekly of myself in comparison to others. Around the people that I have encountered through and in this life that I have led, never have I felt that I truly fitted in because in some way they were all better than I was. My only downfall is my reaction to when I fail to meet these self-imposed higher standards. My God reminded me that I, along with the rest of His creation, are fallible. God expects us to, for He knows that we all will fall (fail) from time to time. He in fact already knows the dates and times of all of our next failures in meeting the mark.

There was, of course, another factor that contributed to my staying away, and that was anger. I am aware that these emotions mentioned are related to the grieving process that I was presently undergoing, again. I began acting foolishly when anger entered the equation. My inability to process my anger, constructively and correctly, has always plagued me in the past. Since I had always been unsuccessful in dealing with a heightened degree of anger in the past, I believed it was best for me not to allow myself to become angry at all. I continued to try to perfect this approach, even though; I continued to fail at it miserably and consistently. Deep down inside of me, I knew that I was simply practicing insane behavior by doing the same thing, expecting a different result, yet I continued still in this manner.

The only thing that I had been successful in doing was placing myself on a deserted island. I found reasons why I couldn't return to my Heavenly Father's House of Worship and in my anger I stopped talking (praying) to God for strength and direction. I had successfully set myself up for a downfall, so I fell back into the usage of drugs, alcohol, and sought out the one individual for pleasure again. This time, I decided I would do it differently I was going to live in both worlds instead of fully being submerged in that behavior, as before. I was able to do just that for a while, but I was increasingly becoming miserable and, I was unable to stop on my own.

Chapter 20

THE REVELATION
OF A NEW BEGINNING

It increasingly became more and more difficult for me to continue to attempt to live a double life. I chose the path of a coward and tried to justify my behavior by telling myself that I was not as bad as before. When in fact I wasn't; I had become worse because the aftermath of my past behavior was clearly present before my eyes. While I was traveling down that pathway through destruction; I was totally oblivious to how my actions affected my sons and my other family members. Now since I became aware of how my actions affected the ones I love the most; my trying to repeat them at even half measure was far worse than what I had done before.

I have to admit that, I made the choice to react the way I did the first and second time. Both times I chose to turn from God; after first choosing to turn to Him. I was fully aware that my God could and would see me through this process. I knew that the pain, anger and all of my other emotions due to the grieving process haven't come to stay, they came to pass. My true issues here was my lack of trust in my God's perfect timing; I of course, felt that I should get through this process more rapidly than it was taking. I was feeling more pain and suffering than I had ever experienced before in my entire life. I am also very capable of reacting very foolishly when I am forced to wait too long; which is something that I am still presently asking God to make me over in this area.

In Retrospect, all those past actions can be linked to my lack of faith (trust) in my God's perfect timing. I usually have enough faith because I would hand those things over to my Heavenly Father to handle and help see me through them. I knew, then as well as now, that He could and would take care of whatever I entrusted to Him. Sometimes my own actions baffled me. In many instances, I could turn things over to God and continue to trust Him to take care of it however long it would take and no matter how bad things looked in the natural. Analytically speaking, my choices that were made when it came to grieving doesn't compute. I could hypothesize that when it comes to matters of the heart, that analytical thinking goes out of the window but that would be an inaccurate assumption.

For in my eldest son, Steven's case for instance; I loved him as much as a father should love his son and I trusted and held on to the faith that my Father in Heaven already had taken care of his freedom, healing, and full restoration. It mattered not how things looked in the natural, I remained steadfast and immovable in my faith. Initially, when Steven passed I became angry with God and went off the reservation, so to speak, but not for long in comparison. A father's love for his son is so different than a husband's love for his wife. I had always expected and anticipated that Steven would leave the nest and one day get married and have children of his own, and they would become his immediate family. I so desperately wanted that for my son as any father should.

In the case of Beautiful, I loved my wife as much as a husband should love his wife; with a love second only to God. I had planned to love and be with her for the rest of my life here on this earth. In my thoughts, we were going to grow old together and see our sons have children and perhaps be around for great-grandchildren. I was incapable of seeing past my own desires, so I saw no possible reason why my God called her home when we still had so much love and life to share with each other. There were still so many experiences we had yet to share, as far as I was concerned.

I began spending more and more time away from my son's, as I became further engulfed with feelings of lust and acting upon them. There was an instance when directly after my desire was fulfilled by this woman; I gazed down upon her and stated "Nothing on this earth should ever feel this good." Upon making that statement, I instantly had an epiphany; that I had fully fallen to the desires of my flesh and that, had to cease right now. I thought about how my relationship with my God had grown, along with the act of communing with Him. I concluded that nothing on this earth can give me more pleasure than speaking to my God, Him hearing me and answering me back.

I decided at that very moment that I would do nothing, intentionally, to jeopardize this relationship with my Heavenly Father. I decided to part presence with this woman, right then and there. While I was in the midst of driving her home the Holy Spirit reminded me that it was Wednesday night, and that Bible study had just begun. Right after receiving this reminder, I was compelled to go to my place of worship Rhema Word Kingdom Ministries. I plotted a direct course for there, it mattered not to me how this woman would get home; all I knew was that I had to go there-straightway. When I arrived in the parking lot, I drove past the entrance and found an empty space to park, a short distance away.

She asked me where we were? I responded that I was back home, where I belonged. This woman pleaded with me to take her home, and then I could come back. I responded to her that she needed to call someone to come and get her, or I would give her bus fare. I, emphatically, informed her that the only place that I was going was inside my place of worship. While we were in the middle of exchanging words my brother in Christ and close friend, Elder DaShaun Blankenship approached the driver's side door of my vehicle to see why I hadn't come in yet. I was pleasingly surprised, and a bit startled to see him standing at my door.

I, immediately, greeted him with a smile and got out of my truck to embrace him. I asked him how he knew I was even in the parking lot, he informed me that he was standing at the entrance to greet people as they arrived and he saw me as I drove by and wondered why I hadn't come in yet. It was divinely purposed that he would be standing at the entrance when I drove by. As previously stated, DaShaun was the first brother that I formed a kinship with when I first started attending Rhema Word. He was, also, the first person the Holy Spirit brought to my mind to call other than my lawyer and parents after receiving the news that my son, Steven had been formally charged with murder and transferred to the county jail.

I began to inform DaShaun what I had been doing, who this woman was that was with me and, finally, how the Holy Spirit directed me to come there. He asked me did she have a way home, I told him she was calling someone right now, but if she didn't I would provide bus fare for her. When she hung up the phone, she stated that no one was able to come and get her. She refused the bus fare I was offering stating that I needed to take her home. DaShaun tried to convince me to take her. I adamantly refused to do so, for I was going to heed the command of the Holy Spirit. Our head trustee, Keith Sanders walked over to my truck to see what was going on. I informed him of what had transpired and how I had reached my destination and the only place I was going was inside. This huge man of God offered to drive her away so that I could do as I was instructed to do. I thanked Keith for his genuine act of kindness and was truly grateful.

This may seem like heartless behavior, especially after the time I had spent with this woman and how we spent our time together. I don't know how else to explain it, other than that this woman had an extremely powerful influence over me; it was as if I was under her spell. The moment I had my epiphany concerning my actions with her the spell was broken and I instantly wanted nothing else to do with her. Only my Heavenly Father could have freed me from this horribly powerful influence (spell) this woman had over me. I had purposed in my mind to rid myself of her by taking her home; but when the Holy Spirit intervened I, instantly, heeded. I was finally freed from the bondage of my flesh that she so easily and exceedingly was able to satisfy. It had gotten to a point that I placed these desires above my God, my family, and everything else; my value system was extremely out of order.

DaShaun and I entered our place of worship at some point in time and we were joined by Deacon Rick Tingling. I began to free myself emotionally with these two men of God. While crying, uncontrollably, I expressed my feelings of despair, anger, loneliness and an inconceivable sense of emptiness that had overtaken me. I told them how gravely I missed my wife, how I didn't know how to live without her and how I wasn't sure if I even could. Rick and DaShaun prayed with me, stayed with me in the office of the Trustees. After we had finished praying, DaShaun a true prophet of the Lord, gave me a prophetic word that strengthen and encouraged me.

He stated that God has another wife in store for me, so I will remarry he went on to say that Tracy (Beautiful) will approve of my choice for my wife. He told me something else that I couldn't understand at the time; but at this present time I do. I have no doubt in my mind that DaShaun is a truly anointed man of God, a true prophet of the Lord and that the Holy Spirit speaks to him. However, when he made the statement that my late wife would approve of my choice for a wife, I instantly thought he got that part wrong. Although, I know in my heart and mind that Beautiful loved me so much that she would want me to be happy, even with someone else, however her approving of my choice was beyond my comprehension.

Rick also encouraged me by telling me how my Rhema Word Family loves me and how everyone had been praying for my safe return. He went on to say, it didn't matter what I had done their love for me hadn't changed. It was suggested by DaShaun that I call my sons to come and join me; they happily agreed and said they were on their way. I was happy to have Tre'mont join me; but I was so disappointed that Centarious only dropped him off when he should have joined us, as well. Upon Tre's arrival, I left from the back office of the Trustee's and joined him. We sat in the back of the church and caught the tail end of Bible Study/Worship Service. I was truly grateful to be back in my Father's House, for it had been far too long.

The suggestion to meet with Pastor prior to my returning fully to Rhema Word was presented to me by some Elders and I agreed that that course of action would be appropriate. I called the church office the following day and talked with Jackie in hopes of scheduling an appointment to meet with my Pastor. I am truly unable to recall when Pastor was available to meet with me; however it was before Sunday's Worship Service. I must admit, I was a bit apprehensive regarding meeting with Pastor because of the level of guilt, shame, remorse and regret that I was feeling.

I must re-state that I truly love this man of God, Gerald L. Glasper that my God chose to be my Pastor. Upon meeting with me, he saw the emotional turmoil that I was obviously in and he asked me, with genuine concern first of all, was I all right. He went on to tell me that they all were very concerned about me during my absence. I was reminded that my actions weren't kept in the dark; they were done in the light of day. I shared in depth with him all of my emotions that I felt and the things I did, so that I wouldn't have to face them, and he shared some things about himself with me. Pastor Glasper asked me point-blank, what were my plans for moving forward? I told him that I have returned to God and will be returning to this, my regular place of worship again. Upon hearing this, he stated that in light of my past actions, that a public restoration would be in order and I agreed.

Also, I was compelled to discuss the fact that even though I did what I had done; I know that my God hasn't changed his mind regarding me. For when God called me to minister to His people He did not make a mistake; nor has He changed His mind and neither have I. Pastor agreed with me. He stated, first, that I must prove myself approved and that will take time. I must get my own house in order. He stated that there will be other classes in the future and in time I can finish what I had started.

Sunday came around very quickly and my sons and I were all back at Rhema Word. I was taken aback by all the smiles, greetings, and hugs that I received from so many people. They truly made every effort to make me feel welcomed back. This first Sunday of my returning was a bit awkward for me, due to the guilt and shame I was still feeling. I was very reserved in my outward display of Worshiping my God. As the time was drawing nearer to the altar call, I began to question my need to have a public restoration.

I know that I had agreed with Pastor to do this necessary act of public restoration; but all of a sudden I began to question the need for it. Restoration is needed when someone has turned their back on God and living in a backslidden state and they feel that God isn't hearing or responding to their prayers anymore. Well part of that was very true for me, because I had definitely turned my back on my God and had severed all lines of communication with Him. However, when I cried out to the Lord (Hallelujah), He not only heard me but also answered my cry. So, I felt that our relationship had been restored already so why should I have to publicly re-do what had already been done in private.

Today, I know that was my pride trying to take control, because in my private meeting with pastor I knew that my relationship with my Heavenly Father had already been restored. Yet I agreed, because I knew that it would be appropriate and necessary to do it in public. When they made the altar call for anyone who wants to give their life to Christ, anyone who needs to be restored or anyone who needs prayer to come forward; I didn't move. I was praying to my God to show me what I needed to do. I was trying also to get Roni's attention to quickly discuss it with her. My God compelled my son Tre' to grab my hand and bring me forth to the altar.

At first I resisted my son's attempt to bring me to the altar, and was a little angry with him. I, of course, didn't realize that my Heavenly Father was using my own son to give me the answer to my prayer. I had never seen Tre' be so persistent; he refused to leave me alone until he brought me by my hand to the altar for restoration. I thought it strange that the Lord would use my son in this manner; but afterwards Tre', not Centarious, was the perfect choice for this assignment.

Tre' had no idea that I had discussed and already agreed to come forth for restoration with Pastor. Also, when I tried to look at Tre' sternly and to pull away from him I could clearly see that something had come over him and I knew that I wasn't heeding to him; but I was heeding to the Will of the Holy Spirit. In this case, it wasn't the enemy trying to sabotage my return, for this enemy was in-a-me; my pride was at work against me. I am grateful that I didn't make up my mind not to do it; but my Spirit Man had enough strength to lead me to pray about it and my God did the rest.

When I approached the altar for restoration, I could feel the enormous weight of my sin and guilt upon my shoulders. My Pastor, whom I love so much, instructed me to ask God to forgive me for all that I had done. So many elders and ministers whom I call brothers had encircled me and were praying over me. The weight had become too much to bear; I fell to my knees and cried out to the Lord to forgive me and the enormous weight was lifted. I then fell on my face in prayer and worship.

I am so grateful that my pride and self-righteousness wasn't able to rob me of being fully restored that day. My pride tried to and was almost successful in convincing me to change my mind. I knew then, just as I still know today that humility is the remedy (cure) for pride. Daily, I perform an evaluation of my actions on a moment to moment basis. For I know that I am capable of justifying some clearly self-righteous and or prideful actions. I purposely make sure that the motives for all my interactions with people are always out of love and genuine concern, because my God is Love.

That was the beginning for me and my family coming back to Rhema Word every week for Bible Study on Wednesday's, Morning Manna and Worship Service on Sunday's. I had begun my grieving process again by allowing myself to feel all of the emotions necessary for grieving uninhibited, in other words. I refused to self-medicate with drugs or alcohol. Since I had interrupted the process earlier it seemed as if I had to start all over again from the beginning. I began to miss Beautiful so desperately all over again, wondering how I was going to live without her. In my mind, I started remembering all the things that I regretted doing and all the things that I should have done differently.

As I pondered back on the last seven or so years we had together, I can recall that spark in our (friendship) marriage had started to fade. I am truly a romantic man at heart; however the desire had been fading over those past years. Beautiful had brought it to my attention on several occasions, stating how terribly she missed that from me. She went on to apologize for not knowing how to properly appreciate, or even reciprocate my actions. For even at the age of 16 years old when we first got together; I had been romancing her and only got better and more intensified as we got older. It wasn't simply something that I did it's who I am, a true lover and a romantic man.

I couldn't understand what was happening to me, to us. I knew that I still loved her as much as a husband should love his wife; but that forever present part of our marriage (romance) was slowly fading away. I prayed, fervently, to my Heavenly Father to fully restore our marriage and I couldn't understand why He wouldn't. Beautiful would ask me over and over, night after night for me to lie in bed with her before she would go to sleep; I would refuse. This went on for the last few years of our lives spent together. I cried, profusely, as I remembered refusing my wife that time of intimacy. I am at this very moment crying as I write this now, because the sense of regret is still ever present. For even today, October 5, 2013, I still regret my selfish actions. In fact I still find myself sitting in the same chair waiting until I am totally exhausted before lying down alone, night after night, and year after year.

Continually, I cried out to my God to see me through this pain and intense suffering I was going through. I wanted him to make it stop. I knew I had to fully experience the whole process and I truly couldn't take starting it all over again until I did it right. Again, I slipped into a deep form of depression preferring being asleep over being awake. I was able to sleep more and more as I was spending time with Beautiful in my dreams. This time I wasn't confused about which state was reality; I knew that I was at least happy in my dreams versus being miserable while I was awake. I knew that I could never be with her, loving her in reality; however in my dreams we were together in love, just as before.

A month had passed since I received that prophetic word from Elder DaShaun. I had grown weary of dreaming I was with Beautiful, being happy and loving her; during one of my dreams, I asked her to stop entering my dreams. I informed her that her presence in this manner was hurting more than helping, for whenever I would awaken my reality was causing me even more pain and agony. Reluctantly, she agreed to stop. When my nightly encounters with Beautiful had ceased to occur in dreamland; I began to, finally, better cope with the fact that she was gone. Also, I was better able to appreciate all the years of love that we shared together from our teenage years to adulthood. I wanted and expected to have more time with her; but, I became much more grateful for the time my God allowed us to have together.

I prayed to my Heavenly Father thanking him for all the years of love that He allowed me to share with my wife, Beautiful. Only after thanking Him did I ask, "Why did You give her to me at such an early age just to take her away from me?" My God answered right away stating that Beautiful was the wife of my youth and that He has a wife for my latter years. This news excited me so much because God had just confirmed what His Prophet DaShaun had told me a month ago. For a while, I couldn't understand why my God answered me this time, and so quickly. I had been crying out asking, "Why Lord why have you taken my Beautiful one away from me?"

The Holy Spirit brought back to my attention; through a word that my Pastor had preached long ago regarding our manner of approach to God. He reminded me that all of the other times that I had prayed I was angry that she was gone and in my anger I showed God no appreciation for allowing me to have her in the first place and the long period of time we were together. In my hurt and anger at the fact that she was gone I only thought of how it affected me. I approached my God like a spoiled brat only thinking of my loss, not considering Heaven's gain. I not once, in those earlier prayers thanked Him or showed even a hint of appreciation; my approach was incorrect, so I received no answer.

It is strange that I was able to receive the Word from my pastor regarding how important it is to approach God correctly. I was even able to pass it on to my sons with a correct analogy; but in my time of heightened emotions I was unable to practice what was preached. This has actually made me ponder on the many times I prayed and received no answer the first few times. It would be impossible, and more over, futile for me to try to review those many, many occasions; however going forward I will be mindful of my approach to my Heavenly Father.

The answer my God gave me brought me so much joy; for I had grown weary of being alone. Then reality set in, I had been with Beautiful for 28 years, since we were both teenagers until our mid-40s. I am unaware of how not to be married and moreover how to go about finding the correct woman to spend the rest of my life with. My life has changed, drastically, since my teenage years and there are more variables to consider, besides just my own personal desires. I am an analytical thinker by nature so I began to consider every variable in this equation, I could think of and came to the decision that I wasn't able to do this, correctly, without the guidance of my Heavenly Father.

After much thought, I came up with eight attributes that the wife of my latter years must possess. I will share the top three with you. First of all, she must love God as much as I love Him; for if she didn't there could be no union at all. Secondly, she has to be capable of giving me a love second only to God; in other words the only one she should love more than me is God. Thirdly, because I have sons she has to be capable of loving them as her own; for loving me means also loving them.

Only after formulating my list of eight attributes, did I asked my God to show me who this woman was that I had chosen. I received no answer right away. I quickly, out of desperation, decided to attempt to formulate my own list of possible candidates. Now in the beginning, I had come to the conclusion that I was ill equipped to make this choice without the guidance of my Father in Heaven, yet I found myself beginning to do it anyway. When I first formulated the list of attributes for viable candidates, I had already decided that she must possess all of them. It was simply all or nothing. I didn't even realize that not one physical characteristic was included; although, it is important of course that I find her attractive physically, as well.

I had thought of some unmarried women that I knew and that met my physical requirements. Wow, I just realized when I tried to do it myself the first thing I thought about was the physical; then I tried to find out if they met my other requirements. That's why the women I had on my list all failed to meet the truly needed attributes; because I was thinking with my carnal mind. When I approached my God with this, I wasn't. Frustration soon set in, I was flooded with thoughts of searching on my own without God's help, and finding woman after woman that failed to meet the mark. I couldn't understand why my God would quickly tell me that he had a wife for my latter years and not show her to me. I know that it states in the book of Proverbs 18:22 "Whosoever findeth a wife findeth a good thing, and obtaineth favor of the Lord."

All I was asking for was that my Heavenly Father reveal to me who I had chosen, I already knew what I wanted and needed in a wife. I was tormented by these thoughts and nightmares for a couple of sleepless nights. Finally, out of desperation, I asked God to show her to me on May 1, 2011; which was on a Sunday. When I saw her that morning our eyes met; she and I smiled a huge smile at each other as if we had never seen one another before. At that very moment I heard the voice of the Lord say "Son behold your wife," and from her reaction, I just knew she was told at that very same moment that I was her husband, because of the look we gave each other. The Lord also flooded my mind with past memories regarding her.

Earlier on in this book I stated that I knew that I was in love with Beautiful because of that time when we embraced I felt my spirit stir and I had never felt that before. Well, my Lord brought an instance of when I hugged this woman and felt the same thing. I released her right away because it scared me. My God allowed me to see this instance as if it were a scene from a movie that I was starring in. He quickly placed a veil over that memory. I then remembered talking to Beautiful about the fact that I can greet every other woman there with a full embrace; but when I embrace this individual it's always with one arm and a space between us.

She is also the only woman that Beautiful and I observed together and conversed about. We had a conversation one day about the fact that we can see that she wants to be married and we both prayed that God would bless her with a good husband. The Holy Spirit brought all of this back to my mind in a flash, right after I heard the words son behold your wife. I was so excited because in that memory flash I received confirmation upon confirmation; so I had no doubt that I had just gazed upon my future wife. The strange thing was that in my thoughts of whom I have chosen, she wasn't even considered.

The reason why she wasn't even considered baffles me because she meets all and exceeds most of my requirements. I could only come up with two possible explanations the first being that she's too perfect for me, because physically I couldn't ask for more. I truly just love her smile, her pretty brown eyes, skin tone, height and her hair, all of which suits my preferences. Secondly, perhaps because God had placed a veil up so I couldn't see her in that way. I was ready to start courting her right away when God told me not yet, for there is a work that he needs to do in both of us to prepare us for each other. My heightened level of excitement dropped instantly; then my God told me to start writing this book.

Then, I couldn't understand why He would show me my future wife, tell me not yet, and to get to writing. I couldn't help but to continue to think about her as my wife and I continued to gaze upon her. I told my Heavenly Father that I must give her a name. When I thought what shall I name her? Lovely, came to mind, for that's exactly what she is to me, simply, amazingly, lovely.

Chapter 21

A New Beginning

My God has shown me whom I had chosen for a wife, in which I am well pleased. In His infinite wisdom He not only told me to wait but also gave me some work to do while He is working us. All I had to do was be obedient to the Will of my Father in Heaven. But I didn't. I not only failed to start the work that he instructed me to write, I also approached her not directly, but definitely prematurely. Every time I am around her I so desperately wanted to approach her; but I keep hearing the voice of the Holy Spirit telling me not yet. My approach to her was inconsistent; which had to make her feel that I was playing games, then I stopped all together and heeded to the voice of the Holy Spirit. Today's date is October 12, 2013, it has now been two years, five months, and 11 days since the veil has been removed; and I was able to gaze upon my future wife Lovely, as still I wait.

It took my feelings getting hurt by Lovely; who told me that I was her brother in Christ and that she didn't see me in any other way than that, before I started writing this book. I was confused by her statement to me so I asked my God how this could be? He simply stated that He told me, not yet. Five months had passed from when my God showed me Lovely, instructing me to start writing before I actually started writing. I sought the counsel of my brother DaShaun of how I should proceed; since he had embarked in starting his radio show after being instructed by our God to do so. He told me the story of how it all came together with a minimal amount of effort on his part, for God had already paved the way for him.

I of course expressed my concerns about my lack of ability in writing and having no knowledge of how to get published or how to advertise. DaShaun told me that I was jumping too far ahead of myself and all that I should be concentrating on doing right now was writing. He reminded me that our God is a God of order, in other words, first things first. I need not be concerned with publishing when I have just begun to write the book; he told me that God has already laid the path down before me so I need to follow it step by step.

Today is Monday, October 14, 2013 (Columbus Day) it has been three years ago today since Beautiful was taken away. This day has become easier to deal with since it is the third annual year of remembering Triscennea's transition from this earth to Heaven. What I find most difficult about this day, this year is the fact that it has been three years since I have had a best friend that I know truly loves me and that I truly love back, a wife. There are only a few people that I could be totally transparent with regarding my true feelings and only one right now that I feel comfortable sharing it all with and that's my friend, my brother, Minister Eric Lee. I truly thank my God for this brother and the position that our God has designated him to have in my life.

I called, my brother, Eric today and left him a voicemail message regarding how I was feeling. He returned my call leaving me a voicemail message reminding me that today was his birthday. I called him back during my break feeling bad about forgetting that it's his birthday and for dumping my emotional package on him on his day of celebration. I wished him a happy birthday and asked him what he did on this special day. Eric told me of how he spent his day with his loving wife, Sharon and how at the end she surprised him by taking him to a restaurant that he had wanted to try for a while now. This wonderful woman of God not only took him there but had a surprise gathering of his family waiting for him and he was totally surprised.

Hearing about his birthday celebration brought joy to my heart, for Eric is a good man and a great friend. I conveyed to him how I missed that; having a wonderful wife out of love would take the time to plan out a spectacular day just for me on my birthday. Equally, I miss doing the same for the woman that I love, my wife. We then discussed what I was feeling and he gave me wise counsel (as always) concerning those feelings and emotions. Eric went on to point out the areas in which he saw growth in me. I expressed to him how difficult it has been in waiting for God to give me permission to approach Lovely. Although, I now have been able to realize that a lot of work has been done in me and yet their still remains so much more to do, before I am ready for her. He encouraged me by saying that my time is soon coming.

I now understand why, my God instructed me to start writing when He did. I am sure that I don't see the whole picture, but what I can see has been revealed to me by the Holy Spirit over time. First of all, He wanted me working after He showed me who my choice was for my wife; since I had to wait He wanted me to have something constructive to do during this time. My God knew after showing her to me, that I would be so taken by her and that it would be difficult to think about anything else. Secondly, since I have been willing to make myself available to be used to write this book, it has been very therapeutic for me. Literally all I do is sit in my room at a folding dinner tray table, with my gospel music playing in the background; which it does 24/7 for I want my home to be an atmosphere of Praise and Worship to my God. I clear my mind and wait to receive what to write.

Truthfully, I can state everything that has been written was given to me by the Holy Spirit, from the title of the book, the chapter titles and content therein, the order in which it is written, and I look forward to receiving the end. Since I began on this journey of partaking in the writing of this book, I have been on an emotional roller- coaster experiencing so many highs and lows. I have literally been walked-through parts of my life that I had forgotten about. Memories have been brought back to me with crystal clarity, the significance of each event has been revealed along with a defined purpose for them. I find that the contents within the pages of this book to be very powerful, and life changing. The Holy Spirit has allowed me to take a step back and look at all the things that my God has brought me through and to see how powerful His presence has been throughout my life's journey thus far.

I have truly been transformed during the course of each of these life events; and have been further transformed during the recording of these events. This life that my God has allowed me to live hasn't been easy; but He never promised me that it would be. However, He did promise me that He would never leave me nor forsake me and that He would be with me always even until the end of time. My God has kept all of His promises to me. During the course of this life, thus far, my God's presence, grace, mercy, favor, love and compassion for me has been overwhelmingly apparent in every situation that I have encountered. My Heavenly Father never turned His back on me even when I did. Now, that's love!

The month of May in 2011 was definitely a month of revelation for me. My choice for my latter year's wife was revealed to me, and my Heavenly Father asked me a monumentally serious question. Allow me to digress for just a moment, my family and I had returned home to Rhema Word Kingdom Ministries in 2008 after Steven our eldest son was arrested and charged with murder. Within the first or second month of our attending Wednesday Bible study/Worship Service and Sunday worship service regularly; my Pastor posed a question to all who were in attendance. He asked "How many of you truly love the Lord and truly desire to serve him?" Dozens of us raised our hands and he said to those of us with our hands raised doesn't it seem like things or circumstances keep coming up to stop you?

He then stated if you truly desire to serve the Lord ask Him to remove anything or anyone that is a hindrance in you moving forward in serving Him. But wait, before you ask God to do that, until you first count the cost. If after you have considered what it may cost you and you still want to, then ask Him. I always take seriously what my Pastor has to say concerning the Lord. This time was no different; except for the intensity of what he said and how he made sure to stress that we take the time to consider the cost. I have the propensity to overthink or over analyze in cases like this. So, I thought of the actual probability of me considering everything that this prayer could cost me. I quickly came to the conclusion that the multitudes of variables were too enormous.

Then, I decided to look at it from another perspective. I know that I loved the Lord more than anything or anybody else and all I want to do is serve Him in any way He sees fit. Since those are my true feelings and desires, it mattered not who or what would have to be removed; because they are only in the way of me fulfilling my heart's desire in serving my first love, God. My Heavenly Father asked me had I known before I said that prayer that it would require my eldest son Steven and my wife Triscennea (Beautiful) to be removed from me; would I have still prayed for it?

First of all, my God caught me totally by surprise with that question; because I never put that together (cause and effect). He asked me at a time when the pain and heartache was still fresh. I was, literally, floored by the question and the timing of it; so I was unable to answer Him right away. It took approximately 3 days and nights before I was able to give my Heavenly Father my answer of yes. Even though, I loved my son Steven as much as a father should love his son; I still love my God more. I loved my wife, Beautiful as much as a husband should love his wife, second only to God, so I still love my God more. Later, the Holy Spirit revealed to me that my God wasn't asking me this question because He didn't know the answer. He asked so that I would know.

Before, I stated that God will never force His will upon us; that's why he's given us free will. We have the choice to believe in Him or not, to love Him, or not and to serve Him, or not. My Heavenly Father asked me that question so I can recall for myself that I asked Him to remove anything or anyone who is a hindrance to me moving forward in serving Him. He wanted me to come to the revelation of what my heart's desire cost me and for me to take the self-examination of whether I regretted it, or not. My God's timing was critical in this instance, because the pain and anguish was still fresh and new. He knew that I would give the most honest answer at this time to Him. I was able to prove to myself that I wasn't just giving my God lip service when I say that I love him more than anyone or anything else; this truth was actually put to the test and I passed.

To be perfectly honest with all of you, each year when the date of Steven's and Triscennea's passing come around I miss them both very much. Still, I have no regrets for my prayer. I still find it difficult to this date to lie in my bed alone without a wife that loves me, to hold and fall asleep in her warm embrace. I know today that the relationship with my God could have never grown to what it is today without them being removed from my life. What's actually so great about all of this is that nothing bad has happened to either of them, because they both accepted Jesus Christ as their Lord and Savior. They simply just went home to be with our Lord; and I could never remain angry or sad about that truth.

I had to be broken before my God could really use me. The process truly began several years before the passing of my son and wife. As a result of me running from God's calling on my life and using drugs as a means of escape, I had lost a well-paying job. I had placed an incorrect value on the position I had within the company and I didn't appreciate the amount of money I was making. The company wouldn't give me a good reference, because of my actions, even though; I had worked there for over 12 years. Since I had no degree, experience was the only thing that I could use and I was unable to even use that. I went from being able to pay the majority of our bills. Especially the larger ones such as our monthly mortgage payment, car note, utilities, and still have money left over. But I never appreciated it at all because I wanted more; to having no job at all.

Beautiful had a well-paying job, as well, so she had to foot the bills as I had to work for much less money than I was accustomed to making. That was an ego breaker for me, for I had thought I was all of that and still I wasn't satisfied. As a result of this initial breaking point and all the events that followed afterwards; I have a new appreciation for this life that my God has given me. I have learned to depend on Him for everything. I appreciate everything, all the more, and all it took was for Him to take everything; so now He's my everything.

My niece Dominique asked me a very interesting and profound question, earlier this year. She asked why is it that the individuals that God chooses to use to do a great work for Him have to suffer so much before being used. I replied to her that her question was very good and that I would answer it to the best of my ability. First of all, I asked her why shouldn't I suffer? For my Lord and Savior Jesus Christ suffered far worse than I ever could at the hands of the people he was sent to save. Since I have accepted Jesus Christ as my Lord and Savior; I have also accepted that this life is not my own. It was bought through the suffering, death, and resurrection of Jesus Christ, my Lord. If I expect to share in the glory of my Lord; I also must expect to share in the suffering, as well.

I have known Dominique all of her life. I am her uncle through marriage; I am still a true uncle through and through. I reminded her of how I used to be and told her some things about my past that she didn't know. She lived with us for a while and would witness me laying out all of the bills, semimonthly, and paying them. I remember in her youth, she thought that was so great to easily be able to pay the full amount asked for every time. She wasn't aware that I wasn't happy; even though, I could do that and still have money left over. My wife, Beautiful had the responsibility of paying one car note and buying the groceries with her pay check. We were living with plenty but it was never enough for me. I had to lose all of that in order to gain an appreciation for it.

The values that I had placed on the things that I had and the position I held at work were terribly inaccurate. I, actually, back then thought that the position I held, my job title, defined who I was. This was so terribly wrong. I had a worldly mindset; yet still I could never really fit in with this world's value system. Today, I acknowledge that I am totally dependent on my Heavenly Father for everything. When I had no means to pay my bills, to buy food and to provide for my family, He made a way out of no way every day, consistently. I truly can say that I depend on my God for my daily bread. My God was giving me everything that I needed, day by day. I didn't wonder or worry about tomorrow or the future; because I realized that all I have is today and my God took care of it already.

Today, I work for one of the largest medical transportation companies in the Midwest; my position/title within the company is Driver. In all the years that I have worked and all the experience I have obtained throughout those years, driving professionally comes in at dead last. I would like to digress again for just a moment. Mentally, after the passing of Beautiful I was truly unable to work. A local car manufacturing plant announced that they were hiring; I stood in a line for approximately 5 hours to fill out an application. My application was chosen and I went through all the testing required to be considered for a position.

Through the Grace of God I was hired. However, the assembly line that I was placed on was more suited for someone half my age. I was trained by a young man in his 20s and I was able to do just about three fourths of the assembly that the position required. Working that line for a shift of 10+ hours had me extremely sore, bruised, and totally exhausted. At the time that I held the position I was suffering from a chronic eye infection that had been going on for three months or so. I also had numbness in all of my fingertips on both hands and started having the numbness in my toes, as well. Part of my assembly process was for me to clip a wire harness on the back of a part that I couldn't see. I was supposed to feel for it in the back, which due to the increasing numbness I couldn't.

I prayed for strength every night that I was on that line and my God gave it to me and saw me through it. A union rep would come by on occasion and asked me how old I was after I told them, forty five, they agreed that I was on a young man's line and they would see to it that I was moved. The numbness and the fatigue became too overwhelming for me to handle anymore. It appeared that I was just receiving lip service from those Reps for I was unable to be moved. I had to quit. Thankfully, while I had that job my symptoms had gotten worse so I could finally address what was wrong with me physically. Some years ago, I was diagnosed with having Grey's Disease (hyperthyroidism). I was treated twice with irradiated iodine which brought my thyroid function from hyper (accelerated) active to hypo (under) active. I was covered under Beautiful's medical insurance, but since she was gone so was my medical insurance.

To be totally honest, I was so distraught after my wife's passing that I wasn't caring for myself, physically, at all. It had actually been a year and some months since I had taken any medication for this condition, I was suffering from. The symptoms were glaringly staring me in the face and had gotten far worse than I should have allowed. Since I had no insurance at the time my parents set up an appointment for me to see their physician. I met him and told him the symptoms I was feeling and that I felt it was due to my underactive (hypo) thyroid. He informed me that it affected my eyes as well. The results of my blood tests confirmed that my conclusion was correct.

My parents doctor truly cares for his patients and is very blunt and to the point when speaking. I had informed him of the passing of my eldest son Steven, in 2009, due to cancer and of my wife, Triscennea's in 2010 due to a brain aneurysm. I went on to inform him of how difficult it was for me to deal with it. My doctor informed me of just how critical I had allowed my condition to become. He stated that in my current condition if I faced any type of trauma that I more than likely wouldn't have survived. He expressed his sorrow for my losses and asked me what I was trying to do? Join them?

When the doctor heard my description of my symptoms, and then informed him of what I thought the problem, was he asked why I waited so long to address it? I couldn't give him a viable excuse or explanation because, except for my eyes, I knew exactly what was going on. Well, the good news was that it wasn't too late and that my condition was still treatable. It would take time to get my levels back to where they should be. Listening to the honest and blunt words, from my doctor, really caused me to reevaluate my mental state. I decided, then at that very moment, that I would do whatever it took, overcome whatever obstacles I had to face, to move forward. My Heavenly Father already showed me whom I had chosen to be my wife He had given me a work to complete, so I had no excuses, anymore.

It took about year and some months, for my levels to normalize. However, I felt significantly better after five months or so. During this time frame, I had plenty of time to make myself available to be used in the writing of this book. Now, as I look back on it, even while I was still suffering from extreme fatigue I could have and should have made time to write, but I didn't. People would ask me what I did for a living; I would state that I was unemployed. I must have stated that untruth one too many times for my Heavenly Father; because He told me going forward when I am asked that question I am to state that I am a writer.

Twice more, I was asked that question and I still gave the same answer; because I didn't feel comfortable enough to state that I was a writer. My Heavenly Father was displeased with my disobedience. He asked me didn't I give you a job to do when I instructed you to write this book? I answered yes, and then He stated that I am no longer unemployed for I am doing a work that He has instructed me to do. I am now a writer and I should make that fact known to whoever inquires as to what's my occupation. When I was asked again, I was obedient and stated that I was a writer. The person went on (just like I knew they would) to ask me what have I written and I told them that I was in the process of finishing my first book. I was asked a multitude of times after that and it became, more and more, comfortable for me to state that I was a writer. First of all, whenever the Almighty God gives you a work to do, that is your occupation, and I needed to walk in it. It matters not that I have never written anything before or the fact that I have never been published.

When God had me enter into this work it was already a finished work. In other words, the footsteps and groundwork had already been laid out. The only thing I have to do is be willing to be used by my God to do this work through me, and make myself available as much as possible. Because it was ordered by the Almighty God it is already a successful work; because my God is incapable of failure. Although, my God had reiterated to me that I was employed by Him, I still felt the need to seek work in the world. I sought to be employed in fields where I had the most experience, also in areas where my experience, skills and knowledge were transferable. I interviewed for position after position that I was qualified for.

I even sought employment at companies that I knew people in, so that could give me the edge to be hired, and was still unable to be hired. All of a sudden, after I applied, there was a hiring freeze or extreme budget cuts. This type of thing doesn't usually happen to me, I am always walking in the favor of the Lord; where doors that are shut for everyone else. They are usually, miraculously, opened for me. What I had failed to realize at the time, was that I wasn't doing the job God had given me to do; there were major time gaps between me making myself available to write. I was really being, blatantly, disobedient and, actually, very disrespectful to my

Heavenly Father by slacking in the work he had given me to do, while diligently seeking employment elsewhere.

Frustration began to set in; then one day I was at my parents building, just returning from the corner gas station when I saw a driver who was employed by my now current employer. This driver had just dropped off one of my parents tenants and was leaving the building returning to his vehicle, that was parked in front of the building. When I saw him I inquired whether his company was hiring, he said yes there are training classes starting just about every 2 to 3 weeks. I informed him that I already possessed a commercial driver's license (CDL) he told me that I should be hired right away and gave me the address to go to and instructed me to apply in person with my CDL in hand.

My experience as a professional driver was less than a year and it didn't even compare to, the over a decade, experience I had in other areas. I truly never wanted to be a driver; but I wanted to work like everyone else and if that was how to get my foot in the door of this company, so be it. I talked with that driver on a Friday, so I went to their base of operation to apply in person that Monday. I was immediately informed that I couldn't fill out an application there and was given the website so I could online. The online application was in the range of the longest job application I have ever filled out online. I just knew that I would be contacted right away from what the driver I had met had told me. A week had passed and I had yet to receive any correspondence back from them; which I found it hard to believe since I stated on the application that I possessed a CDL already.

It was nearing the end of the second week when I finally received a call from their human resources department inquiring of my availability for an interview. I was instructed to obtain a copy of my driving record from the Department of Motor Vehicles and to bring it with me for the interview. Finally, they called and I was about to have another interview!!! My mind instantly brought to my recollection all of the other jobs that I applied for recently in fields where I had more experience and still wasn't hired. In one or two cases I never even obtained an interview. I couldn't help but wonder would this be the case again because none of this was making any sense to me. The Holy Spirit just gave me a revelation in this matter as I am giving an account of it now. Earlier, I stated that I was instructed by my God to stop stating that I was unemployed and to tell anyone who inquired of my occupation that I was a writer. Bottom line is that, my God was reminding me that He had already provided me with a job, and please believe me that my God pays His workers very well.

Instead of me just doing the job that He had given me; which I wasn't dedicating enough time to do. I was spending my time looking for job as if I was still unemployed. I even did this after, I myself, acknowledged that I was a writer and felt comfortable stating that truth. By my actions, I was telling my God that the job He had provided me with wasn't good enough. I wanted to have a job in the world like everyone else did, so I could fit in. I also added insult to injury by hardly even showing up for work; I simply was exhibiting a lack of faith and trust in my God, which I didn't even realize at the time. My God was supplying me with everything I needed daily. I wasn't in need for anything. If an additional need would arise, I would pray for and receive provision. I was being sustained so I could do this important work.

My God was giving me just what I needed daily at this point in time, despite this I obviously felt I needed, and wanted more. My Heavenly Father wanted to bless me with abundantly more, but I had not yet proven myself to be a good steward with what He had given me in the past. It was a necessary process that I had to go through in order to become ready for the abundance of blessings that my God has in store for me, spiritually, as well as financially. I was in such a self-absorbed state that I couldn't see why my God was blocking me from getting job after job. There was a concern that I had brought to my Lord, in prayer, regarding temptation. Throughout my 20+ years of working experience I primarily worked with women, side-by-side, earlier on, then in supervisory positions of authority.

There have been many ladies which I have encountered who have been taken in by my acts of kindness, attention, and genuine concern for their well-being. Some of them formed emotional attachments to me due to my natural personality traits, that were, of course, unwanted. Due to my marital status, only a few ever attempted to cross that threshold; however, the few that did came very forcefully and boldly. On many occasions, I had to perform a self-evaluation of my actions to ascertain whether I sent out the wrong messages. Since I worked with and supervised, primarily, women I had a few close female friends (that Beautiful was fully aware of) that I would seek counsel from. Their insight proved to be invaluable. They informed me that I gave these ladies attention that they weren't getting at home from their spouses or boyfriends. I was told that when I would complement them daily on their clothing, hairstyles, or their appearance in general and noticed when they changed something about themselves, that it would uplift them for the day.

Some of these ladies actually looked forward to me coming to their work area every day for this uplifting experience. This confirms the truth that is written in the book of Proverbs 18:21 "Death and life are in the power of the tongue: and they that love it shall eat the fruit thereof." The words that I would speak to these ladies were uplifting. The attention that I gave them was what they were lacking at home my actions and words, brought life to them. My words sparked emotional responses in them that were dormant (even dead) for a while and some would misconstrue my actions for advancements; this was truly unintentional on my part, because I wanted nothing from these ladies.

Please understand, by no means am I trying to convey to anyone that I believe myself to be irresistibly handsome or anything of that nature. For I am truly aware that the attraction that members of the opposite sex have to me is to the Christ in me. Since Christ is in me and I am in Him; I have a love in me that illuminates through my very being. That light and that love is naturally attractive; I know it is to me. There is no woman more attractive than one that truly loves and worships the Lord, to me.

Before going on this interview, I asked the Almighty God would I be hired for the position I had applied for; He instantly answered yes. I was just about to ask why yes for this job, when He told me point blank why. My God told me that in this position I would have the opportunity to witness and minister to a multitude of people. I thought that would be wonderful, because this job would allow me to make His presence known in this earthly realm through my love and the words of my testimony. For many years, throughout my career have I participated in the interviewing process as both an interviewee and as the interviewer, never have I asked my God to speak through me in these processes. I was compelled to do so this time; since I have never asked prior to or been informed prior to an interview that I would receive the position.

I was scheduled to meet with a gentleman from human resources but he was still conducting another interview, so I was interviewed by one of the trainers. To my knowledge, it was uncommon to be interviewed by a trainer, but not unheard of. I was trained many years ago on how to properly conduct myself, professionally, during an interview. There were many do's and don'ts that were instilled, or ingrained, in me. Needless to say, because I had, invited my God to speak through me, all of the years of interview etiquette went out of the window. All of the answers that I gave were based in my faith and belief in the Almighty God. Never in the multitude of interviews that I have participated in have I felt the presence of the Lord so strongly in the room.

If this interview would have been judged or critiqued by the standards of corporate America they would have found me to be totally out of order, and all of my answers to be inappropriate. I spoke of my past losses and how I had been strengthened and made over and better because of the experiences. I conveyed how that would make me better suited for this position. I have no idea how this interview would have turned out had it been conducted by anyone else. I do know it wasn't by chance or mistake who I ended up being interviewed by. When I was asked, did I have any questions concerning the position that wasn't covered in the interview? I asked the standardized questions. Then, with the Holy Ghost boldness, I asked when I could start.

My interviewer stated that he didn't see any reason why I wouldn't be hired. With that being said, I asked could I possibly take the physical required prior to being hired right away, so that no time would be wasted. He appeared to be very surprised at my request but answered, "I don't see why not, let me check for you." A few moments later, I was handed the necessary paperwork along with the address of where I needed to go. I left the base on such a spiritual high because I had just experienced my God moving in a way like never before.

Since I already had a Commercial Driver's License with a passenger endorsement; which simply meant I was certified to transport passengers in a commercial vehicle. I wasn't required to take the first training course. I joined in a class that had been formed and in session for several weeks already. The first session entailed training new potential employees and preparing them for passing their CDL exam. The second session entailed training us in passenger safety, professionalism, etiquette, proper procedures, paperwork, proper use of equipment etc. they instilled in us to always perform our duties in a professional and courteous manner. We were instructed in the proper way to assist our clients in and out of our vehicle, and how to assist them according to their particular disability.

We were tested vigorously, via written exam and actually performing particular functions; such as, loading a client in the vehicle that's in a wheelchair and or power chair/scooter. Our performance was rated on several scales such as our appearance, pleasantries and properly securing our passengers who are in a wheelchair, power chair/scooter or seated in the standard van seat. Everyone was assigned a trainer to drive with for three days as we picked up and dropped off clients. Some trainers drove one or two of the three training days; my trainer had me drive all three days. This was very beneficial for me. He had the full three days to critique, advise, and correct me when necessary. I am grateful that I had an excellent trainer who prepared me as best as he could be for this job. He prepared me for many instances that may arise; but no one could ever prepare anyone for everything. He came as close as he possibly could, I think.

Towards the end of our training, we were told what types of schedules they were running currently. We were asked what our ideal schedule would be, I, of course, stated that I would love to have the weekend off; but had to have Sunday off. Our trainers informed us that we would be unable to pick our own schedules; they would be assigned to us. Depending upon how many schedules were available some of us may even be required to work a floating schedule meaning no set days or set hours. Today, I have been working for this particular medical transport company for just under a year. I have had three different sets schedules, all of them included having Sundays off; for that is my Heavenly Father's day. The first schedule I was assigned entailed me working three, 13hour days Wednesday through Friday; which took some getting used to.

After a few weeks of doing this schedule, I was used to it, in theory it was perfect for me I was off work Saturday through Tuesday. I worked three straight days and had the opportunity to write for three days excluding Sunday of course. The 3 ½ months that I had this schedule, I wrote maybe once or twice, which was ridiculous. My first job is now and should have been then, was to finish the work my God had given me to do. I had gotten complacent with the other job; which was a big mistake, because now it was time for my God to disturb me. It was now time to be on another schedule and since the first bidding goes in order of seniority; I found myself in the bottom hundred out of approximately 500 total.

Needless to say, there weren't many schedules left to choose from especially with Sundays off. I went from working three 13-hour days to four 10 hour days Wednesday through Saturday hours 1:15 PM to 11:45 PM. I was truly no longer happy with my work schedule, I prefer mornings and, I had to sacrifice my Saturdays so that I could have my Sundays off. I was so disturbed by my new schedule that I began making myself available to write again. I love my Heavenly Father so much. He didn't become angry with me for not writing and seeking other employment in the first place. My God allowed me to apply for job after job gently leading me to a position where I can make His presence known here on earth. My Daddy even made sure that my work schedule wouldn't interfere with the work he had already given me to do. When I still operated outside of His Will; then He had to become my God, the Disturber. My Heavenly Father knows just what to do to ensure that I got my priorities back in order.

Time and time again, I have taken a look back to examine how far my God has brought me over these past four years. My focus has been particularly on the time since my Heavenly Father gave me this assignment and revealed to me my choice for the wife of my latter years. I am amazed at myself for actually thinking I was ready for Lovely even though God stated that we both weren't ready yet. I remember attending Greg and Tasia's baby shower; I had helped them to transport some of their many, many gifts home. They actually did very well in the gift department for their car was fully loaded up, along with my Chevy Tahoe. We were finishing up unloading the vehicles at their home when Tasia told me to wait, she said she has something for me to read and that I would enjoy it.

She came back out and handed me a book written by Daryl O'Neil expertly titled "And To The Unmarried I Say.... "Things To Consider Before Saying "I Do". My first thought was, what is this still newlywed woman of God thinking about when she gave me this book to read. She already knows that I had been with Beautiful for 28, years and that we had been married for 22 of them. Tasia reminded me who Apostle Daryl O'Neil was saying that he had visited our church on many occasions, and that he was friends with our Pastor. I took the book from her, and thanked her for letting me see it; although I just knew this book couldn't give a previously successfully married man of 22 years any new insight or ideals regarding marriage. I received the book from her in the spirit in which it was given to me, friendship.

I began reading this book that very same night with the premise that it could in no way enlighten me at all. Wow!!! I don't think that I have ever been so wrong before in my life. When I started to read this anointed piece of literary genius, I found it hard to put down! If I had not been so tired that night I would have read it all. This book is a must read for anyone seriously contemplating getting married. It should be read by men, as well as women. I would go as far as to say even if you are married, buy this book it will surely be beneficial to your (friendship) I mean marriage. I was and still am so impressed by this book that I've read Tasia's copy twice, and written about how great I thought it was on Facebook. Tasia sent my comment to Apostle O'Neil. He was glad that I enjoyed it; especially, adding that not very many men see the importance of it.

I sent him a friend request on FB, he accepted and we have been friends ever since. I was made aware of the monthly Unmarried Bible Study that he conducted, usually on the first Saturday of every month. I attended the aforementioned Bible study and purchased my own copy of his book. Then and only then did I give Tasia back her copy. Of course you know I had to read my copy, with my pen and highlighter in hand; this book is just that great. It was no mistake that Tasia was compelled to give me her book to read by Apostle Daryl O'Neil. His book was so informative and helpful to me that I just had to hear whatever he had to say regarding the unmarried. I chose to sit in the front row when I attended the unmarried Bible study because I didn't want to miss a thing.

The biblical truths that he revealed in his book and during Bible study are thoughtful, informative, and very powerful. He explains the difference in the term "single" that society uses versus the biblical term "unmarried." If you want to learn more, I strongly suggest that you buy a copy you will be very glad that you did. When my Heavenly Father stated that there was a work that he needed to complete in me before I can move forward in serving him and before I could marry Lovely; I had no idea how much work needed to be done. By no means am I stating that I fully know what all it would take to prepare me; but I do see a definite improvement thus far.

The behavioral tendencies and prejudgments that we, as people, act upon were pointed out by Apostle D. It mattered not at first how many times he said it before we enter into a relationship (friendship) we take with us the preconceived notion that there is something wrong with them. We quickly seek to find their faults; however, when we self-examine ourselves we always give ourselves an A+++. I listened to this man of God make that statement, over and over again, but never saw myself in it. It took about a year for some of the truths, that he was teaching about to sink in. With my analytical way of thinking, I just knew that Lovely was the cause of our delay in getting together because there was nothing wrong with me. I know what it takes to be married, stay married; for I had done it already for 22 years.

Never did I realize the level of arrogance, self-righteousness, and haughtiness that I possessed. My mind was totally closed to even the possibility that these character traits were within me, blatantly, at times. Now, let me reiterate, when I saw that Lovely was the one I had chosen, I was and still am, well pleased. I found nothing wrong with her. My Heavenly Father stopped me from moving by stating that he needed to do a work in her and me. Ever since then I couldn't find a thing wrong with me (so I thought) so it had to be her. I began to study her more closely still at a distance. I soon started to find the behavioral tendencies and character flaws all in her personality. Not once, at first, did I perform an accurate examination of myself.

Last year towards the middle of 2012, in the midst of my desperation and frustration, I asked my God when would Lovely be ready to start a life with me. Just to make this perfectly clear, I already knew that my God wouldn't tell me about another person's faults, He only talks to me about me. Somehow, I figured he would tell me since I am waiting on her anyway; as you can see my arrogance was blaring. I was simply a new kind of crazy to think that my God that changes not would go against how He operates to answer my question.

My God gave me an answer right away. At the time, I didn't realize that it was the answer when I would be ready, not Lovely. I was given a new revelation on the meaning of the movie Thor, which I had seen several times already. Thor was the son of a King and he possessed several character flaws such as immaturity, self-righteousness, arrogance, and haughtiness. He had been given a hammer that only he could wield. Thor only needed to outstretch his arm and open his hand and it would come right to him, no one else could even pick it up. Due to Thor's disobedience, arrogance, self-righteousness, and disrespect to his father, the King; he was stripped of his superpowers and his hammer was taken from him. He was banished to Earth and his father, the king, gave a directive to Thor's hammer. The directive was if anyone was found worthy they too could have the hammer and wield the power of Thor. After issuing the directive he sent the hammer to earth as well.

Thor found himself on Earth without his superpowers. He was as weak as any other human being, which was a humbling experience for him. Thor's hammer was found by several men, and people came from miles around trying to pick up the hammer and couldn't. When Thor heard of his hammer's location he went to retrieve it but even he was unable to lift his hammer, this devastated him. The king had given the hammer to Thor, so it belonged to him no matter how many men who tried to possess it, they couldn't possess it. At the present time, Thor was unworthy to have it he couldn't possess it either. As the movie progressed, a transformation in the person of Thor was occurring. He had become humble, after all he knew and was, had been stripped away from him.

A destroyer was sent to Earth to the location where Thor was after his friends (fellow warriors) had come to retrieve him. This giant destroyer began to wreak havoc upon the small town and its inhabitants even Thor's warrior friends were no match for it. Thor could no longer watch the destruction of this town and of its people. He, selflessly, gave himself up to be sacrificed for the lives of the townspeople and his friends. This destroyer was a giant metal robot, of sorts; its giant hand took one swat at Thor and mortally wounded him. Everyone gathered around Thor as he was about to die. When he took his last breath, the hammer of Thor took off like a rocket from its location to be reunited with Thor's outstretched arm and open hand. Thor was brought back to life upon being united with his hammer, and all of his superpowers were restored.

In my arrogance and blinding stupidity, I believed that Thor represented Lovely and that the hammer represented me. I even had support for my irrational thinking, years ago Beautiful and I attended a married couple's function for Rhema Word. Each spouse was asked if they had to describe their mate as a tool what it would be. Beautiful described me as a hammer, because I so often would hammer my point across like driving a nail into concrete or wood. I described her as a screwdriver; because she claimed to have the ability to tighten me up in the areas I was lax or loose in.

I find it hard to believe that, it took a whole year for me to receive what my Heavenly Father was telling me about myself. I was so full of pride that I couldn't see that I truly represented the person of Thor. I possessed all of his character defects just as depicted in the movie. In short, my Father in Heaven, the King of Kings was telling me that I couldn't have Lovely yet, because I was unworthy of her. My God in His infinite wisdom, also told me what it would take to be worthy; all I needed to do was to die in my flesh (my carnal self) and be reborn again. He was also telling me that whom I have chosen is who he has for me. While I go through this process, I need not fear, no one else can have her no matter how hard they try.

The dilemma I am facing now is that I can see all that is wrong with me and I wonder when I will ever be ready. It's funny, when God revealed to me who I really am; I was totally undone it was truly a humbling experience. I can also now see some of the other purposes for working in my current position, such as service. When my Daddy (the Almighty God) told me that I would get this job He only revealed part of the purpose it will serve. I have not only had the opportunity to witness and minister to individuals, but on many occasions, I have been witnessed and ministered to as well. I have on occasion had the opportunity to be belittled, cursed out, and blatantly, disrespected on many levels, also.

I remember on one occasion, I was called a stupid, new driver. The passenger even called into the office and repeated the insults to them. She just knew I was going to make her late for church. My God showed himself mightily in me on this occasion. He kept me in perfect peace; I returned her insults with kindness. I responded to her yelling at me in a calm and caring manner. There was another passenger that I had to pick up; he was located directly in the route I was taking for her; so I asked my dispatcher for permission to pick him up on the way. She became infuriated once again calling into the base stating that this stupid, new driver was picking someone else up and was going to make her late for church.

This client didn't even address me with her concern. However, I assured her that she would arrive on time. As soon as I pulled up to the building that the gentleman resided in he came out. She was still on the phone speaking ill of me when he entered the vehicle. She was so irate she didn't even acknowledge his presence. I picked him up four blocks before reaching her designation and she wasn't late.

She was in a wheelchair so I had to remove the restraints that held her in place, and then wheeled her into the church. I made sure she was situated and told her goodbye and have a blessed day. Believe me, during this whole exchange, my flesh did rise up and demanded that I respond differently to all of the insults. Through the grace of God, my flesh was placed under submission. I was always going to remain a professional in my response to her even if I would have gratified my flesh. For example, I wanted to point out that I still got her there in time even though I was new. I was also tempted to tell her that I would pray for her which in both these instances would have particularly satisfied my flesh; but would have also yielded a negative response from her.

As a born again Christian, I have recognized and accepted that this life is not my own, it was paid for with a price. My Lord and Savior, Jesus Christ suffered while being tortured by men and died in excruciating pain by being nailed to the cross for my sin and the sins of the whole world. So this life I am allowed to lead belongs to Him that saved me. My Jesus was ridiculed, spat upon, falsely accused, and never said a word in His defense; so why should I behave any differently. It is my responsibility to make his presence known in this earth through my love and the words of my testimony. If I were to have sought gratification for my flesh at the time of my encounter with this client; I would have missed the Golden opportunity to suffer for Christ's sake.

After my encounter with this client was over the Holy Spirit gave me a Revelation on the importance of how I reacted to her. He assured me that her reactions to me had nothing to do with me. She was suffering, physically, emotionally, and spiritually. She had just begun to seek God and her issues have increased so she felt overwhelmed and is wondering did she make the right decision, by seeking help through Jesus Christ. I had made a great impression on her by returning her anger with love and her impatience with patience. This job as a driver, that my God had allowed me to have had truly been an opportunity for me to decrease, and allow the Spirit of Christ to increase in me. Even though, I have always had a genuine love and concern for others, I found that it has increased, exponentially. I have also noticed an increase in humility and the placing of other people's needs and desires before my own; it has truly been incorporated into my nature.

Unless there is a power outage or some momentary glitch in the system, gospel (praise and worship) music resonates throughout my home 24/7. I always want my home to have the atmosphere of praise and worship to my Heavenly Father; for He is worthy of everlasting praise and worship. The great thing about this secondary job, which I have as a driver, is that I play my gospel CDs all day while at work. There is a power in music, now depending upon what type of music it is, it can have a negative influence or a positive one. I always choose to set the tone on a positive note. When I first started this driving job, I worked the shift of three days on and four days off. During those very long three 13-hour days it was one CD that I played the most, it was by Marvin Sapp titled "I Win". I never did, and still haven't become tired of listening to, it over and over and over again.

This magnificent copulation of songs ministered to me and still does, today, like no other CD ever created by any other artist. The anointing on Marvin's life and his God-given talent kept me going through those early 13- hour days. I would allow his CD to play, over and over again, and never got tired of hearing a single song. All I can say, is that every song on this particular CD speaks to me and my current and past situations. I remember the first time I heard "I Win," playing while sharing a part of my testimony to a client. She asked me if that music I was playing and singing along with was by Marvin Sapp; I told her, yes, and expressed how much this whole CD ministered to me, so strongly and completely.

She informed me that we suffered similar, back to back, losses the last one for both of us being our spouses. Upon hearing that information, it all made sense to me. I can't say that any one song touches me more, spiritually, than another. The song titled "My Testimony" may be his testimony, but it is certainly mine, as well. I look forward to meeting and talking at length with Marvin soon and giving him an autographed copy of this book and having him autograph my personal copy of his CD "I Win," because, I truly have won.

What I am about to state may sound incredibly strange too many of you; but please believe me that it is one hundred percent true. I am so grateful to my Heavenly Father for bringing me through all of these experiences, challenges, storms, and trials that I have had the opportunity to face. My God could have chosen anyone else to go through all the things that He appointed and or allowed me to go through; but He chose me to go through this perfecting work. My God was there with me in the fiery furnace the whole time not for one moment, or instance did He ever leave me or forsake me, even when I turned my back on Him. The enemy flooded my mind with thoughts of self-condemnation for the ways that I reacted on several occasions; which kept me painfully in a state of unforgiveness and extreme sorrow. I stayed in that state for far too long.

I had already asked for forgiveness from my God, from my family and forgiveness was granted, in which I had no doubt of. My issue was that I didn't know how to forgive myself. The Holy Spirit brought me back to the word of God in the book of Romans 8:1 "There is therefore now no condemnation to them which are in Christ Jesus who walk not after the flesh, but after the Spirit." The Holy Spirit reminded me that I had already been forgiven and revealed to me that I handled and reacted in the way that I was called to. In other words, I had to react in the way that I did in order for me to be in the place that I am today. The things I was appointed to go through was designed to break, shatter, and ground the old me to dust; so that my God could make me all over again.

With every fiber of my being, I can honestly state that I am grateful for everything that I have been chosen to go through to get me where I am today. My faith, trust, total dependence and love for my God has gotten so much deeper than it ever was before. I thank God for everything that I am still going through today; even though, it hurts so badly at times, but I know that I am experiencing growing pains. Sometimes, I am very tempted to ask my Daddy God to take the pain away by stopping what I am going through; but I know if He stops the pain, the growth stops also, and I don't want that. In faith I know that everything that I am going through is according to His plan and purpose for my life. I know that it won't last a moment longer than it is necessary and that I will become so much better because of it. I thank my God for everything that he has allowed me to share with you within these pages. I pray that everyone will be blessed from reading my testimony!!!

The man who finds a wife finds a treasure,
and he receives favor from the Lord.
Proverbs 18:22 (NLT)

I have been blessed to have found
two treasures in one life time.

On June 6, 2015
I married a "Phenomenal" woman of God.

Our journey continues and the best is yet to come.

To God Be The Glory!

Printed in the United States
by Bookmasters

Printed in the United States
By Bookmasters